NIETZSCHE AND THE SPIRIT OF TRAGEDY

Nietzsche and
the Spirit of Tragedy

KEITH M. MAY

MACMILLAN

First published 1990

Published by
THE MACMILLAN PRESS LTD
Houndmills, Basingstoke, Hampshire RG21 2XS
and London
Companies and representatives
throughout the world

Typeset by Vine & Gorfin Ltd,
Exmouth, Devon
Printed in Hong Kong

British Library Cataloguing in Publication Data
May, Keith M.
Nietzsche and the spirit of tragedy.
1. European literatures. Theories of German
philosophy. Nietzsche, Friedrich, 1844–1900
I. Title
809
ISBN 0–333–45372–7

For Nadine and Steve

Contents

Acknowledgements

Appreciation is gratefully expressed for the opportunity to make use of the following editions of Nietzsche's works: *Beyond Good and Evil – Prelude to a Philosophy of the Future*, translated with a commentary by Walter Kaufmann (New York: Vintage Books, A Division of Random House, 1966); *The Birth of Tragedy* and *The Case of Wagner*, translated with commentary by Walter Kaufmann (New York: Vintage Books, A Division of Random House, 1967); *Daybreak – Thoughts on the Prejudices of Morality*, translated by R. J. Hollingdale, introduction by Michael Tanner (Cambridge University Press, 1982); *Dithyrambs of Dionysus*, Bilingual Edition, translated and introduced by R. J. Hollingdale (Anvil Press Poetry, 1984); *The Gay Science*, translated with a commentary by Walter Kaufmann (New York: Vintage Books, A Division of Random House, 1974); *On the Genealogy of Morals*, translated by Walter Kaufmann and R. J. Hollingdale and *Ecce Homo*, translated with a commentary by Walter Kaufmann (New York; Vintage Books, A Division of Random House, 1967); *Human, All Too Human – A Book for Free Spirits*, translated by R. J. Hollingdale, introduction by Erich Heller (Cambridge University Press, 1986); *Philosophy in the Tragic Age of the Greeks*, translated with an introduction by Marianne Cowan (Chicago: A Gateway Edition, Regnery Gateway, 1962); *Selected Letters of Friedrich Nietzsche*, translated by A. N. Ludovici, edited and introduced by O. Levy (Soho Book Company, 1985); *Thus Spoke Zarathustra – A Book for Everyone and No One*, translated with an introduction by R. J. Hollingdale (Harmondsworth, Middlesex: Penguin Books, 1980); *Twilight of the Idols* and *The Anti-Christ*, translated with an introduction and commentary by R. J. Hollingdale (Harmondsworth, Middlesex: Penguin Books, 1978); *Untimely Meditations*, translated by R. J. Hollingdale, introduction by J. P. Stern (Cambridge University Press, 1983); *The Will to Power*, translated by Walter Kaufmann and R. J. Hollingdale, edited with an introduction by Walter Kaufmann (New York: Vintage Books, A Division of Random House, 1968).

*Are you perchance thinking of comparing
yourself with the ancients who saw gods
everywhere? Gods, my dear modern, are
not spirits; gods do not degrade the world
to a semblance, and do not spiritualise it.*

Max Stirner

1
Apollo and Dionysus

Nietzsche's use of Apollo and Dionysus in *The Birth of Tragedy* shows that he thought of them not as exclusively Greek gods but as gods of all humanity. By 'gods' I mean commanding psychological principles. The duality of Apollo and Dionysus expresses an unalterable feature of the human condition.

The two deities signified to Nietzsche something other than their apparent ancient meanings, but we should not therefore conclude that he falsified them. Rather he perceived their defining qualities which were obscured in the days when these gods were worshipped. After all, historians generally claim to know a time more fundamentally than it knew itself, and they are right, for they know what the time led up to as well as what preceded it. However, there is a clearer resemblance between Nietzsche's Dionysus and the ancient god of vegetation than between Nietzsche's Apollo and the Apollo of mythology. Dionysus was indeed a fertility god whose adherents and orgiasts temporarily surrendered their separate identities. In the early 1870s Nietzsche apprehended Dionysus in a similar way, but during the next decade he came to see Dionysus as the principle of supreme affirmation. In *The Will to Power*, under the dating March–June 1888, he observes that the word 'Dionysian' means 'an ecstatic affirmation of the total character of life'.[1] Nietzsche's later Dionysus is a development of the earlier, not a markedly different conception. It is fair to say that the philosopher merely clarified his youthful insight.

Apollo meant many things to the Greeks, prominently including health, light, the law and protection against evil. In *The Birth of Tragedy*, and later, Nietzsche simplifies Apollo but does not, I believe, misrepresent him. He consolidates Apollo's various functions into one quality and refers to this quality as though the Greeks themselves contemplated Apollo in the same inclusive way. In fact no Greek would have been capable of saying, as Nietzsche says in *The Will to Power*:

1

The word 'Apollinian' means: the urge to perfect self-sufficiency, to the typical 'individual', to all that simplifies, distinguishes, makes strong, clear, unambiguous, typical: freedom under the law.[2]

Nevertheless this is a convincing *psychologist's* definition of the Apollo we encounter in Greek literature. So far as Nietzsche was concerned, the question to ask of any culture was: what need does it satisfy? Nietzsche's Apollo is not a piece of culture, but culture itself in the widest sense. He is the deification of man's power of sublimation.

It will aid our understanding of Apollo and Dionysus if we briefly consider two modern analogues. The first of these is Freud's division of the psyche into ego and id; the second is Sartre's 'nauseous' vision in *La Nausée*.

The Freudian unconscious is the mind-body process that remains outside our linguistic capacities. Ideas are unconscious when they cannot be expressed in words. The id is composed of such wordless activities. Consciousness is emphatically verbal and, being so, must also be selective and superficial.

Freud believed that the extent and power of the id would gradually diminish. The egos of modern individuals are more efficient than the egos of our remote ancestors, which were indeed scarcely developed at all. Thus the unconscious was regarded by Freud as territory to be increasingly and profitably annexed.

But Freud was a nineteenth-century scientist and therefore had faith in the acquisition of firm knowledge. On the other hand, Nietzsche supposes the god Dionysus to stand for the entire realm of the unknowable. To be more exact, Nietzsche sees knowledge itself as a series of codes and conventions beyond which reality begins.[3]

Nietzsche's influence on Freud is conjectural, while his influence on the early Sartre is perfectly clear. Sartre's expression, 'nausea' is taken directly from Section 7 of *The Birth of Tragedy*. Sartre's hero, Roquentin, sitting in a municipal park, becomes aware that existence normally escapes his grasp. As a rule he perceives only appearances and these are differentiated and labelled. But beneath or behind the veneer of the world is undifferentiated fluidity. Everything seeps into everything else. Nietzsche sees will to power in this flowing quality, while Sartre sees a yieldingness. Nietzsche therefore emphasises energy, and Sartre a sort of weakness and helplessness. But that distinction probably indicates two sides of the same coin and is not important for us anyhow. The point is that nothing exists in its own right, since the division of the world into specific items is a human mental activity – or, rather, it is *the* mental activity. It is what minds do.

Sartre's Nietzschean observation is of a kind that readers peruse with keen interest, or possibly amazement, and then abandon. It is purely a feature in a story and the everyday scene does not remotely resemble Roquentin's perceptions of the park. But if we think of *La Nausée* in this fashion we wrongly diminish Sartre's thesis to the effect that outside the human mind there is nothing but endless and pointless movement, mere activity. In fact this is Sartre's own thesis to the extent that it is an elaboration upon some remarks of Nietzsche.

For the moment, then, we might say that Dionysus means the world 'as it is', outside human reckoning, and Apollo means what we humanly make of the world. However, at the beginning of *The Birth of Tragedy* these two are described much more simply as 'art deities of the Greeks'.[4] At first the terms are thus restricted. Originally sculpture was the Greek Apollonian art, and music the Greek Dionysian art. In the course of time the Greeks developed an art form which combined the two tendencies: Attic tragedy. It is important to remember that to begin with the Apollonian and the Dionysian appeared as not merely distinctive but opposed tendencies. The factor of opposition is vital: tragedy is the brief reconciliation of contradictory impulses.

So far this will not have been of much help to one who wishes to reach the heart of Greek tragedy. Accordingly Nietzsche proposes that we provisionally think of Apollo as representing dreams and Dionysus as representing intoxication. This is not an arbitrary proposal since, according to Nietzsche, there is a close connection between the sphere of art and our experiences of dreams and tipsiness. Dreams are the very foundations of Apollonian art because when dreaming we create images of beings and events. Presumably the earliest narrative artists found means of expressing in the waking state visions which had first appeared to them in dreams. They modified the dream material, but not excessively. So the first story-telling came about. It follows that primitive stories were not 'lifelike', were not about insignificant daily doings, but were idealisations – as dreams are idealisations.

In addition (Nietzsche observes) dreamers often feel that their visions are mere appearances: even while dreaming, someone may know that he is experiencing only a dream. Very well, says Nietzsche, this is true of art as well. It is composed of ideal images, in the sense of images shorn of irrelevancies. More remarkable, there are some 'philosophical men'[5] who intuitively grasp that everyday life is mere appearance. Such people have a glimpse of what both art and life meant to the Greeks. The Greeks of the tragic period did not suppose, as Christians suppose, that our experienced world is grossly inferior to a 'back world', but, on the contrary, apprehended abysses falling away just over the horizon of their senses and their understanding. Without that knowledge of how limited and potentially misleading our knowledge is, there can be no tragedy.

Here it is necessary to comment upon Nietzsche's rather haughty attitude in *The Birth of Tragedy*. Perhaps, in fact, it is not so much haughty as brimming over with confidence. He himself later called the book 'very convinced and therefore disdainful of proof, mistrustful even of the propriety of proof'.[6] These words are sometimes quoted with approval even by commentators sympathetic to Nietzsche, yet he may have been unwontedly self-critical. Certainly the words are liable to be deceptive, since all his works are, by the usual standards of philosophers, disdainful of proof. He never stopped mistrusting the propriety of proof, but continued to see it as a rhetorical and somewhat forensic requirement beloved both of 'philosophical labourers' and laymen. Admittedly, *The Birth of Tragedy*, quite unlike most of the later works, looks like an ordinary essay, but omits the evidence that many readers need.

Nevertheless detailed arguments and some sort of proofs can be provided by readers who see what Nietzsche is getting at. For example – and this is not only an example but a vital part of our theme – Nietzsche states that Apollo is the 'glorious divine image of the *principium individuationis*'.[7] What does this mean and what scholarly evidence is there for it? There is no evidence for it, because Nietzsche is relying on an elementary principle to the effect that one can know only something other than oneself. In other words, to the extent that there is knowledge there must be differentiation. To know an element of the self it is necessary to differentiate it from other elements, and in particular from the knowing element. To see things, oneself included, as a blur, which happens, for instance, in extreme drunkenness, is precisely not to know them. Apollo, as the god of sublimation, of medicine, prophecy, light, protection and justice, must necessarily be the god of knowing too. Who but he could stand behind man's capacity, uniquely well developed among the animals, to know? Therefore, it is Apollo through whose agency we discern individuals, for how else could we know anything and be other than brutes? Such is the sort of argument that Nietzsche cavalierly omits.

But note: the capacity to perceive individuals is delusive, and none the worse for that *provided we do not altogether lose sight of the fact that it is delusive*. We see the items that we see because we are human beings, extraordinarily refined creatures, not because they exist in the relative isolation that our vision confers upon them. We have been practising our discriminatory powers of perception for so many millenia that we find it almost impossible to contemplate what alone truly exists, namely quanta of energy. Apollo is therefore the agent of delusion, though he is a glorious agent without whom we would be brutish.

Our world is as a stormy sea (this is Schopenhauer's simile, recalled by Nietzsche), upon which each person sails trustingly in his vulnerable bark. The trust, the sense of relative security, is due to Apollo, but we are at the mercy of the waves. All our prophylactics, plans, analyses of cause and effect; all our societies and, of course, religions, form a kind of screen behind which the sea rages. We peer through the screen but may use only one aperture at a time and therefore notice only segments. The panorama normally escapes us and this is as it must be.

However, people sometimes receive intimations of the panorama; they realise in ecstasy and terror that all is flow, meaningless force and, from our point of view as ordering creatures, frankly chaos. This is the encompassing realm of Dionysus.

> Under the charm of the Dionysian not only is the union between man and man reaffirmed, but nature, which has become alienated, hostile, or subjugated, celebrates once more her reconciliation with her last son, man . . . Transform Beethoven's 'Hymn to Joy' into a painting; let your imagination conceive the multitudes bowing to the dust, awestruck – then you will approach the Dionysian.[8]

'Charm' may seem an odd word to use here, but Nietzsche is

suggesting that to be reconciled with nature is charming as well as terrifying. Charm also implies bewitchment, and the Dionysian reveller was 'bewitched' or 'beside himself'. He further thought of himself as godlike because he was part of a world that continually re-makes itself. Thus the godliness that he resembled, or shared, was not other-worldly but purely natural: he was at one with a divinely natural world. If we modern people look through a telescope at a distant galaxy, or consider the fact that the universe is continually expanding, or peer at bacteria with the aid of a microscope, we appreciate instantly, without theoretical proof, that nature is never-endingly self-creative and self-destructive. The drugs L.S.D. and mescalin sometimes produce similar, if richer, visions. The point is that these are presumably visions of the 'truly existent' beyond our symbolising and discriminatory minds. Such is the non-moral, fertile sphere to which the Dionysian was certain he belonged.

Yet he was not certain as a lower animal may be said to be certain. Merely to be sure as a human being implies one's awareness of other attitudes. The animal knows no other conditions, but a human being who is briefly a votary of Dionysus will return to ordinary social life and may therefore compare his Dionysian with his normal un-Dionysian existence. When he is apart from the Dionysian frame of reference he thinks of himself, erroneously, as an individual, only accidentally and inessentially connected with his environment.

In fact the cult of Dionysus first developed in lands other than Greece, and the early barbarian worshippers were savage and unrelenting. When the cult spread to Greece it encountered formidable opposition in the form of Apollo. It was the force of this struggle and the fact that the struggle was not at all one-sided that gave rise to tragedy. Apollo just barely held the Dionysian impulses at bay and his defences were continually threatened. The Greeks were fully aware of this. Easy repression of Dionysus is incompatible with the reality of Dionysus: he is a god, not a concept to be taken up and, then again, discarded.

When we remark that the Greeks acknowledged not Apollo alone but a range of supernatural beings, the Olympians, we should remember that they thus idealised the pains and pleasures of existence. The gods were not good, since goodness in the unqualified Christian sense is a defiance of existence. Nietzsche remarks in *Human, All Too Human*, that the Greeks saw the Homeric gods as 'only the reflection of the most successful exemplars of their own caste, that is to say an ideal, not an antithesis of their own nature'.[9]

The Olympian theology means, so Nietzsche says in *The Birth of Tragedy*, that 'all things, whether good or evil, are deified'.[10] Nothing is perfectly good, most things are imperfect, but everything is sacred. This is the reverse of our secular mode. What gives the ancient tragedies their awesome power is the fact that no word or object of reference is other than deified. We still praise our modern literature, even Renaissance and medieval literature, for the inclusion of banalities and the quality of verisimilitude, though this is the quality that the Greeks effortlessly surpassed. They did not rigorously exclude ordinary matters, but on the contrary gave them divine significance. For example, Creon is the king in the Theban plays of Sophocles but he is not therefore to be likened overmuch to a modern ruler. The tendency to praise Sophocles on the grounds that he excellently portrayed the struggle of power versus principle can be misguided. The chief significance of Creon is that, in common with everyone else, he belongs to a fated, tragical world. We are anachronistic when we censure him for condemning Antigone or praise him for wishing to deliver Thebes from civil strife. In fact Creon is not a wicked, and therefore theoretically corrigible man, but simply a figure who is 'divinely' what he is and so contributes to his own and Antigone's tragedy.

Similarly, the words uttered in a play, of which a play very largely consists, signify universal deification. When it is reported that Clytemnestra has used a sword to kill Agamemnon and Cassandra, the sword in question is itself a sort of sacred implement. It is no longer a mere murder weapon in the unholy modern sense. It is *the knife that killed Agamemnon*, a vastly more potent and magical thing.

Nietzsche does not exaggerate when he points out this aspect of early tragedy. The people who watched the first performance of the *Agamemnon* naturally distinguished their troublesome and comic everyday lives from the sphere of the play, but must have believed that the latter gave meaning and justification to the former. Their own market-place words were distinctly different from the words of an Aeschylean chorus, for instance, since the chorus always speaks in solemn, urgent or elevated tones. But this means that the spectators' words were not wholly secular either. To be exact, they were secular 'in themselves' but formed parts of a sphere that was tinged, as it were, by the colours of divinity, or else its very ordinariness was exalted by the regular proximity of stage diction.

Nietzsche mentions that Greek religion did not offer to most people a compensatory other world. A few virtuous dead, favoured by the gods, were destined for Elysium and the majority were translated to the utterly listless realm of Hades. No one before Socrates seriously thought in terms of a future that might be better than the present. Therefore the gods enabled people to accept the pains of living. This was not 'resignation' in the usual doleful sense of the word, but was actually exuberance in the midst of suffering. Even now I am giving a false impression by placing exuberance on one side of the scales and suffering on the other. In fact, the Greeks contrived to relish a sorrowful life, because it was shared by their radiant and immoral gods.

Here it is necessary to venture into metaphysics: Nietzsche himself (whom Heidegger regards as occupying the '*last* fundamental "metaphysical" position in Western thought'[11]) unapologetically does so. Nietzsche seems to believe that nature requires 'redemption through illusion'. He writes that he is 'impelled to the metaphysical assumption that the truly existent primal unity, eternally suffering and contradictory, also needs the rapturous vision, the pleasurable illusion, for its continual redemption'.[12]

These are startling words, since we are prone to imagine nature without us. Thus we wonder how on earth the primal unity might require redemption and illusion. Is not the unity actual and everlasting, while we have simply and temporarily devised our illusions? And how is the primal unity to acquire its vital illusions, hence its redemption, when the illusion-creating human race has departed? Nietzsche can only mean that we are usually obliged to think of nature in human terms: Dionysian frenzies (like the modern use of psychedelic drugs) cannot be sustained, and have little to do with 'thought'. For this reason our normal habits of mind, including 'pleasurable illusions', provide the link between us and the rest of the world. To try to deal with the world as it is, or will be when our race has died, is perhaps the most ridiculous undertaking imaginable. We cannot be certain that whatever we catch in a net of human symbols is not altered by the net.

Nietzsche is arguing that the cosmos is ultimately a unity, and, secondly, that we, as parts of nature, make our unique contribution to the whole by providing illusions of art and knowledge. Our scientific understanding of nature is still but a kind of illusion; we must finally get rid of the notion of objectivity, or as Nietzsche remarks in *Beyond Good and Evil*, 'It is perhaps just dawning on five or six minds that physics, too, is only an interpretation and exegesis of the world (to suit us, if I may say so!) and *not* a world-explanation . . . .'[13]

Since the ability to form interpretations has been naturally implanted into mankind, we may legitimately regard the interpretations themselves as required by nature. There is no finally correct interpretation, for all that matters is that the primal unity be explained in some fashion – as God's creation, or as the expanding universe, or as something else.

It is possible to re-phrase the point as follows: because only people conceive things, nature without people is inconceivable. So by a marvellous paradox, if we saw the universe 'correctly', that is, without scientific or mythological conceptions, we would see only chaos; and yet, strictly speaking, the universe cannot finally be chaos, since it is an inescapable sequence of occurrences.

As human beings, then, we are normally obliged to apprehend the world in Apollonian terms, and this means that we must observe Apollo's one unchanging law. This law states that the individual may not overstep his bounds. Nietzsche does not here use the word 'hubris', but nevertheless explains what hubris is. This tacit explanation seems to be derived from Heraclitus, for no other philosopher, ancient or modern, before or after Nietzsche, has viewed the cosmos in the same way. Moreover, as we shall see, the Heraclitean–Nietzschean belief is more 'scientifically' satisfactory than other beliefs. When we contemplate it, we appreciate what gives tragedy its character and power. No one else provides the clue. Aristotle analyses tragedy as drama and poetry, but not much, and not persuasively, as psychology. In the opinion of the modern American scholar, G. F. Else, in his *The Origin and Early Form of Greek Tragedy*, the structure of tragedy was simply invented in stages, more or less without spiritual incentive.[14] Many contemporary writers concentrate upon societal and historical influences (for example, the position of women in Greek society) without noticing that these matters, however important, are still superficial.

Nietzsche alone is radical and convincing. And as usual he offers no explicit proof. His answer, in brief, is this: in order to survive, human beings must regard themselves, falsely, as individuals, but beyond a certain point doing so is self-destructive. Tragedies were composed because the Greeks of the sixth to the fourth centuries understood perfectly what we have failed to understand ever since: that our power to create is inexhaustible, but that our power to create harmlessly is negligible.

Nietzsche writes as follows:

> And so, side by side with the aesthetic necessity for beauty, there occur the demands 'know thyself' and 'nothing in excess'; consequently overweening pride and excess are regarded as the truly hostile demons of the non-Apollinian sphere, hence as characteristic of the pre-Apollinian age – that of the Titans; and of the extra-Apollinian world – that of the barbarians.[15]

Taken by themselves these words give the usual impression that hubris means nothing other than excessive pride, as we today understand such a phrase. But, for the Greeks, where did acceptable pride end and hubris begin? In fact tragic heroes and heroines often suffer for deeds which we find unexceptionable and even praiseworthy in the highest degree. Nietzsche is suggesting that *in nature* hubris attends upon every piece of individual self-assertion and that it is often a mistake for us to apply a socio-moral code to behaviour in tragic drama. Such a code is always misleading in some degree. In our eyes Prometheus is a mighty hero and his stealing the fire is not an act deserving of punishment. Prometheus must be torn to pieces by vultures 'because of his titanic love for man', as Nietzsche puts it.[16] By Greek standards the deed of Prometheus, which inaugurated the arts and sciences of mankind, was monumentally hubristic. The legend of Prometheus expresses how the Greeks of the Apollinian and tragic periods apprehended knowledge: they presumed that learning itself, or the acquisition of learning, was a sort of arrogance for which mortals were inevitably punished. It is foolish for us to smile at this superstition, for we too must grow to appreciate the danger, as well as the glorious necessity, of seeking knowledge. Knowledge of the highest quality entails spiritual danger and alarms the researcher as he or she works.

Then, what of Oedipus? In what sense does he merit his dreadful destiny? It is not convincing to assert, as H. D. F. Kitto does, that Oedipus kills Laius unnecessarily because 'his temper gets the better of him'.[17] And while it may be true that 'lack of prudence'[18] has led Oedipus to accept the crown and marry Jocasta, such behaviour is not much of a defining trait. Nor were these presumptuous acts, since crown and queen were urged upon the young man by the grateful citizens. Such explanations of the tragedy occur only to one in search of explanation, a modern person who must find a cause for every effect. The one wholly characteristic deed of Oedipus that helps to determine his subsequent career is his solving the riddle of the Sphinx. Only he has been able to do this. Thus he has exercised unfettered intelligence, which is by definition hubristic behaviour. But fundamentally Oedipus suffers because his family was cursed before he was born. The lineage of Oedipus and his actions are offensive to the gods. There is little reason in this, because reason is itself inadequate and always will be so. Tragedy exceeds reason.

Behind these examples of Prometheus and Oedipus which Nietzsche offers lies his appreciation of the early tragic attitude, or, to be exact, of the central doctrines of the Greek philosophers who taught in the period of the rise of tragedy. These men indeed contemplated the nature of the universe, but tragic thinking was connected with certain universal conceptions. The conceptions are discussed with exemplary clarity in *Philosophy in the Tragic Age of the Greeks* which, as Nietzsche mentions in his 'Later Preface' to that work, is a deliberate simplification of confused teachings. Nietzsche's principal theme is to the effect that philosophers from Thales to Parmenides were concerned with the reduction of multiplicity to unity, of discord to harmony, of the many to the one. The nature of hubris is illuminated in Heraclitus and is mentioned by Nietzsche in Sections 6 and 7 of his book. Heraclitus' celebrated assertion that the one is the many means that there is no unity other than an ultimate concord of all cosmic things, but things as such come to be and pass away. In other words, there is no being apart from becoming, and we can contemplate absolute being, should we wish to do so, only as the totality of acts of becoming. Being is not separate and ideal, as in Plato.

The ephemerality of existence applies to moral qualities and activities of the psyche, including ideas, as well as to objects. There are many injustices and forms of sorrow in the world, but these are reconciled in – and only in – the invisible harmony of the whole. They are like pieces of a picture or snatches of a symphony, imperfect in themselves yet making sense in the entire composition. Therefore hubris, or alternatively selfhood, is vital for all organic things, though it entails what human organisms apprehend as wickedness and pain.

This is, certainly, the belief of Heraclitus, or a belief imputed to Heraclitus, not an idea consciously shared by all Greeks. Nevertheless it is a reasonable imputation and it seems likely that the same understanding lay buried within the Greek psyche. Hubris is attendant upon living, so that tragic instances of it – exceptional instances to be sure – strike a universal chord.

All things 'suffer' according to their nature as an integral feature of existence. To superstitious people such as the Greeks this is interpreted to mean that things are penalised for extending their limits. But such limits are whatever must have been exceeded whenever there is suffering. So hubris is not codifiable and is scarcely avoidable, though the means of avoiding it are clear: 'know thyself' and 'nothing in excess'. Needless to say, the Greeks did not censure tragic hubris in the manner of a Christian moralist; rather they saw it as prodigious. It was both blasphemous and inspiring.

At this point I should make it plain that I am selecting some of Nietzsche's main observations and enlarging upon them, not randomly but with one end in view: to delineate the spirit of tragedy. The spirit (or determining quality) is to be found not too far from the orgination of tragedy, for the course of cultural development has been anti-tragic. We have striven for centuries to deny tragical insights by means of religion, science and the urge to social betterment. This means that tragic dramas produced within the Christian and meliorist schemes have generally been different at their roots from pristine tragedy. To the extent that they have been tragical they have not been Christian.

So far, then, Nietzsche has given us a clear idea of the Apollonian–Dionysian dichotomy, but we are still a long way from seeing how the dichotomy works and its relevance for us today (which is not the same as its scholarly relevance).

Perhaps the key assertion of *The Birth of Tragedy* is its most famous remark: 'for it is only as an *aesthetic phenomenon* that existence and the world are eternally *justified*'.[19] This memorable utterance has nothing to do with the doctrine of aestheticism. We must bear in mind also that, so far as we are concerned, existence in general needs to be justified, since we could not otherwise endure it. Perhaps 'justification' is almost synonymous with Nietzsche's earlier use of 'redemption'. At all events, existence is partially rescued from its cruelty and wantonness by our imaginative grasp of it. If we call existence 'cruel' we thereby help to make its pains endurable, for we have defined and qualified them; that is to say we have applied a whiff of anaesthetic to them. When Macbeth declares that life is a tale told by an idiot he still cannot grasp life's total lack of intelligibility. An idiot's gibberish still has a sort of meaning for us, since we ourselves have labelled it, or in other words commandeered it, and we apprehend it in relation to normal sense.

Explanations are often, perhaps always, justificatory and redemptive. For this reason Nietzsche means that while our observations are sometimes obviously justificatory and sometimes *technically* condemnatory, 'existence and the world are eternally justified' – not justified according to a particular civilisation or a merely historical set of values – when we cast them in an aesthetic mould. If the mould includes values, then plainly the values are subordinate to the mould. No doubt Homer believed that the values of his time ('bronze-age' values, as we call them) contained the *Iliad*, but now we know that the truth is the other way round.

Here we come to what matters above all about the earliest tragedies, that aspect which has been consistently misunderstood by later generations; according to Nietzsche it was already misunderstood by Euripedes. We are told by Aristotle that tragedy derived from the satyric chorus. It passed out of the satyric phase, acquiring dignified tones. In our time many scholars believe this to be true, while others follow A. W. Pickard-Cambridge who maintains in his *Dithyramb Tragedy and Comedy* (Oxford University Press, 1927) that the dithyramb, tragedy and the dance of satyrs each developed independently from the early forms of worship of Dionysus. None of the three grew out of another. Nietzsche, however, is in this respect a neo-Aristotelian. In addition he, like many others, seems to identify the less undignified, more mesmerically potent sort of satyrs with the wise variety of Sileni. The important point is that the proto-tragic chorus consisted of men dressed as semi-animal creatures, mediators between human beings with all their powers of artifice and the Dionysian world beyond artifice. We can certainly infer that to Nietzsche the essential quality of a satyr was not his lecherous or buffoonish character but his hybridity. This is an important, if somewhat subtle shift of emphasis, since it stresses, justifiably, that tragedy, by means of the satyric 'missing link', reminded spectators of their natural, unregenerate condition.

The satyr-chorus did not deliver a commonsense commentary upon some action (for, apart from anything else, there was then no action and 'the spectator without the spectacle is an absurd notion'[20]); nor did it represent an ideal observer. If the chorus was 'ideal', it was so only in an odd specialised sense which runs counter to our prejudices since Plato. From Plato onwards the ideal has been higher or purer than the visible factors of which it is the abstract or, in a few cases, the apotheosis. But the early chorus was in no sense higher than the listeners. The original function of the chorus was to nullify the feeling of distinction, of apartness, which normally afflicted each of the listeners. Everyone, watching or performing, felt re-united with the rest and with all material things. No one was now distinguished, either by talents or by shameful deeds.

Since the chorus often spoke of cruelty and horrors, natural occurrences, the entire theatre was joined once more with physical nature. Thus the earliest tragic forms were not compensatory in our regular sense of offering an alternative, relatively painless vision, but, strange though it may seem, they 'compensated' by articulating both pain and joy, dismemberment and rebirth, indivisibly. Suffering was welcomed because it was then seen as essential, utterly inescapable. We say that life is worth living 'in spite of' problems and sorrows, and while a Greek of the tragic age might have made a similar remark, he would not have been capable of the same implication, namely that bad things are ugly excretions on the fair face of life. The modern way is to imagine that living is enhanced by the absence of suffering, while to the Greeks such a supposition would have seemed eminently ridiculous. The gods themselves suffer and so do all sensitive beings.

Nietzsche's contention is that mankind, a species divine simply because the world as a whole is divine, once used its unique capacity for symbolical representation in order to confront what is irreducible to symbols. The chorus, and from the time of Thespis an actor also (followed by the two actors introduced by Aeschylus and the three introduced by Sophocles), chiefly represented something other than superficial events, gestures, chatter, the 'paraphernalia', as one might say, of realism. They pointed towards the reality far beyond mere realism: a painful–ecstatic world of growth and death, of constant change, of tearing down and building anew, in short of Dionysus himself.

It is plain that this original Dionysian character must have been modified to some extent by the introduction of dialogue. However what had been lost by the time of Aeschylus' *The Persians* was a kind of crudity, in the sense that an embryo is crude. The true

Dionysian dynamism still informs the plays of Aeschylus and Sophocles, and is not quite transformed into Apollonian manipulation in Euripedes.

At one time, therefore, the spectators of tragedy themselves became Dionysian creatures and, as such, temporarily incapable of proper social activity. The Dionysian state cannot be sustained, since its continuance must entail bestial apathy or self-destruction. For people to act in the ordinary fashion of society it is necessary for them to be deluded. Nietzsche points out (throwing off sparks of insight) that such is the point of *Hamlet*. The prince cannot act, not because he is a dreamer but because he is anything but: he is without self-preserving dreams – about the honourable code of revenge, for instance, or the maidenly sweetness of Ophelia. Hamlet resembles Dionysian man in his 'nausea', his realisation that his actions cannot 'change anything in the eternal nature of things'.[21] Nietzsche does not, however, emphasize that Hamlet's brilliancy of mind is also Apollonian in the highest degree.

Hamlet is aware of the gulf between the unutterable truths of nature and the masks of culture. On the other hand, the purest tragedies are signposts to the heart of nature. Therein lies the power of Aeschylus and Sophocles. Watching their plays, a contemporary spectator was not so much wrestling with moral problems as half imagining himself changed into a Silenus-like figure. At least some of the sombre wisdom of Silenus had rubbed off on to him. He, the chorus and the actors were more or less merged, excluding workaday matters. But this flowing-together of human beings was only part of the story, for everyone present was touched with a religious sense of belonging, not to the crowd but to the world.

In contrast to this sense of merging, this melting of the boundaries of individuality, the diction of Aeschylus and Sophocles is precise and clear. By means of their words, nature, far from being imitated, is exposed and dissected. The celebrated 'Greek cheerfulness' (of which much was made in the nineteenth century) was not therefore simple lightness of heart. For example, Oedipus is the wretchedest man on earth and the Athenians 'cheerfully' observed his woes. It should go without saying that no sadism was involved: however much cruelty or aggression we might Freudianly suppose to lie behind the story of Oedipus, it has been completely sublimated in the Theban Plays of Sophocles. How, therefore, was a contemporary of Sophocles made cheerful by these dramas, and how is it that they have the same effect on us today?

The answer can best be approached in a roundabout way. Oedipus ends (at the close of *Oedipus at Colonus*) by being capable of blessing King Thesus and the kingdom of Athens. No one less afflicted than he could do this. That is Nietzsche's assertion, which we had better consider for a space, since it is very remarkable and also germane to the theme of this book.

Oedipus is unique, not just a sufferer but *the* human sufferer who has, so to speak, 'broken the code' of nature. He is the great lawbreaker too, since the laws against incest and patricide are grounded not in social preferences but in the very processes of animals and plants. Accordingly, pain is not just what Oedipus happens to undergo, nor is it somehow a 'fitting' punishment for his crimes. It is his destiny and his 'calling', as it were. Note: although Oedipus spreads a power of benediction, there is no suggestion here of the forgiveness of sins. There are no sins in anything resembling the biblical sense, and no forgiveness in that sense either.

Oedipus suffers on behalf of the Athenians (and perhaps, as it has turned out, for the sake of a wider humanity) but he is a purely fictional personage who, furthermore, never intended either to suffer or to redeem anyone. Christians believe that the Son of God was incarnated in order to redeem mankind from sin, which is to say from the mere process of living in this world, while on the other hand Oedipus completes the link between human beings and natural things.

Thus he annihilates the idea of sin. Nietzsche does not here draw attention to the utter discrepancy between the tragic and the Christian spirit, though it is important for us to bear this discrepancy in mind. Certainly this is much what Nietzsche meant when at the end of his career he closed *Ecce Homo* with the words '*Dionysus versus the Crucified*'.[22] Christ aimed to break the link which Sophocles, through Oedipus, contrived to celebrate.

Something similar must be said about the love of Oedipus. Having suffered hideously, he is able to love and bless *actuality*. Here there is no trace of yearning for a higher world or a generally better future, though Oedipus has naturally wished for an end to his particular woes. The future of Oedipus himself is the unending gloom of Hades. Almost his final message to his daughters, Antigone and Ismene, is (in the Loeb translation): '. . . one word / Wipes out all score of tribulations – *love*'.[23]

To appreciate this we must expunge the notion of a 'higher' love that seems almost to release the lover from fleshly ties and ultimately, as in Dante's 'Paradiso', outsoars the flesh. To Sophocles there is no loving God. The meaning of life, the truth (*aletheia*) is not love. Love has the following characteristics: it is involuntary rather than willed; it is a lasting bond between individuals, and it is *incidentally* a means of wiping out tribulations.

So Sophocles presents love as in part a consolation for sorrows, and it is clear that in a painless sphere, heaven itself, there could be no love. Our dream of celestial saturation in love is eternally impossible, and indeed nonsense to all eternity. The reason for this is that love is stimulated into being precisely by the conditions of life. It is not 'pure'. To Sophocles, love is quite other than Christian agape; neither is it eros. We should also remind ourselves that Sophocles is not remotely a prey to guilt, though he is acutely aware of injustice and cruelty. There is only torment decreed by the gods or the Fates and often produced by mortals. This might be lightened by a correlative quality of loyalty and affection which we call 'love'.

Yet sharing Sophocles' vision helped to make Athenians cheerful. The reason has grown steadily plainer and, despite some repetition, might now be summarised: each individual transcended his Apollonian individuality, not in the direction of a human community (the modern dream of Marxism and secularised Christianity) but by flowing outwards to the world as a whole. Thus the boundary was crossed between the human race and all natural processes. The boundary actually vanished, for it was purely manmade. So the Greeks in their tragic age looked for guidance to Apollo (through whose agency the boundary was erected), but they 'went home' at regular intervals to the fundamental realm of Dionysus.

The Birth of Tragedy is not in the usual sense a scholarly work but a refutation of scholarliness as a means of discovering origins. The origin of something usually lies beyond facts, documentation, empirical reason. Nietzsche admires science and some quasi-scientific procedures, yet does so with proper reservations. He certainly regards science as braver for modern people than caprice, wishful thinking and blind faith. However, value lies in courage, not in the truths that courage enables us to discover. What is termed the 'truth' about something, meaning a view of it that is at present irrefutable, is apparent in its make-up. For instance, the will that informs tragedy, that wears the mask of tragedy, is clear if we look closely at the mask.

If, alternatively, we look for facts about the beginnings of tragedy we shall find little more than hearsay. Aristotle says that tragedy 'certainly began in improvisations – as did also Comedy; the one originating with the authors of the Dithyramb, the other with those of phallic songs, which still survive as institutions in many of our cities'.[24] This is interesting and may well be true, but it is not proved by the standards of modern scholarship.

The arguments and the known facts about Nietzsche's views in relation to Greek studies are assembled in *Nietzsche on Tragedy* by M. S. Silk and J. P. Stern.[25] These authors are fair-minded about Nietzsche, yet as one would expect, give precedence to the solid work done since his day. They say that *The Birth of Tragedy* is a 'major contribution to the appreciation of ancient Greece . . .' because of its 'insights into the religious outlook before Socrates and . . . its elucidation of the spirit of tragedy'.[26] Towards the close of their study Silk and Stern remark that 'the brilliance *and* the exasperation of this extraordinary book stay with the reader to the end'.[27]

I suggest that a reader is liable to be exasperated as well as impressed by Nietzsche if, for professional or temperamental reasons, he is not in a position to give enough weight to Nietzsche's 'genealogical' method. To take the plainest example, *On the Genealogy of Morals* convincingly traces morality, as we understand the term, back to the slave revolt in morality that began among the Jews three to four thousand years ago. Yet clearly this is not a process that can be in any proper sense documented, and Nietzsche's own pieces of scholarship, amounting to four pages of etymological comment, rather casually support the case. The thrust of the argument is, once again, psychological. Our kind of morality springs from what Nietzsche famously calls *'ressentiment'*, a re-active, slavish pattern of feeling (even when it occurs in those who are officially masters).

Nietzsche's view of 'genealogy' is not confined to cultural, or even to human, movements. Rather it more generally involves tracking the forces that lurk behind perceptible events. A force is more or less successfully camouflaged by appearances, though it can be detected by one who reads back from the appearances: what drive thus finds its expression? Gilles Delleuze analyses this Nietzschean attitude in his *Nietzsche and Philosophy*, saying for instance that

> We will never find the sense of something (of a human, a biological or even a physical phenomenon) if we do not know the force which appropriates the thing, which exploits it, which takes possession of it or is expressed in it. A phenomenon is not an appearance or even an apparition but a sign, a symptom which finds its meaning in an existing force.'[28]

Let us note one striking example, which will later be shown to have a bearing on our theme of tragedy. In *The Anti-Christ* Nietzsche conjectures that the 'psychological type' of the redeemer may be perceptible in the Gospels, though none of the Evangelists understood the type. Jesus was repelled by every reality, by *reality as such*; consequently he created his own inner world which he called the 'kingdom of heaven'. His aversion was the result of an extreme capacity for suffering. So he denied the world, replacing it with a pure spirit of love. 'The fear of pain, even of the infinitely small in pain – *cannot* end otherwise than in a *religion of love.*'

The ground was prepared for Christ, as has so often been remarked, by the social circumstances of Galilee, expectations of the Messiah and the simple idea of heavenly bliss. But he poured into these existing conditions a new ideal of instantaneity: 'take therefore no thought for the morrow', and in this way (not in distant hopes) obliterated every pain. So Jesus soothed his own exquisite sensitiveness and this is the 'news', so to speak, that lies beneath the texts of the Gospels. This ultimate origin of Christianity is apparent even in the practices and pronouncements of the modern Church, although we cannot hope to find evidence for it of the sort that scholars require.

Conversely, if we look at the extant tragedies of Greece, we find, before Euripides, ritual celebrations of suffering. In Nietzsche's opinion the ritualistic element of tragedy was intolerable to the young Euripides. Watching the plays of Aeschylus and Sophocles this irreligious youth was above all puzzled. Nothing made sense; no effect had a proper cause, or at least the assigned cause was never properly investigated. The plays were religious mysteries and Euripides despised mystery; everything makes sense if you think about it. Some deeper analysis and a more developed dialectic should have accompanied Clytemnestra's murder of Agamemnon. Why wasn't the background of every play expounded at the beginning, so that everyone would understand the plot as it unfolded? Above all, the personages of the dramas should have better resembled actual persons, betraying little real-life preoccupations.

As a young man Euripides failed to understand that the early spirit of tragedy declared individuation to be the sole and inescapable cause of suffering. To be exact there are no separable causes and effects, since everything flows together. Nature is all one, a unity deified as Dionysus. Dionysus dies and is reborn, constantly. That is to say, parts of nature put out their little shoots, try to scamper away from the mass, and so suffer and die. The mass is not solid but composed of quivering elements. These absolutely belong with one another and with the whole, yet cannot help asserting themselves. Dionysus himself is a single god, though he appears in countless guises and dies countless deaths.

Prior to Thespis this Dionysian myth was fading, then Thespis introduced an actor into the performance and gave the myth what Nietzsche calls 'its most expressive form'.[30] At first classical tragedy was the resuscitation of a dying belief, and the belief recovered its strength as, for a few decades, it was more completely expressed than ever before.

Now Euripides came along as the new force, the new will. Naturally he assumed the mantle of tragedy, but for most of his career he scarcely believed in Dionysus. So far as Euripides was concerned the apparent was the real. Passions accompanied specific goals and frustrations, almost as if they were parts of a mechanism – however violent and unruly they appeared to be. Now everything was a matter of *comprehensible* human behaviour in relation to social customs. This might now seem to us to be common sense, because we are heirs of Euripides. Alternatively, Nietzsche implies that genuine (Dionysian) passion is scarcely understandable. When a dramatist appears to account for the feelings of a character he is foisting a bag of tricks on the spectators. People indeed copy the antics of fiction, but when, to the contrary, their feelings are whole-hearted they cannot even relieve them, let alone explain them, by theatrical gestures. As we shall see later, such genuine and mystifying passions are represented by Aeschylus and Sophocles, while Euripides, on the other hand, brings actions and emotions into the light of day, making them thoroughly accountable.

Nietzsche says to Euripides, or as it were, to his shade: 'And because you abandoned Dionysus, Apollo abandoned you.'[31] This is a subtler and more far-reaching observation than it seems at first. It implies that without the Dionysian base of our passions they become artificial. The feelings of Euripides' characters (even of Medea and Alcestis) are brilliantly coloured rather than real. Each set of emotions is a firework display well above the earth. A firework is more dazzling than a plant or a clump of ground yet it is only a device. Reality dwells in the tones of Aeschylus' Cassandra and Orestes, in those of Sophocles' Ajax, but Euripides contrives only 'copied, masked passions'.[32]

The psychology that we meet in Euripides is all too human and therefore comprehensively expounded. Medea 'knows her own mind', as we might say, and no mystery is left over. Human actions even of the most appalling or outlandish sort are quite consciously motivated. Euripides discarded instinct, replacing it with fully developed consciousness. The people of Euripides have clear reasons which can be, or in fact must be, clearly debated. Indeed, these characters have no other stimuli, and *no other being*, than the reasons they so lucidly express.

So the spectators of Euripides beheld upon the stage eloquent versions of persons like themselves. These were not religious but secular performances which in the course of time encouraged people to imagine that their own obscure emotions might be expounded. Such were the dramatist's objectives: to bring the spectator down to the orchestra, and provide him with motives. As we know, the spectators were not pleased by this development, since it was clear to them that Euripides was bent on destroying religion. He was denying Dionysus, not merely showing one or more of Dionysus' innumerable deaths (in the masks of the tragic personages) but striving to replace the god permanently with the god Apollo. Nietzsche's radical point is that Apollo cannot subsist without Dionysus: when we pretend that he can, we fail to write tragedies. Nietzsche means in the first place that tragedy proper cannot be purely Apollonian. But he also means that the notion of Apollo without Dionysus became, after the fifth century, the general human deviation. The attempt to exclude Dionysus is the basis of nihilism. Nihilism is not, as modern people often believe, just a denial of moral values; indeed these values are themselves potentially nihilistic. Nihilism is the denial of all fruitful meaning as an end result of trying to determine all meaning.

Towards the end of his career as a thinker (that is, a year before his insanity), Nietzsche wrote as follows:

What does nihilism mean? That the highest values devaluate themselves. The aim is lacking: 'Why' finds no answer.[33]

'Why' finds no answer because myth has capitulated to science, and science surveys only specific fields. In 'Schopenhauer as educator' Nietzsche makes these remarks:

Nowadays, however, the whole guild of the sciences is occupied in understanding the canvas and the paint but not the picture; one can say, indeed, that only he who has a clear view of the picture of life and existence as a whole can employ the individual sciences without harm to himself, for without such a regulatory total picture they are threads that nowhere come to an end and only render our life more confused and labyrinthine.[34]

In other places Nietzsche speaks as if the partial truth of any scientific discovery or law means that it amounts only to another human fable. At any rate the threads of the sciences go on and on through the labyrinth, endlessly leading nowhere. So there are now no reasons in the sense in which we are accustomed to think we need reasons. It is not a great exaggeration to say that pre-Euripideans already knew this, for their myths were grounded in obscurity. Certainly they did not ask for explanations beyond the tales of their gods and heroes, and these were a sort of dreadful pastimes, ending in disaster for some noteworthy people. The very pointlessness and injustice of sorrow were the qualities that people had never doubted.

It is clear enough that, in his day, citizens of Athens saw Euripides somewhat as Nietzsche sees him. The Euripides of Aristophanes' *The Frogs* (produced in the year after Euripides' death) calls Dionysus an 'idiot', boasts that he has made the drama democratic, and that he has turned contemporary problems into dramatic situations. His whole motive, he now claims, was to cause ordinary persons to question their lives. To this Nietzsche adds, in effect, that Euripides wanted the citizens to ask questions because he had not grasped the rhetorical nature of questioning. He failed to realise that our show of finding solutions gives us just a semblance of control. It is possible, for instance, that in our day someone has written a psychiatric treatise on Medea – as if this might help to 'cure' the Medea personality-type.

Euripides was not so highly regarded as his predecessors. He was contemptuous of the people, and, for a while, they of him. It is a backhanded compliment to Euripides that in *The Frogs* he is preferred to Aeschylus by the inhabitants of Hades, and the author, Aristophanes, allows Aeschylus to retain the Chair of Tragedy. Euripides' point of view, which seems to us to have favoured the ordinary spectator, was not that of the ordinary spectator. He was not in that spirit a 'democrat'. Nevertheless, he built his hopes, according to Nietzsche, on 'civic mediocrity'.[35] 'What strange consideration for the spectator', Nietzsche asks, 'led him to oppose the spectator?'[36] It seems that Euripides was desperately perverse; he first made to lead the people away from Dionysus and then, when they were beginning to be reconciled to the absence of the god, or at least to his derogation, wrote the *Bacchae* which *in terror* reaffirms the power of Dionysus.

The question here involves a distinction between what one is interested in and what one admires. We have a modern European example in Ibsen, who noticed mannerisms more closely than any other dramatist yet gave his regard to the hero who turns his back on society, such as Brand and, at the end, Rubek in *When We Dead Awaken*. Euripides produced no heroes in this fashion but for long enough gave his allegiance only to the power of criticism. Nietzsche puts this matter dramatically, though the observation is meant to be taken literally as well. He says that Euripides wrote for just two spectators: himself in his alternative capacity as critical observer, and the great contemporary dialectician, Socrates.

Socrates was not so much the inventor of the dialectic as the one who made it respectable, and even, by the manner of his death, heroic. Up to that time argument of the sort in which Socrates excelled had been considered ill-bred. Certainly no well-bred person would have undertaken to defend his way of life in the fashion that Socratic questioning required. Note that Nietzsche does not suppose Socrates to have defeated the spirit of tragedy by introducing 'thought' into the proceedings – as if no one before Socrates did any thinking. The author of *Philosophy in the Tragic Age of the Greeks* knew as well as anybody that Socrates was scarcely the first thinker. Nor of course did Nietzsche imagine Socrates, a hero at Potidaea, and a praiser of Achilles and other legendary heroes, to have been automatically opposed to the heroical, or the specifically tragical world-picture.

According to Nietzsche, the innovation of Socrates was to make dialectical reason itself into an heroic or admirable procedure. We might call him a 'martyr for truth', as others have done, if the word 'martyr', were not significantly misleading. The question remains: why did Socrates promote dialectical reasoning? As he makes plain in the *Apology*, such argumentation was his vocation, and he necessarily had to pursue it to the death. To have done otherwise would have been a deplorable self-betrayal. There would have been no Socratic influence upon the world, since there would have been comparatively little upon Plato, if Socrates had tried to grovel his way to an acquittal. In Socrates' view he was at most merely technically guilty, but not guilty at all in a moral sense, because his procedures were noble rather than sinful.

Nietzsche's idea is as follows. Once you question a set of values (the Homeric, the Jewish, the tragical, the Christian; it doesn't matter which) you begin to destroy them. *No values whatsoever can stand up to persistent questioning.* The spirit of science itself could not withstand severe interrogation by philosophy. Likewise it is by now fairly obvious that philosophy cannot retain its value in the face of scientific enquiry. It follows therefore that Socrates was one of the originators of the long process leading to modern nihilism. He yearned for truth, but failed to see (perhaps did not wish to see) that positive truth is not left over when the questioning has finished, for by that time nothing of consequence is left over.

It is important to remember that the Socrates we meet in the *Dialogues* is not a neutral investigator; that is just his mask. He uses words as weapons. The distinction is not between myth and poetry on the one hand and rational discussion on the other, since rational discussion, no less than the other, non-rational forms, is a mode of *will*.

Socrates probably did not set out to destroy tragedy, but his cast of mind was non-tragical. He wished to 'correct existence', as Nietzsche puts it. The Socrates of Plato is one who, on behalf of our race, judges existing beliefs, showing the faults in them. Despite the genuine respect for valour, there is no important criterion other than the intellectual: which belief can best be defended by skilful discourse? Socrates deliberately and famously makes no attempt to postulate another standard, such as 'value for life'. To him the best is not the healthiest or strongest, but that which can be most ably supported by argument. In other words, the processes of living, which include thought-processes, are subordinated to thought-processes; the whole is judged by one of its parts.

Therefore, let us not suppose even for a careless moment that Socrates was a champion of the wholesome against the constrictions and infidelities of society. Sometimes he appears to be that because he is scornful about liars and has robust appetites. Furthermore, he listened to his daemon, his non-rational inner voice which warned him against certain courses of action. So he sounds 'natural' enough.

Nietzsche has no doubt about the rebellious power of Socrates' instincts, and accordingly, in *Twilight of the Idols*, contends that no one whose instincts were not so strong as to threaten his reputation, his wellbeing and, possibly, his sanity, would have placed such emphasis upon reason. Or, to be more precise upon logic, since he displays a 'superfetation of the logical', as well as 'barbed malice'.[37] It is one thing to be logical and quite another to enthrone logic as Socrates did. Inwardly he was a chaos of warring passions; hence, because he was also prodigiously clever, he produced the formula, reason = virtue = happiness.

We must accept that Socrates was never the pure voice of intellect probing the deceptions of belief and custom. For this assumption presupposes that Socrates had no desire for power and no vengefulness. His public stance is unquestioned and we take his side because he has won. He is not supposed to have wanted power in any sense, merely because he did not want official or recognised power. We certainly should not doubt that he was a hero of the intellect and of character also, since he mastered himself so well. And, as we have noted, he was also a hero in the orthodox military way. For all that he wanted a different sort of person to rise up, his own essential sort, the 'theoretical man'. Nietzsche intends to bring home to us that the man of reason should not be accepted as the arbiter of our lives, since reason is no more than another type of combat. Not necessarily a better type, except on those occasions (such as occur even in the *Iliad*) when reason breaks a log jam of passions and is invigorating.

Often enough, however, reason takes us further from Silenus and the satyrs, from Dionysus, from creatures and plants and the superabundant earth. Principally it causes things to be classified together according to what is perceived to be their kind. This is a convenient, perhaps a necessary way of thinking, and one that increases our sense of control. But it leads to quasi-mechanistic assumptions and to the tendency to believe that behind perceptible things there are, in Plato's terminology, 'Forms'. Thus as Socrates argues in *The Republic*:

Then what about the man who recognises the existence of beautiful things, but does not believe in beauty itself, and is incapable of following anyone who wants to lead him to a knowledge of it? Is he awake, or merely dreaming?[38]

Glaucon's answer, of course, is that such a man is dreaming. This expected response leads in turn to the metaphysical assumption that underpins *The Republic*, namely that only the Forms, such as beauty, are real, because they do not die. Each single beautiful thing flourishes and dies; hence it seems to the Platonic cast of mind unreal. The opposite, tragic assumption is that the ephemeral is the real. More exactly, to Plato being is reality, while to the tragic thinker there is no reality outside the world of becoming. At the time of *The Republic* these two beliefs were poised against each other. On the Socratic–Platonic side was the new faith that reality, whatever it is, must forever survive intact. On the tragic side was the old myth that reality is Dionysus, endlessly dying and coming to life. Each masked figure, which is to say each phenomenon, is Dionysus, and reality is the 'flesh' or physical world. But Socrates follows neither Apollo nor Dionysus, taking ideas to be stages en route to the spiritual reality which is God. For Apollo, despite his property as the light-bearer, belongs to the tragic picture, while Socrates and his one God fall as a screen or shield between us and the ancient response to nature. The great contest is between Dionysus and the human wish to reform existence by means of righteousness or intellect. Today it seems that a long phase in that contest is drawing to a close.

2
Aeschylus

Nietzsche anticipates twentieth-century literary criticism, since he emphasises the distinction between a work of literature and the actual spheres of nature and society. He is not impressed by mimesis either as a principle of art or in the practice of individual artists. However, as we have remarked, he goes much further than that, contending that everyday life, no less than a piece of art, is to all intents and purposes a man-made structure, for we reduce life to the contours of our vision. That the world overwhelms these contours is the basis of tragedy. Further, Nietzsche is sure that the world as a whole is best understood as an assemblage of 'artistic' processes: 'the world as a work of art that gives birth to itself—'.[1]

Nietzsche suggests that 'one does best to separate an artist from his work, not taking him as seriously as his work'.[2] More than that, whatever an artist conceives and expresses must be other than his normal self: 'a Homer would not have created an Achilles nor a Goethe a Faust if Homer had been an Achilles or Goethe a Faust'.[3] When an author derives a character from his earlier self (Stephen Daedalus out of the young Joyce, Paul Morel from the younger Lawrence) he presumably creates a fresh character, even if there are many superficial – and not so superficial – correspondences. There is an elementary law at work here: the maker of something must be other than what he makes.

Despite similarities between Nietzsche's ideas and some latter-day assumptions, he, unlike many of our contemporaries, stresses the will of an artist as the cohesive and determining factor. Rather we should say that he never forgets that the product constitutes the author's will to power, so that any attempt to interpret it in another way is to work with unsuitable tools. When we accurately discern an author's will we do not submit to it, but, on the contrary, fend it off, or even cause it to submit to us, by holding aloft its own reflection. In discussing this matter we are not flirting with the 'intentional fallacy'. Nietzsche never cared what an artist's surface intentions were, but he did care about the goal of an artist's personality. This is what the work progressively reveals. The goal subsumes all mere intentions or makes them irrelevant, and is only dimly apparent to the artist himself, because it lies ahead of him and cannot be clearly foreseen.

To Nietzsche, therefore, such features as the tactical uses of language and the manipulations of myth are integrated by a force provided by the artist, or indeed a force which essentially *is* the artist, though, as a rule, it cannot be found in his biography. This attitude towards art is only foreshadowed in *The Birth of Tragedy* and is developed in later works; hence Greek scholars tend to overlook it. After *The Birth of Tragedy* art in general and the attitudes of individual artists are by implication seen as forming one class out of numberless universal procedures: all is will to power.

The tragic dramatist, then, came upon a scene composed of certain forms and values and infiltrated that scene until he had made it his own. In order to do this he needed not to reject the ways of his predecessors but to incorporate and amend them. The new dramatist took it upon himself to think and feel his way into the attitudes of other people: his immediate forbears, his rivals and the spectators. I do not mean that these attitudes were a set of questions to be answered, as in an examination, but that the dramatist alone knew when an attitude had ceased to puzzle him and so had been 'solved'. More than that, he would exercise the best kind of creative power to the extent that he assimilated the behaviour of evil or hostile people. For whatever is now rejected as wicked, or at least 'unacceptable', is that which must sooner or later find its way into the pattern of an artist or original thinker. Its inclusion contributes the modification of values which the creative individual sets out to create.

An artist's power is not publicly recognised; it is unperceived or patronised or misunderstood by contemporaries. Admittedly, artists like to be esteemed, and, according to Nietzsche, they shamelessly sought esteem in ancient Athens.

Artist's ambition. – The Greek artists, the tragedians for example, poetized in order to conquer; their whole art cannot be thought of apart from contest: Hesiod's good Eris, ambition, gave their genius its wings.[4]

Even so, it was one person's peculiar genius that was given wings:

one could not gain credit in one's own eyes by emulating others. Nevertheless some disguise, some camouflage was necessary, for one's naked meaning would have been too startling and objectionable.

Nietzsche thinks that genius is a notably specialised form of will to power. It is not a mysterious gift bestowed upon the infant at birth; it is certainly not genetic. He argues against the biologists that 'Life is not the adaptation of inner circumstances to outer ones, but will to power, which, working from within, incorporates and subdues more and more of that which is "outside" '.[5] For our present purposes here is as neat a defintion as can be found in Nietzsche. (It will not do equally well for all purposes.) Wagner, for example, set himself an exalted task and invented the means of carrying it out. Wagner's genius was not an innate quality from which his ambition sprang, but developed in tandem with the ambition.[6] So the artist takes the pieces of the world that interest him and builds them *as a process of self-definition, self-discovery and self-enlargement* into his art. We must remember that all artistic techniques from the starkest realism to the wildest fantasy are means of appropriating the environment. There is no question of copying for the sake of copying, no pure mimesis, and likewise no question of reproducing external 'truths'. Thus will to power, which in the words of the Nietzsche scholar, Richard Schacht, 'has the character of an ordering transformation',[7] is most ably exercised by the artist or the thinker. Such people transform pieces of nature into images or ideas which take their places in larger compositions – themselves determined as much by their authors' creative– transformative aims as by rules of structure. 'Imitation' is the wrong word to use for this procedure.

The narrative artist, for instance, more or less skilfully produces thin, contrived characters who, so Nietzsche says, 'are in no way living products of nature'.

> In reality we understand very little of an actual living person . . . There is much illusion involved in these created characters of the artists; they are in no way living products of nature, but, like painted people, a little too thin, they cannot endure inspection from close to.[8]

This extract from *Human, All Too Human* incidentally testifies to the different quality of the will to power of an artist from that of a man of action. Nietzsche apparently told Lou Salomé that men of action are harmonious and homogeneous; they suffer little internal conflict and use their powers of reason only so far as to assimilate the little that is necessary or favourable to themselves.[9] The thinker to the contrary, and it seems the artist as well, is the more pleased with himself the more he can take in. (A 'thinker' in this sense, is not necessarily an academic specialist.) The perceptions of this second type are numerous, diverse and, above all, conflicting. The artist Homer, has a more commodious will to power than a warrior of the kind of Achilles, since Homer readily, or even eagerly, acknowledges his awareness of the warrior, and by this means enlarges himself. Perhaps we can roundly say that poets, for example, according to their stature and accomplishments, have greater will to power than soldiers. Conversely, an 'Achilles', meaning some actual man-at-arms of the Bronze Age, could scarcely begin to assimilate Homer. Just the same, Homer's artistry and our admiration for it depends upon *his* admiring Achilles, as well as poetically mastering him.

This fact about the *Iliad* will serve, so it seems to me, to illustrate Nietzsche's remark: 'The will to power not a being, not a becoming, but a *pathos* . . .'.[10] The argument at this point in *The Will to Power* is to the effect that outside the field of mechanics (and Nietzsche believes mechanistic theory to be no more than a useful fiction) there are no things in nature, but only forces which affect others, or exercise power over them, to the extent that they are 'in a relation of tension to them'. The word 'pathos', in the above quotation means something like 'experience': the will to power is not primarily a matter of deeds, since it is felt rather than done. A pathos is 'suffered', though of course there may be a pathos of pleasure or joy. So will to power in the individual seems to consist somehow of highly organised impressionability. It is true that the epithet 'impressionable' is generally applied to those who absorb impressions too readily, as we suppose, lacking defences or self-assertion. Yet there is no other word for what I have in mind, namely the capacity, at its best, to receive multiple, finely discriminated impressions, thus enhancing oneself. For it is not possible to absorb impressions without moulding them, creating new patterns and an ever-growing self. This is why human beings are more powerful than lower animals, since animals, comparatively speaking, take in next to nothing, and harmonise the little they do take in in a correspondingly rudimentary way. A person exercises power to the extent that he or she receives imprints of the surrounding world, causing them to coalesce in a satisfactory design.

The organisation, the pressing into service of one's impressions is paramount and, except in madness, unavoidable. It is not always sensible to compare artists according to the number and variety of impressions they reproduce, since much depends upon the style of the artist's period. Shakespeare is the observer *par excellence*, but who knows how much Aeschylus managed to apprehend? The latter's objective was to mix the colours of his original impressions into a uniform tone.

The Aeschylean quality is obviously the result of compression. It is not single but multiple; nevertheless the multiplicity has been fairly thoroughly fused. If it were single the effect would be thin rather than rich. As it is, a slow drum beats throughout a play of Aeschylus and everything contributes to one end or 'doom'. In *The Persians* Poseidon, god of the sea, punishes Xerxes for bridging the Hellespont, and the Persian empire is desolate. We cannot tell how far in their daily lives the first spectators of this play felt triumphant and condescending towards their former enemies or, alternatively, how prone they were to shiver in awe whenever they recollected the might of Persia. Aeschylus seems to have ensured that the crowd carried away at most the residue of triumphant feelings. Nor is the play particularly moralistic: so lofty an aristocrat as Aeschylus would not have stooped to the pleasure of perceiving a *moral* lesson in an enemy's downfall. By our usual modern standards Xerxes simply aimed high in making his chain of boats across the Dardenelles, thus taking his vast army from Asia into Europe.

In the terms of Greek thought, the pride of Xerxes has unsurprisingly turned out to be a grave defect. The pride of course lies in the deed and is not a disposition prior to all deeds. Also, the pride must have been offensive to the god, since the Persians have been horribly beaten. It is the effect rather than the ambitious motive that conclusively proves the wrongness of the enterprise. The Greeks were still quite primitive in their modes of thought, which means that they had a great and superstitious dread of evil – meaning whatever causes harm. It was necessary to propitiate evil itself, as though evil (of all kinds, including a good many accidents) were a person, or had personality. Therefore one way of fighting against evil was to regard it as deserved. In general it was less threatening if it was merited. So Nietzsche writes that primitive people justified evil as punishment.[11] Such evil, for instance that of Xerxes, does not evince guilt. Or, to be precise, the word 'guilt' has also changed its meaning; obviously Xerxes is 'guilty' in the sense of owing a debt of shame, but he is not guilty in anything resembling the theological or damnable sense.

At some stage (perhaps even at the outset) Aeschylus began to detach himself from this traditional pattern of thought. He developed a somewhat Heraclitean belief to the effect that the keener one's desire and the more ardent one's pursuit of it, the greater the counterblow that must sooner or later fall. As Heraclitus says, 'It is hard to contend against one's heart's desire, for whatever it wishes to have it buys at the cost of soul'.[12] This seems to mean that while heart's desires are hard to resist, pursuing them destroys peace of mind. From our vantage point this is only a variant of the vulgar ethics but it is a sophisticated variant, especially when, as in the attitude to life of Aeschylus, high ambition is also seen as the best part of humanity. The most vital people are thus defined, even if they are, for the same reason, designated as evil or reckless.

Neither the popular nor the aristocratic idea is acceptable to us, for we see the first as superstitious and the second as disheartening or cynical. We also convert the hamartia of a Xerxes, for example, from its aspect as error of judgement to its aspect as moral flaw at the drop of a hat. At the same time we preserve a sharp distinction between the two. Nor in the present chapter have we reminded ourselves that mistakes and moral flaws were once brought together in a single category, since they were both signs of unwonted individuality. In *Daybreak* Nietzsche explains that

> Originally all education and care of health, marriage, cure of sickness, agriculture, war, speech and science, traffic with one another and with the gods belonged within the domain of morality: they demanded one observe prescriptions *without thinking of oneself* as an individual.[13]

Individuality was thus felt to be the root of both error and suffering. Xerxes separates himself from others, from humankind, in defying the god of the sea. Everyone knows that thousands of men cannot, with impunity, be transported across the Hellespont, that the sea cannot be 'chained'; therefore he who does this is a gambler to the point of lunacy. The shame of Xerxes implies behaviour that fifth-century Greeks found offensive because it was demonstrably offensive to Poseidon. We cannot view Xerxes in any way other than the tragic, for he has bound his life to a single fateful task. He is not exactly 'to blame' for this, for how could he be other than Xerxes? And how could he be other than ruined by the Fates through their divine agent, Poseidon?

Aeschylus all but confines himself to the tragic pattern and provides a comparatively brief chronicle of Salamis. The Messenger's speeches describing Salamis and Psyttalea, graphic though they are, scarcely change the tragic measure. These accounts would have been wonderfully exciting to the spectators (many of whom had fought in the battle only eight years earlier), yet the play moves on its course to the dialogues of Atossa, first with the ghost of Darius and then with her wretched, dishevelled son. It is instructive to seekers after the meaning of tragedy that Aeschylus has been able – effortlessly, it seems – to abandon his personal recollections of screams and smells, of hacked limbs and bodies piled high. Physical sensations, which contribute to our immediate experiences of the world around us, must be pushed to the edges of the mind before their significance can be grasped. It is the mind that grasps or, properly speaking, *invents* the significance. And the point about tragic meaning is that it remains tied to the earth, affirming that we are moments and fragments of an ever-changing world.

But what is the peculiar purpose of Aeschylus, since it is not panegyric, historical or conventionally doctrinal? Perhaps we had better mention something else that it is not: so far as we can judge, neither the dramatist's intention nor his main effect is catharsis of pity and terror. Although this psychological process incidentally occurs, Aeschylus sought something else, something in the strict sense *metaphysical*. That is why the play is also not a character-study, even to the small extent that the *Oresteia*, fourteen years later, may be so described. The figures of *The Persians* are less characters than embodiments of forces. Therefore when the first spectators had watched the play they were not so much purged of painful feelings as exhilarated and eager for life, in spite of pity and terror. For they were at that moment convinced of the inestimable value of living. Some of them, the most percipient, must have vaguely sensed what Aeschylus was then, in 472, beginning to teach: that human life has value because human beings can conceivably cast the dice along with the gods. Even today, if this attitude is fully grasped, it still seems amazing and sacrilegious.

Here it is necessary to proceed very carefully because the prejudices of the ages are against us. So, for that matter, is the immediately apparent meaning of *The Persians*. Xerxes has cast the dice and lost; the Greeks, who on this occasion were forced into gambling, have *on this occasion* won. Yet even that assertion is hackneyed and no more than partially true. Poseidon is a great god, but he too is subject to stronger universal forces. The gods themselves habitually lose as well as win; Zeus himself cannot control the Fates. In *The Libation-Bearers*, second play of the *Oresteia*, Electra says to her brother, Orestes, 'May Might and Justice, with Zeus the third, supreme over all, lend thee their aid.'[14] Either Zeus alone is supreme over all or Zeus, Might and Justice rule as a triumvirate. Might and Justice are certainly not regarded as mere attributes of Zeus, who is 'the third'; either Zeus is the senior partner or the three, the god and two qualities, are roughly equal partners. Zeus does not dominate over the Fates (*Moirai*), though they are his daughters. By the stage of Aeschylus' *Prometheus Bound* he cannot even compel, though he can constrain, the Titan Prometheus.

In the eyes of Aeschylus, Electra properly invokes Zeus, Might and Justice: it is not simply a dramatically functional or misguided invocation. It indicates Aeschylus' own criterion of hierarchy. Justice means satisfactory requital. Evil should be repaid with 'evil', but in such a way that human feelings are gratified. 'Might' of course means great efficacy. The interesting point is that Justice should have been placed alongside Zeus and his unparalleled (but not unlimited) powers, for this indicates that Aeschylus thus breaks with tradition to the significant extent of advocating, not recompense alone, but a sort of recompense that is felt to be fitting. Aeschylus himself requires Justice as a universal power and boldly casts his own dice, along with the gods.

This then is the will to power of Aeschylus, just coming into view at the time of *The Persians* and fully developed in *Prometheus Bound*. Aeschylus is his own Prometheus. But notice that by the date of the later play, when the aim of Aeschylus has been fully revealed, he expects Zeus to be his enemy, and the Fates to be whatever they arbitrarily choose to be. In short his power is self-created and self-proclaimed. He does not suppose that it will be ratified by other people and especially not by the powers that be. It is this gulf between the yearning of Aeschylus and the nature of things that makes him pre-eminently tragic.

In *The Persians* Xerxes, though cast down, is not censured. Aeschylus is neither magnanimous nor condescending towards the defeated enemy; on the contrary, he quite appreciates why the Persians sought to conquer Greece. Xerxes' outrageous conduct was not ignoble. The Ghost of Darius sees his son as the victim only of conceit and ignorance; no doubt the young man was led on by some mighty being. Atossa, the Queen Mother, feels maternal pity for Xerxes. The closing part of the play is an antiphonal exchange between Xerxes and the chorus of Persian Elders, each bewailing the miseries of Persia but neither imputing guilt. Xerxes assumes that the Fates have turned against him. There is nothing moral in all this, and Aeschylus, the Greek aristocrat who fought at Marathon and Salamis, accepts the downfall of Persia as the sort of thing done to aspiring mortals by higher beings. There are no sinful ones exactly but only struggling people, of whom Aeschylus bids fair to be champion.

He will be their champion purely in a Promethean fashion, out of pity for the human race but also as a means of gambling and creating along with the gods. Now, if one asks what, in a word, Aeschylus wished to create, the answer will plainly be 'Justice'. He wanted to replace the haphazard ways of fortune with coherent ways. If a person commits crimes, retribution should normally follow. On the other hand, sufferings should not befall innocent people. An eye for an eye, in other words, but not the kind of excessive or 'misplaced' catastrophe that people sometimes suffer.

To further his aim Aeschylus firmly and repeatedly puts Justice beside the god's gaming table as a prize to be won. Sometimes the fortunes of people will be felt to be deserved and this should be the unvarying pattern. At the conclusion of the *Oresteia* Aeschylus allows himself the supposition that the Eumenides have been permanently pacified, though, as *Prometheus Bound* suggests, this cannot have been more than a moment of exultation. Such triumph cannot last; no one knows this better than Aeschylus, whose pride and joy lie solely in his audacity of his endeavours. Here is his 'heart's desire', in the words of Heraclitus, for which he knowingly exchanges his peace of mind, or 'soul'.

It is readily possible to detect this motive in the selection by Aeschylus of the theme of the *Oresteia* from the dreadful and complex history of the house of Pelops. In its 'raw' state, so to speak, we have here a sequence of atrocious crimes, one begetting the next, and in truth it is hard to see how Aeschylus, or the most merciful modern humanitarian, could wish to intervene at any point to suspend the workings of retribution. For each crime *demands* retribution. That is, until the final murder has been committed by Orestes. The standard progressionist view of the trilogy is defined by Simon Goldhill as the dramatisation of an historical movement from the notion of justice as retribution to our notion of legal justice. Goldhill does not personally see the matter in this light, but later remarks that

> Tragedy's challenge is precisely to the sense of the secure and controlled expression of the order of things that for so many critics in their different ways has constituted the end of the *Oresteia*.[15]

These words point to the vital quality of tragedy, its controlled imitation of an uncontrollable universe. They also point to the characteristic modern error, for we should remember that modern people have a far greater sense of security than the ancient Greeks. All our talk about the frightfulness of contemporary life is still superficial, coming as it does after centuries dominated by the idea of progress. That is the idea which must be relegated before tragic philosophy can be understood and the tragic drama seen in something approaching its original religious light.

Aeschylus introduces into his sublimely dreadful world a sense of meaning which goes beyond the aesthetic and the mythical, but he is emphatically not a progressionist; he does not seek to get rid of suffering. At this point let us briefly recall the sequence of events of which the *Oresteia* is the conclusion. Tantalus killed his young son Pelops, and served him up as a meal to the gods. Pelops was brought back to life, grew to manhood and fathered Atreus and Thyestes. In due course Atreus set before his brother a dish containing the flesh of Thyestes' children. In consequence Thyestes cursed the house of Atreus. Thyestes then married his own daughter, from which union Aegisthus was born. Thyestes and Aegisthus, father and son, eventually contrived the death of Atreus. Subsequently Aegisthus became the lover of Clytemnestra after her husband Agamemnon, King of Mycenae, had sailed away to Troy. Agamemnon was the son of Atreus and had been marked out for further revenge by Aegisthus upon the family of Atreus. That Clytemnestra and Aegisthus have together plotted the murder of Agamemnon is the starting point of *Agamemnon* and the *Oresteia* trilogy. As for Clytemnestra, she has long waited to kill her husband only partly because she has taken a lover during Agamemnon's absence, but also because he sacrificed their daughter Iphigenia, in order to gain a favourable wind for the Argive ships.

Now the self-appointed task of Aeschylus is to bring this ghastly series to a just conclusion. He takes it upon himself to challenge even the gods and the Furies in order to present the spectators with what we, today, call a 'fair' outcome. 'Fair' means that no one properly feels aggrieved: what happens is what, taking everyone's natural feelings into account, 'should' happen. This attitude and this drive of Aeschylus explains why Clytemnestra is a fascinating rather than a repellent woman. Kitto calls her 'a woman of intellect and intellectual courage', but nevertheless, he says, she does not constitute a character-study.[16] We can readily agree with this. 'Intellectual courage' seems to be the right phrase, because, for all her *social* duplicity, Clytemnestra thinks straightforwardly. From the perspective of this play (though not elsewhere) she is superior to Agamemnon. He is majestic but deficient as a thinker, intellectually cumbersome. At the opening of *Agamemnon* the Watchman calls Clytemnestra a 'woman in sanguine heart and man in strength of purpose'.[17] In truth she is sanguine, or hopeful, since she confidently expects to determine her own destiny, and her strength of purpose is allied to an unusual capacity (unconnected with her gender) for cutting through the web of belief and custom. When the Chorus of Argive Elders suggests that Clytemnestra's news of the fall of Troy might have come to her in a dream, she rightly replies, 'I would not heed the fancies of a slumbering brain.'[18] Nor would she and yet, by some unexplained means, she has come to know of the events of Troy.

Clytemnestra' skill in the devices of persuasion is connected with her efficiency of perception: she is adept at exploiting the fancies she does not share. Her greetings, courtesies and the use of the purple carpet are a predator's contrivances and camouflage. In this regard she too, like the artist who conceived her, makes use of tradition and ideology for her own ends. I do not think that Aeschylus could have imagined his Clytemnestra except as a version (a degraded version, if you will) of his own contempt for the simpler forms of conventional belief.

In contrast, Agamemnon is kingly in the awe-inspiring style of the ancient world. For all his crime in killing Iphigenia (and his less than engaging conduct in the *Iliad*) he is thoroughly regal in outlook and accordingly one who implicitly believes in customs – even when he breaks them. The Queen is the creator here, the 'artist', while the King is a customary being. He genuinely respects the will of the people over such a matter as stepping on the purple tapestries; he does not wish to be envied overmuch by others and it is Clytemnestra who manipulatively remarks, 'True, yet he who is unenvied is unenviable.'[19]

Throughout *Agamemnon* the underlying conflict is between custom and accepted notions on the one side, and the individual will on the other. Cassandra, whom Agamemenon has taken as slave, is powerful – or, better, she is electrifying – because she sees through the devices and screens of social intercourse to the excoriated reality. Where everyone else observes manners and surfaces, Cassandra observes flesh, bones and palpitating organs. Her foresight is really penetration into the here and now. Likewise her sense of the past consists of hallucinatory images, precisely those images from the past whose reality is now determining events. Cassandra can 'see' (for she constantly visualises or otherwise hallucinates) the 'human shambles' of the house of Atreus. Coming to the palace at Argos and observing Clytemnestra, Cassandra knows that Agamemnon and she herself must join the row of butcher's-shop corpses. This is not a matter of probability, even of very great probability, for to Cassandra past, present and future are more or less indivisible. The house reeks of 'blood-dripping slaughter' before blood has been shed.

Cassandra is a mortal and horrified herald of the immortal Fates. On the other hand, the Chorus is comprised of the sort of people who merely and sorrowfully receive such messages as Cassandra's: there is nothing to be done. Here is the uncreative response which Aeschylus himself, the Promethean, surpasses. Certainly Agamemnon must now, in the words of the Chorus, 'pay the penalty for the blood shed by others before him, and by dying for the dead . . . bring to pass retribution of other deaths . . .'[20] (the other deaths will be those of Clytemnestra and Aegisthus.) Here the Chorus correctly refers to the workings of the Fates, the fundamental fact of life which Aeschylus will in due course (in the *Eumenides*) contest. He will contest it, not in the regular modern sense of trying to alter it (as if it were no more than an idea), but as one copes with an unalterable natural force. The Chorus, as a conventional group, can see no way but resignation, while Aeschylus, as a unique creative being, wishes to defy tradition and experience on this very score. Meanwhile, however, Clytemnestra is a force in the hitherto uncontested proceedings of the Fates, yet she is a clear-sighted force, not clairvoyant like Cassandra but percipient in everything pertaining to her will. Clytemnestra is nothing but will, while Cassandra is virtually without will, and therefore scarcely possible as a realistic figure, acceptable only as a (terrible) fantasy.

Clytemnestra finally tells the unutterably horrified Chorus that she glories in her deed. All her linguistic tactics are thrown aside now, as she proudly proclaims herself to be an agent of 'Justice', meaning Ate, the Avenging Spirit. She notes with scorn that the Chorus, for want of better thought processes, manages to blame Helen even for these latest murders. The Chorus thus consists of the sort of men, common enough in our day, who hold people responsible for events such people could not have anticipated, let alone caused. How is it possible for us not to see that Aeschylus stands behind Clytemnestra rather than the pieties of his time? Clytemnestra acted, she says, to avenge Iphigenia; Agamemnon deserved to die, but the Chorus cannot appreciate that anyone, any mortal soul, can act without at least desiring the approval of society.

Aeschylus himself, creator of Clytemnestra, stands behind and above her. She has a narrower vision than he, of course, since he appreciates both the justification of her deed *and the narrowness of that justification*. Thus Aeschylus has greater will to power than he represents in the figure of Clytemnestra. Nevertheless she proceeds from within him and is not an alien creature acting out a morality, or a devilment, to which he is opposed.

It is important to see this matter rightly: Aeschylus has the genius to understand Clytemnestra as the gods, and more especially, the Fates, do not. The latter, who rule the world, are quite without the human power of understanding and Aeschylus does not regard the gods as his superiors in power of assessment of motives and meanings. Apollo himself plainly cannot possess shrewder psychological insight than Aeschylus. Neither can Athena. The knowledge of Aeschylus provides the basis for his own, as opposed to supramundane criteria of justice. In other words, Aeschylus attempts to subject both gods and human beings to his conception of justice. He is arrogant enough to say to the gods that he knows better than they. He does not expect the gods to yield to him, for they are stronger than he, but as a brave and clever man, he can do nothing other than propose – or rather, postulate – his more discriminating and therefore more just mode of justice. Further, Aeschylus sets out to fashion people, dramatic figures, who shall be judged by him and by this means he will make an Aeschylean sphere within the Dionysian world. Certainly he will suffer for this, but what of it? What else is there for him to do? As soon as human beings realise they are cleverer than the gods, they are obliged to prefer their own opinions.

Nevertheless, in the opinion of Aeschylus Clytemnestra must incur the penalty due to her. He cannot find a good reason to exonerate her. Aeschylus is her creator and judge; so he both understands and punishes her – through the medium of Orestes. Clytemnestra in her pitiless audacity has assumed that she may choose her deeds and their consequences. Certainly we must not view her murder of Agamemnon in the light of a modern society governed by a body of laws. In theory she might readily escape the consequences of her crime, for she is the Queen. But she has a nightmare in which she gives birth to a serpent and, as she suckles this frightful offspring it draws clotted blood rather than milk from her breast. Now Clytemnestra fears she cannot escape. Even so, she sends her daughter Electra, and servants with libations to Agamemnon's tomb in the hope that the spirit of Agamemnon might be placated.

In *The Libation-Bearers* Clytemnestra has dwindled almost to a nonentity beside the potent figure of *Agamemnon*. Likewise, she is now, just before her death, of little consequence or worth in comparison with the shade of Clytemnestra who scorns the Furies in the third play of the trilogy. Here, however, she is still cunning, as in her reception of the false tale of Orestes' death, but for the most part she is simply a woman in terror of her son Orestes, come to murder her. When Orestes has done the deed, the Chorus praises him, but he must flee, for behind the figure of the Chorus he can see the Eumenides determined to pursue him to the end.

Once again Aeschylus means that the mere success of one's enterprise is neither here nor there; 'the balanced scale of Justice', as the Chorus terms it,[21] takes no account of success. But this is still the old Justice of vengeance, mere reaction against a deed, having no regard for the intrinsic quality of the deed. Everyone assumes that blood spilled in murder pollutes the scene, giving rise to yet another murder. The problem for Aeschylus, as the *Eumenides* begins, is how to distinguish in terms of value between one murder and another, how to replace the old culture of actions breeding crude reactions to all eternity with a new culture in which a nicely comprehended action meets with a nicely matched response. That is Aeschylean Justice, human justice, which no forces in the world other than human beings could ever invent, because no others have the same intelligence. As we have suggested, Aeschylus expects that in trying to establish this human sort of justice people must be followers or imitators of the tortured Prometheus.

The murder of Clytemnestra by Orestes is different in kind from Agamemnon's murder by her. We can all see that, yet in the twentieth century we have advanced but little towards the notion, not of two degrees of murder (which is still too rough and ready), but of many gradations of murder from the utterly base to the wholly justified.

To be still more exact, each murder should be judged on its peculiar merits. But then, so should every piece of human behaviour; that is the Justice for which Aeschylus is distantly reaching. The argument of the *Eumenides* ('argument' both as theme and proposition) amounts to a human demand that the Furies cast off their foul forms, change their malevolent natures, and, as it were, come over to the human camp. At the outset of this play, Orestes, the matricide, is a suppliant at Apollo's shrine, and the Eumenides are asleep, exhausted, in front of him – between him and the spectators. At the end they are 'venerable goddesses' escorted in a torchlight procession to their subterranean home.

Soon after the opening of the drama the Ghost of Clytemnestra appears and rails at the Erineyes until they awake. They in turn now upbraid Apollo for seeking to save Orestes. These introductory events quickly lead to the trial of Orestes, complete with jury appointed by the calm and wise Athena. Apollo is Orestes' advocate, though he is also the witness for the defence, acknowledging that he incited Orestes to kill Clytemnestra. This amounts to saying that human beings, despite their highest wisdom and deepest soul-searching, cannot see anything wrong with the murder. Apollo wished it to take place, the god of light encouraged it. Yet how can Aeschylus find an argument for this? The reasoning he gives to Apollo is scarcely watertight and has often enough been seen by modern critics as absurd. In truth this is not a dialectical matter and cannot be reduced to dialectics. There is a discrepancy between our powers of perception and our powers of analysis. At one extreme there are the loathsome Eumenides, who have no judicious capacity to distinguish cases; they are age-old, traditional, hate-filled and vengeful. At the other extreme we note the desire of Aeschylus that retribution should be in harmony with knowledge. Our feelings about Orestes have yet to be scrutinised and defined. He has 'done wrong', but somehow he has not done wrong at all. The vision of the most far-seeing people always outstrips the range of knowledge in their day, hence it outstrips the possibilities of argument. But at this point in *The Eumenides* we are faced with a matter which, perhaps, will always outstrip argument, so long as argument relates individual cases to general rules. It is the general rules themselves which are misplaced; can we ever dispense with them? At any rate, Aeschylus aspires to replace rules with a fresh, creative, non-dialectical, *Promethean* vision of life.

Still the war is between human beings, who must be defined as clever natural forces, and other natural forces which are powerful though blind. It is not that we are 'objectively speaking' superior; we are not actually lords of creation or – after the teaching of Shaw and others – pioneers of the process of evolution. All these are modern ideas and therefore qualified, limited, *wrong* ideas. We are simply gifted with quick, ranging, symbolising minds and cannot help expecting deeds and consequences to match.

Here we come to what I prefer to regard as the culmination of Aeschylus' development. I say 'prefer to regard', because while we know that the *Oresteia* was first performed in 458, two years before the author's death, we do not know whether the play we shall presently consider, *Prometheus Bound*, was produced before or after the *Oresteia*. This matter has been thoroughly discussed by scholars and, anyhow, can only be pondered in relation to one's understanding of the Aeschylean will to power. It all depends upon whether one thinks the attitude to life in *Prometheus Bound* is more or less ripe, *as an expression of Aeschylus' will*, than the attitude in the *Oresteia*. Regrettably, this question is often confused with the question of development in dramatic skill. As most will agree, the *Oresteia* is a technically more remarkable work than the *Prometheus*. Thus the former seems to be the 'cleverer' play, but this is to regard drama predominantly as technique, as if, for instance, *The Master Builder* 'ought' to come after *When We Dead Awaken*.

On the other hand, one theme of this chapter is that Aeschylus should be seen as progressively breaking free of old ideas, old pieties. Above all I am sure that we should not imagine an Aeschylus who entertained ideas and attitudes largely for the sake of their dramatic use. For that would be to grant him only malleable ideas, while contemporaries insisted that he was a sternly religious man. No one thought him conventional and he angered people by profaning sacred rites, but he was supposed to possess an exceptionally religious temper.

'Art is feebler far than Necessity', Prometheus tells the Chorus of the Daughters of Oceanus.[22] Here the word art (*techne*), means all human skills, and by extension, animal skills as well. Prometheus means that no devising by creature or god can take precedence over Necessity. All beings, all worldly forces are subject to Necessity. The latter is enforced, Prometheus states, by the Fates and the Furies. Enthroned above Olympus are the Fates: all that happens is in accordance with their will, administered by the Furies.

To make the point once again, this is not just a theatrically appropriate sentiment, but what Aeschylus must personally have believed with deeper certainty than many of his contemporaries. But how may we express the belief in twentieth-century terms? A useful way of putting it would be to say that everything develops according to its nature as part of an endlessly moving whole. Development includes decay. The Necessity of which Aeschylus has Prometheus speak is a law of being, or rather, of becoming. In the strangely metaphysical sense in which the words are often understood, there is neither freedom nor unfreedom, for what one 'freely' chooses to do is simply an inclination which arises prior to the processes of deliberation. Things and especially animals may be said to be free to be themselves, but really the term 'free', is not very sensible here. People evade or falsify themselves, though in this connection too, the concept of freedom seems inappropriate. It is simpler and better to say that people either persist in their own line of growth or copy the prevailing pattern – even in respect of memories and desires. However one's line of growth cannot be selected from a range of options, since it is original, new to the world. According to Nietzsche, it is a 'law that every man is a unique miracle . . . uniquely himself to every last movement of his muscles . . .'.[23] Here is not the place to promote a discussion about this particular point which, in any event, will probably command widespread *theoretical* agreement, but to stress that each such 'unique miracle' is, so to speak, 'given' and is not subject to freedom of choice. No doubt it would be accurate, though possibly misleading, to speak of 'predetermination', indicating that such fundamental character is settled before the processes of social and conscious determination begin. What we must note at this stage is that for Nietzsche 'choice' is, on the one hand, insignificant (a choice of tie to wear, of chocolate from a box, of drink at a bar) and on the other hand, when significant, already determined by one's unconscious and basically somatic make-up. The rest is a priestly fiction designed to make people feel guilty and utterly responsible for their actions.

The will itself is a myth, if by 'will' we mean a unitary mental agent. Nietzsche states that 'the will is not only a complex of sensation and thinking, but it is above all an *affect*, and specifically the affect of the command'.[24] He also remarks that 'in all willing there is, first, a plurality of sensations, namely, the sensation of the state *"away from which"*, the sensation of the state *"towards which"* . . . and then also an accompanying muscular sensation . . .'.[25] If this complex is indeed the so-called will, it follows that the will of Aeschylus to write plays, and not only plays but exactly *his* plays rather than others, is neither free nor constrained in the usual sense of these words. On the other hand, the Aeschylean will is one sign or instance of what the dramatist calls Necessity.

And this small piece of Necessity must clash with other pieces, hence tragedy and the tragic world-picture. The Necessity of Prometheus unavoidably collides with that of Zeus, or, to speak generally, the whole, the World, is an endless contrariety of wills and that *fact* is the comprehensive Necessity which governs all things.

We are urged, though not compelled, to believe that under the rule of Necessity evolutionary improvements have taken place. Likewise we tend to assume that homo sapiens might, centuries hence, conquer all vicissitudes except death. A few people are so intoxicated with scientific advances that they contemplate (rather shamefacedly as yet) the conquest of death itself. Now at this point, before we comment upon *Prometheus Bound*, it is necessary to mention Nietzsche's view of progress. On the one hand, he thinks, there is progress of a sort, but on the other hand there is no progress in our usual sense.

Man represents no progress over the animal: the civilised tenderfoot is an abortion compared to the Arab and the Corsican; the Chinese is a more successful type, namely more durable, than the European.[26]

In other words, species and subdivisions of species each have their own perfection and limitations. The better members of the human species do not come later than the earlier and homo sapiens is not a better sort of ape. For all that, it is undoubtedly a progress that people no longer have to go in dread of wild animals and that, according to Nietzsche's own interpretation of Aeschylus, people will push aside the Olympian gods, even as those gods disposed of the Titans. At the time of *Prometheus Bound*, namely 'mythical', the grand enemy is seen by Aeschylus to be Zeus, who is immensely powerful, cunning and full of rancour towards the human race.

What is really happening here? The answer is that human beings have split their own talents and proclivities into two classes. In the first class we have placed all the elevated qualities, meaning not virtues but impulses of power, of command. These have thus been deified, becoming, for example, Athena or Apollo. The Olympians are ourselves writ large with impotent elements subtracted. Not only that, but whenever a 'mere' mortal is seized by an overmastering impulse he or she ascribes the source of the impulse to a god, and so the gods are repositories and symbols of our fateful urges, for good or ill. Further, since human beings are continually at the mercy of natural forces, these forces are often agencies or expressions of the wills of gods. All this amounts to saying that what remains when passion and grandeur have been taken from mortals is an impoverished humanity. The procedure testifies to the shame and modesty of our forefathers, for they disowned their own impressive powers. The modesty was in turn a product of fear, for, as Nietzsche convincingly states, 'man has not dared to credit himself with all his strong and surprising impulses'.[27]

Now Aeschylus in his pursuit of Justice has grown aware that Zeus – and accordingly every lesser god – must be opposed whenever Justice is denied. He, the tragic poet, sees further and more subtly than Zeus. Aeschylus cannot, however, straightforwardly acknowledge his superior vision and so he ascribes it to the Titan, Prometheus. Prometheus can openly oppose Zeus, and must do so, since that is his *raison d'être*.

Yet there is far more to this question than we have so far discussed, for the unparalleled capacities of the human race require explanation. How has it come about that people use language and by this means make finer distinctions than other animals? Language also enables us to store and bequeath our knowledge. Thus we collate the evidence of our senses and erect structures of understanding. That the structures might topple is neither here nor there, since each serves its purpose for generations. Similarly we have devised numbers and can calculate quantities. We have also discovered or concocted medicines and have built societies and whole epochs upon the skilful use of metals.

These unequalled achievements (and I am speaking only of developments to the fifth century B.C.) may not be attributed to human genius, because any talk or even thought along such lines invites the blows of the Fates and the derisive anger of the gods. Even as late as the Renaissance, human ingenuity had to be given a Mephistophelean source and to this day is commonly justified on the grounds that it benefits the human race. But an overlap is suddenly visible; we have now begun to discard justification also, only to find ourselves in danger of extinction. This is the extreme case of what the ancients meant by the Fates (the always-concealed, always-to-be-dreaded consequences). And yet Aeschylus never seems to say 'Hold back'. He is fascinated by our possibilities, knowing, *tragically*, that they lead to vile things as well as good. To Aeschylus and his contemporaries it was clear that we could not possibly have done what we had done unless we were helped by a figure both superhuman and tortured beyond human endurance. Prometheus is this figure, the Titan who still sympathises with our predicament and once stole fire from heaven so that we might realise our potentialities. It cannot be stressed too strongly that Aeschylus (like Heraclitus) already knew this to be a dangerous, if exhilarating, course.

Let us carefully consider the early psychology of human inventiveness. The creative genius of individuals was disavowed and was able to function only on that condition. In the course of time, among the Greeks, the source of all genius was named: Prometheus, meaning 'forethought'. Possibly this suggests that the root of our capacities lies in the ability to anticipate and make plans, including the power of hypothesising. Leaving that aside, the point is that our most remarkable gifts are allocated to Prometheus. In fact Prometheus is ourselves at best. But this 'at best' includes the hideous tortures as well as the forethought. Thus is crystallised man's sense of being 'up against it', the essential feeling of opposition to one's self without which, it seems, no human creation would take place. That Prometheus in Aeschylus' drama has an *unseen* antagonist perfectly represents this aspect of the human condition, for the opposition which people detect takes an infinite number of forms and is therefore virtually without form, the nearest thing to an essence. But here comes the most intriguing fact of all:

the antagonist, Zeus, is also a projection of homo sapiens: *naturally*, for what else could he be? Prometheus is our creative power, while Zeus is our apprehension, not of the universe 'as such', but of a synthesis of all universal forces, which seems to us – to our inescapably egoistic minds – to exist for the express purpose of arousing our creative zeal.

When Aeschylus writes a play, exerting himself against not merely local, social difficulties but an image of sovereign power, he gives that image the character of injustice. The superiority of Prometheus over Zeus means our mortal superiority over Zeus, and this in turn may be defined as the superiority of human intelligence over other modes of power. This superiority lies in forethought, in the capacity to bring plans to fruition. Zeus himself lacks forethought, hence the astounding contempt of Prometheus, which is to say Aeschlyus, for the god of gods. Prometheus declares that Zeus has 'empty-headed purposes',[28] and these shall be his undoing. Specifically, Zeus will make one of his characteristically lustful and mindless matings and produce an offspring who will overthrow the father; that is the secret Prometheus jealously guards. Prometheus prophesies that one day '. . . he shall at last come into bond and amity with me, eager no less to welcome him'.[29] In brief, human beings will sooner or later gain god-like capacities. Alternatively, people will realise the abilities that were always potentially theirs. Aeschylus himself cannot see so far ahead, but I suggest that we may agree with Nietzsche when, in *The Birth of Tragedy*, he contends that Aeschylus offers an 'intimation of the twilight of the gods'.[30]

Prometheus Bound is a profoundly serious play with a greatly suffering hero, therefore a tragedy. But there is more to its tragical nature than that, for it emphasises as no other work of literature before or since that god-like powers do not bring relief from sorrow. Aeschylus proclaims that distant posterity will, like himself, welcome the talents and the sorrow. Prometheus gave us 'blind hopes',[31] by which means we alone, of all the world, project our designs into the future and gloss over the rational calculations that would destroy our hopes. In other words, if we do not survive it will be through excess of zeal, not rational despair. The quality of an experience, or its affective tone, is always different from what we expected, sometimes bitterly so. And there are always additional, unforeseen consequences, for people as for the Olympian gods. In this exact way Aeschylus predicts that we shall one day live and suffer like gods – beneath the sway of Necessity.

3

Sophocles

In *The Birth of Tragedy* Nietzsche draws the following contrast between Aeschylus and Sophocles:

> The splendid 'ability' of the great genius for which even eternal suffering is a slight price, the stern pride of the *artist* – that is the content of Aeschylus' poem, while Sophocles in his *Oedipus* sounds as a prelude the *holy man's* song of triumph.[1]

We have come to understand the artist's pride of Aeschylus but perhaps it will be harder to apprehend Sophocles or his Oedipus as a holy man. At the time of his death Oedipus reaches a state which might be described as 'holy', and Sophocles is reputed to have possessed a generous and lovable nature – though that is a far cry from holiness. As for Nietzsche himself, when he refers to holiness he usually does so with disdain and even downright hostility. In *The Anti-Christ*, for example, he calls it an 'idiot-fanatic' condition.[2] Similarly in *The Case of Wagner* he mentions his ambivalence towards *Parsifal*, which opera, he maintains, is a stroke of genius and degenerate also, because of its moral and religious absurdities, in a word, because of its holiness. Nietzsche says that the holy ideal is the higher value for the masses, even as philosophy represents higher values for the few.

It is not that Nietzsche changed his mind on this score between *The Birth of Tragedy* and the later works, but rather that he recognised a certain supreme quality among the Greeks which he, the classical philologist, chose to call 'holiness'. Nietzsche was then still under Schopenhauer's spell to some degree, yet at the same time he perversely adapted one of Schopenhauer's cardinal terms. Section 49 of *Beyond Good and Evil* (1886) begins as follows:

> What is amazing about the religiosity of the ancient Greeks is the enormous abundance of gratitude it exudes: it is a very noble type of man that confronts nature and life in *this* way.[3]

Presumably this capacity for gratitude is connected with the holiness that Nietzsche in *The Birth of Tragedy* attributes to Sophocles and Oedipus. It is utterly distinct from Schopenhauerian holiness which, as the loftiest stage of human development, is composed of asceticism, self-surrender, renunciation of the world and repression of the instincts. Thus on the one hand Nietzsche eagerly discovers a life-affirming Sophocles, while on the other hand he remains somewhat under the influence of a philosopher who reserves his highest praise for those who manage, through virtue, to 'outgrow' the world. We can be sure, also, that Nietzsche has already detected in the New Testament hatred of the world masquerading as love of humanity.

We need to recognise the strangeness and novelty of Nietzsche's valuation of the Oedipus plays. Further, if the attitude to life of Sophocles is accurately represented, Nietzsche also hints at a fresh philosophic corollary of that attitude. At the time of his death Oedipus (in *Oedipus at Colonus*) becomes a mystic benefactor to the kingdom of Athens, and this final development is completed off stage, being reported by the Messenger. It is the consummation of a life of error and crime. Apparently Sophocles, in his nineties, came to see the life of Oedipus as the perfect soil in which the gift of benefaction might grow. And this benefaction is quite different from seemingly similar deeds in the lives of the Christian saints. The difference has been obvious enough down the centuries, but, so far as I know, no one has dwelt on it with the object of emphasising the conflict between the spirit of tragedy and the sphere of Christian or 'post-Christian' ethics.

At this preliminary stage it will be best if we try to explain why the manner of Oedipus' death (as the fruit of his life) constitutes a 'song of triumph' and a 'prelude'. I suspect Nietzsche means that Oedipus is the first figure in Western literature to come to terms with nature, to 'conquer nature', as it were, through the sheer holiness of his mature temperament. This affirmatory sort of holiness has little or nothing to do with goodness, since Oedipus, far from forgiving his enemies, curses his son Polyneices, consigning him to Tartarus. Not only that, but we must also note that Nietzsche implies, as early as *The Birth of Tragedy*, that holiness is not an escape from this competitive world but another avenue of triumph. The holy man too aims to conquer – though in a most remarkable way. In fact the time is overdue when I should try to define this divine quality: it is the capacity to acknowledge one's assimilation to a *divinely material* world and, correlatively, to relish one's unique destiny. That is to say: materiality is not 'mere' materiality, but, on the contrary, is to be venerated in its own right. Therefore the holy person treats himself and all things as sacred, but he is careless about customs and creeds. Holiness is an exceedingly rare kind of nobility; one is above society but still no more than a natural force.

Nietzsche certainly means something 'beyond good and evil', something supramoral and possibly nihilistic in a specific sense. A highly noble person cannot be concerned with moral praise or blame. This is exactly the tendency of Sophocles' work, not just of the Oedipus plays. All the plays are *nobly* non-moral. Everyone is forgiven in Sophocles, or, rather, they are conspicuously not forgiven because they are not held responsible in the first place. Sophocles 'redeems the world'; he does not set out to correct existence (the usual tendency of authors great and small) but to redeem it. Now here we come to the striking fact about Sophocles, which Nietzsche suggests but typically omits to labour: this ancient Greek poet redeems our world *without reference to any other world*. The divine principle is in no sense apart from or opposed to the frightfulness of nature. Sophocles 'perceives God' (as we might say) precisely by gauging the abyss of nature. God is purely a response to nature and is neither an overlord nor a promise. He is a compensation certainly, but a completely natural, non-ideal compensation, rather as shade compensates for the glare of the sun. Above all, there is no suggestion that death, or life after death, is preferable to life. In short the Sophoclean redemptive quality is different at its roots from the Christian variety, though here and there in Christian culture (for instance in the paintings of Raphael) we see a like reverence for the natural world. Sophocles, who was born nearly seventy years before Plato, is, from our point of view, thoroughly 'anti-Platonic'; that is the fundamental point.

The phrase 'redeem the world' is taken from Nietzsche's *Twilight of the Idols*, in which context, however, the author is commenting not upon the noble ethos but upon the task of modern philosophers. They must emphasise the '*innocence* of becoming', bringing home to their readers that an individual is an extricable part of the whole, in exactly his present form. The innocence of which Nietzsche speaks is blamelessness: blame is seen as an obsolescent device. So one link between *The Birth of Tragedy* and *Twilight of the Idols*, sixteen years apart, is the view that morality must be surpassed. Innocence, holiness and the highest nobility are closely allied qualities and might in the end be one quality. In *Twilight of the Idols* Nietzsche declares that no one is accountable and this is the insight earlier ascribed to Sophocles.

> One is necessary, one is a piece of fate, one belongs to the whole, one *is* the whole – there exists nothing which could judge, measure, compare, condemn our being, for that would be to judge, measure, compare, condemn the whole. . . . *But nothing exists apart from the whole!* – That no one is any longer made accountable, that the kind of being manifested cannot be traced back to a *causa prima*, that the world is a unity neither as sensorium nor as 'spirit', *this alone is the great liberation* – thus alone is the *innocence* of becoming restored. . . . The concept 'God' has hitherto been the greatest *objection* to existence. . . . We deny God; in denying God, we deny accountability: only by doing *that* do we redeem the world.[4]

Naturally Sophocles did not deny God, but he came as near to doing so as his theistic or polytheistic age permitted, for he denied accountability far more thoroughly than we do even today. Nietzsche implies that while modern people hold one another socially accountable at every end and turn, these are purely herd inclinations. Few now believe they are *truly* accountable to God, or to the universal order. Our relatively sophisticated argument is that the human mind itself necessarily constitutes or contains a moral arbiter, but this is certainly a last-ditch position for moralists.

The key to the above comments of Nietzsche seems to be the word 'fatality'. 'The fatality of his nature cannot be disentangled from the fatality of all that which has been and will be.' The idea is associated with the formula *amor fati*, as that is defined in *Ecce Homo*.

> My formula for greatness in a human being is *amor fati*: that one wants nothing to be different, not forward, not backward, not in all eternity. Not merely bear what is necessary, still less conceal it – all idealism is mendaciousness in the face of what is necessary – but *love* it.[5]

So in *Twilight of the Idols*, written (in 1888) a few months before *Ecce Homo*, Nietzsche indicates the real nature of the world, namely a vast interplay of forces and processes. Next, in *Ecce Homo* he states that his formula for greatness in a human being is the ability to accept the world's real nature. Rather, the great human being *loves* what is necessary – what is eternally necessary. 'He *is* in the whole' and can have no separate being. Our regular mental dodge is to accept such an existential observation in theory but then to speak and act in defiance of it. We still fancy that most of the facts of our lives were not strictly necessary to our development (we say 'If I had been born ten years later . . .'). Nietzsche is sure, to the contrary, that one is a chance collision of worldly events which could not have happened otherwise, even in respect of the smallest detail, and (notwithstanding a questionable interpretation of eternal return) will never happen again. Conversely, each action I perform ultimately affects everything else in the world. Every deed entails consequences which in turn entail others, and so on to infinity. Hence tragedy, which lies in the illimitable interconnectedness of things.

The natural order boils down to the necessity of one's own nature. Great human beings recognise this fact and accordingly practise a sort of all-embracing but not ignoble egoism. They appreciate that they cannot be less significant than the whole, since the whole is nothing other than an interaction of forces such as themselves. The whole is falsely conceived as a body superior to its parts. And there is nothing outside the material world which could judge or measure our being. (This, incidentally, is exactly the egoism of Max Stirner's remarkably interesting book, *The Ego and Its Own*, 1845, against which Marx and Engels railed.[6])

I propose to consider Sophocles as one who already, in the fifth century, saw life in the same extraordinary way, or at least received intimations along such lines. Sophocles accepted people and happenings as fortuitous; 'caused' no doubt, but not in any way that implies the possibility of correction or the wisdom of regret. Such is the foundation of Sophoclean tragedy: an incorrigible world contains incorrigible people such as Ajax, Antigone, Oedipus and Creon. Sophocles is plainly not a fatalist in the 'Turkish', or utterly submissive, sense; nevertheless he believes that what is done is necessarily done and its consequences are – whatever they are. There is no meaning in the world-process and one answer to it is the 'holy' man's answer, namely love. But this is still a tragic, not a moral response.

For example, it would be wrong to describe Sophocles' Ajax as a 'flawed hero', if we meant thereby to suggest that Ajax should be, or theoretically could be, other than the man we encounter. The impulse behind such a view of Ajax is therapeutic: it implies that this hero had the potential to take a more 'balanced' view of Odysseus and need not have been driven mad by Athena. In other words it lay within the power of Ajax to possess only minor flaws inoffensive to the gods. This is exactly the kind of speculation that tragedy proper is designed to refute. Thus the Ajax who passionately believes himself to merit the arms of Achilles is the one and only Ajax. The Ajax who slaughters the flocks, taking them to be the Atridae and their entourage, is not one possibility of Ajax but the whole man. That he has other possibilities at other stages of his life means not that he amounts in the end to a sum of possibilites, but that at any moment the entire Ajax is whatever he does there and then. The rest is strictly non-existent. In this way tragedy means that what happens must happen.

A tragic world is full of will, intense and exceptional will, but – to say it again – there is no *free* will. So the tragic world-picture matches Nietzsche's observations about moral psychology.

> *Unaccountability and innocence.* – The complete unaccountability of man for his actions and his nature is the bitterest draught the man of knowledge has to swallow if he has been accustomed to seeing in accountability and duty the patent of his humanity. [As regards actions] he can admire their strength, beauty, fullness, but he may not find any merit in them . . .[7]

Presumably it follows that in watching a tragedy we may, or indeed should, admire, but should also refrain from praise and blame. Moreover, it is mistaken in a tragic context to set up a model of conduct by which to measure the hero or heroine. Such a model is of no consequence except perhaps in terms of the hero's goal; it does not realistically exist. R. J. Winnington-Ingram in his *Sophocles: An Interpretation* argues that the Ajax of Sophocles 'carries the implications of the heroic code to the extreme possible point . . .'.[8] Commenting upon this and similar remarks, Goldhill suggests that 'the Sophoclean hero [Ajax] does not simply reflect a Homeric model but offers a specific distortion, distorted in its extremism'.[9] Yet even these comparisons would be misleading if we did not remember that narrative or Homeric heroism is a code rather than a reality. I mean that it is not even a 'literary reality' since in Homer himself Hector adheres to it while Achilles, hero of heroes, could probably be said to break it. The model from which Ajax deviates is more accurately a theoretician's idea or a dreamer's dream, at any rate an abstract from Homer, and it is only an expedient for those who wish either to moralise or account for a catastrophe. Sophocles, however, desires just to portray the end of Ajax – a noble end, it goes without saying – and is absolutely not interested in trying to explain it. There is no Sophoclean diagnosis of the hero; we alone provide a diagnosis because we cannot bear to leave Ajax where he is: a mighty warrior fallen for reasons *which are not explanatory*. It is all a matter of scholars' references and futile contrasts to consider the Ajax of Sophocles against the Ajax of Homer, or Ajax as against Achilles.

Ajax compares himself with Achilles; that is, he implicitly regards himself as at least Achilles' peer. For so long as Achilles is more highly esteemed than Ajax, the former is, in a sense, the 'quarry' of the latter. But it is not for us to see Ajax as a sort of lesser or more extreme Achilles. Ajax resents to the point of insanity the fact that his deeds have not even gained him the arms of the dead Achilles. He set out from his home of Salamis with the aim of being the greatest Greek warrior, and it must be confessed that it is a kind of accident (in other words, a piece of fate) that Achilles has been held to occupy the first position and Ajax the second. So we are dealing with the bubble reputation, and Ajax (who fought Hector to a standstill in Book VII of the *Iliad*) is possibly 'justified' in his anger. The point is that Sophocles' play is not dialectical but tragic; arguments as such have only subordinate status within it. Not being dialectical, it is not moral either, for its first purpose is to celebrate a hero.

I believe Sophocles wishes to say that the sheer ambition and hubris of Ajax, even if it contradicts almost every estimate of him by others – *because* it does so – makes him especially noble. He is noble to the extent that his self-estimate (not a fantasy but a claim supported by deeds) exceeds the social estimate. And Odysseus in his speech in defence of Ajax acknowledges this very point. Ajax will not accept that anyone is his superior; hence both his madness and his stature in the eyes of Sophocles. To be exact, Ajax has been driven temporarily mad by Athena as a means of preventing him from killing Agamemnon and Menelaus, but we are justified in interpreting this rather more in the terms of psychopathology. From our point of view Ajax became insane because his self-estimate was cruelly refuted by the Atridae. On the other hand, our interpretation should not imply that the madness might have been prevented. Might-have-beens merely constitute a false style of thinking.

As it is, Ajax arouses respect at every turn, and sometimes awe. Moral considerations have no place here. For instance, it is notable that when thinking of how to cancel out his shame Ajax rejects the idea of dying in a vain onslaught on the Trojan walls – the very course that centuries later would have appealed to a medieval or Renaissance man of honour (a Hotspur, say). Instead Ajax opts for suicide on the grounds that such a course will rob the Trojans of a sense of triumph. The rule is simple: one must never be beaten. I suppose such an attitude was already atavistic in Sophocles' time and may have been fading at the time of Homer. Therefore it is a measure of Ajax' pride: he has bound himself to a 'stern rule of life'[10] and bids his infant son, Eurysaces, to do the same. This is a self-imposed rule for Ajax and his son, not for others. This exclusivity is another sign of nobility, for it will not do to possess a common virtue. The stature of Ajax is actually enhanced by the fact that he acknowledges no duty to the gods, and that on leaving for Troy he told his father, Telamon, that he would be victorious without heaven's help. Likewise his dying wish that the Greek host should perish puts the last touch to his Bronze Age grandeur.

The appraisal of Ajax as an 'excessive hero' seems to be ours, not that of Sophocles. The pronouncements of Odysseus at the end of the play should not be read as a gesture of forgiveness and peace-making but as a wholehearted reminder that Ajax is one of the 'mighty dead'. Odysseus points to the never-failing bravery of the spirit of Ajax, counting this as far exceeding the social virtues. There are thus two values in the play: the warrior courage of Ajax and the magnanimity of Odysseus. The latter properly belongs to Sophocles himself.

It is necessary to emphasise that Sophocles did not advocate the golden mean. The nature of his heroes and heroines shows that he admired precisely those who, for other than contemptible reasons, break social and ethical rules. The plays are not moral exempla (not lessons, for example, that one should be more careful than Oedipus or less fanatical than Antigone), but glorifications of persons who carry their unethical virtues to excess; hence in the end, of the 'excesses' of nature itself.

By imputing our own didacticism and caution to Sophocles we

obscure his superior, affirmatory nature. He chiefly discovers a creative–destructive world which must be loved for what it is. There is no such thing as excess in nature, and among people it is just a cautionary idea. The final words of Teucer, half-brother of Ajax, 'Since time began / There lived on earth no nobler man'[11] are meant to be less an exorbitant funeral sentiment and more a piece of truth, for who indeed has been specifically *nobler* than Ajax?

Here is the place to question two related assumptions often made about tragedy. Both are implicit, never brought out and openly examined. The first is that tragic dramatists, despite their admiration for their heroes and heroines, still judge those figures by ordinary standards, by a social ethic, by virtues accessible to the common man, or by the mean. Aristotle implies something along these lines, and so do modern Marxist critics such as Raymond Williams. The second assumption is that we prudential modern commentators are certainly wiser than the principal persons of tragedies and, often enough, wiser than the dramatists themselves, whose world-pictures we have outgrown. So at one and the same time we admire Sophocles' Antigone (perhaps with reservations) and rightly judge her incapable of sharing our reasonable attitudes. Creon, her antagonist, likewise pushes his view 'too far'. In brief, by confining ourselves to a mediocre vision we reduce our admiration of Antigone to the level of theory and sentimental indulgence.

We fancy that Sophocles personally thought as we think now. His work supports our caution and common sense, teaching us lessons which we have absorbed so completely that watching the *Antigone* is not much more than a recapitulation. The view in this chapter is, to the contrary, that Sophocles continues to remind us of what we would rather forget, or indeed tells us – always, as it were, for the first time – what we have never grasped. This lesson is to the effect that awe-inspiringly creative deeds are done by a few individuals. Such deeds are always destructive as well as creative and do not *fundamentally* advance the human race, being self-justifying, like bursts of energy on a distant star.

Antigone is more impressive than we ourselves, since otherwise her play is little other than a moderately realistic study of a clash of psychological types, each adhering to a typical ethical standard. That is what the play has often been taken to be, but how can it also be a tragedy (not far removed from the birth of tragedy), except in a trivial, formal sense? As we shall see in the next chapter, Nietzsche believes Euripides to have written precisely such pseudo-tragedies, representing persons too real and commonplace to bear tragic destinies.

The root of our error lies in judging the *Antigone* by criteria which Sophocles only adumbrates, which Euripides significantly develops and which the history of narrative technique has consolidated. These criteria have to do with the prior importance of foreground, of psychological cause and effect, and, correlatively, with the value in some plays of debate, which, so we imagine, is the *raison d'être* of even a tragedy in which a serious debate occurs. Considerable Greek scholars are not immune from applying the first standard, praising realistic elements in a fifth-century work. As to the second standard, the significance of the debate, perhaps we are tempted to read back into Sophocles literary and intellectual priorities which were introduced by Plato. In Sophocles debate exists for the sake of tragedy, while in Plato debate is plainly all-important as a social mechanism and way of life. Platonic argument replaces tragedy and was designed for that purpose. Just the same, we are inclined to see Sophocles as something of a dialectician in his *Antigone* partly because Western culture has been dialectical since Plato.

Antigone tempts us to such an inference: it *appears* to be dialectical in both the Socratic and Hegelian senses. Looked at through the lens of Socrates the *Antigone* contains for the most part a dispute theoretically capable of solution yet pushed, as we say, 'to extremes' and therefore flowering into tragedy. It is a tragedy because one of the disputants, Creon, has the power of life and death over the other, Antigone, and the question between them is not argumentatively resolved. (I do not see how the debate could reach a philosophically satisfactory solution, as opposed to a political compromise.) If, on the other hand, we accept Hegel as a guide (basing our conclusions on *Aesthetik* and *The Phenomenology of Mind*, Parts V and VI) we see two ethically justified points of view colliding to the point of catastrophe because, while each is intrinsically sound, it is also exclusive. In Hegel's eyes tragedy is the representation in an heroic society (not elsewhere) of the incompleteness – and therefore in the last analysis the wrongness – of even the most watertight case.

Hegel regards Antigone herself as admirable and also heroically undivided; that is to say, her personality coincides with her ethical consciousness. There is no possibility of her doing wrong in her own eyes; she could never experience shame. Further, Antigone's belief in the priority of the brother–sister relationship over all other relationships is correct, since a brother and sister may form a purely ethical bond, 'unperturbed by desire',[12] without frustrating the 'individual existence'[13] of either.

The above is the briefest of summaries of Hegel's observations (of which a much fuller yet still inadequate account is given by A. C. Bradley in his *Oxford Lectures on Poetry*),[14] but I have indicated just enough to satisfy our requirements without misrepresentation. As for the dialectic of Socrates, it is clear that sophistical arguments were designed to give the death-blow to tragedy. With these considerations in mind, should we not rather see Sophocles, the tragedian, as antedating all metaphysical and value-laden theories that run counter to tragedy? He desires tragedy, not the reasonable solution of problems, because he has looked as far as possible into nature and finds it best represented by tragic drama. He also believes tragedy to be unsurpassable, not a form peculiar to an heroic period. Since there are no progressionist notions lurking in Sophocles and no ideals, we post-Hegelian people can appreciate him only by putting aside any faint belief that the world is moving towards the goal of Absolute Knowledge (Hegel) or indeed towards any goal. We are in a better position to do this than our immediate predecessors because we, unlike them, find it relatively easy to contemplate a world without purpose. We can bear in mind Nietzsche's contention that if the world 'had any kind of goal that involved duration, immutability, the once-for-all (in short, speaking metaphysically: if becoming *could* resolve itself into being or into nothingness), then this state must have been reached'.[15] Likewise we may recall the wonderment of many latter-day physicists and their increasing tendency to believe that knowledge, even of the most empirical kind, belongs to the realm of human creativity. These changes now cause the ancient Sophocles to seem more convincing than the modern Hegel, tragedy less of a deception than 'progress'.

Antigone herself is perenially admirable since her value has nothing to do with this or that society, with one creed or another. The reason for this near-universal enthusiasm is that Antigone speaks to the individual, linking him or her not with society but with the world. She obeys what she calls the 'eternal laws of heaven',[16] but, since she is no thinker, does not explain what she means. We have to provide the explanation, which must take some such form as the following. Societies, collectives of all kinds, are expediencies by means of which the lone person thinks to preserve herself and advance her cause. In reality she is liable to lose herself therein, because she is fundamentally a nonpareil whose character and spirit are subject to the laws of heaven, not those of the nation. 'Heaven' in this context should be interpreted as the source of personal ethics – *emphatically not social ethics*. Antigone is connected in this way with the larger world to which we all belong, a world which encompasses all human times and places. Her line of connection obviously bypasses Thebes. Therefore what is right for Antigone is right *per se* and the rules of society are of secondary importance at best.

Now it is necessary to specify ambiguities in both Antigone and Creon. From one point of view she, not he, is the traditionalist, because his decree against burying Polyneices sweeps aside the customs of the ages. Creon is thus quite radical. On the other hand she, not he, is the radical champion of individuality, a new attitude to life and indeed a new phenomenon. People have been essentially customary, tribal, and here is a girl whose being affronts the tribe. Admittedly the feeling of the people is for her and against the king, but this is because they do not see the full implication of Antigone's conduct. They possibly sense it but cannot formulate it. Antigone, whose entire personality consists in her beliefs, means that *I*, I alone, decide what is right and wrong, and, for example, put my feelings about my brother above the community. Antigone is doing far more than holding to an ancient law, for she is also ushering in a fresh understanding that, were people not so abject, might rock society to its foundations. Her attitude – to put the matter bluntly and perhaps shockingly even by the standards of today – is that Polyneices was *her* brother, not a brother, not a mere specimen of brotherhood.

Antigone does not fight for any cause or movement; in fact, she does not exactly fight at all. She does not want companions; hence the cross-grained rejection of Ismene, her less ardent sister, when Ismene finally comes round to Antigone's side. Nothing in Antigone's behaviour connects her with liberation movements or with feminism, for she merely refuses, as a solitary person, to mould herself to a social requirement. She takes precedence over the king and any conceivable sort of society. Each law of heaven is applicable to a person and a place, not a group. The fact that this particular heavenly law coincides with an old social law does not affect the supremacy of the former. Remember also that Antigone is faithful not to an idea and perhaps, in the final analysis, not even to Polyneices, but to her own peculiar and alien nature. The ethic in question is her ethic; in fact, as Hegel emphasises, it *is* her. She acknowledges, as she is led towards the cave, that neither god nor man will help her. What I wish to bring out here, and will continue to imply later on in connection with Oedipus, is the apolitical or even anti-political nature of the Sophoclean hero.

The other figures of *Antigone* are mundane. Creon is, at worst, technically 'evil' as opposed to malicious, and simply gets out of his depth, as many people might in dealing with so inflexible a subject as the heroine. Ismene is a purely social creature, not cut out for heroic deeds. Haemon, Creon's son betrothed to Antigone, proves to be fearless and mature as he first pleads for justice and then goes off to kill himself beside Antigone. But Haemon's reasoned argument shows that he doesn't understand the matter for which his loved one is prepared to die. Eurydice is a distraught mother, neither more nor less, and Teiresias fails to rise above the wiseacre level. The Chorus of Theban Elders laments in such a way as to incite Antigone to her most stirring words. The burden of these old men is that mortals may not do as Antigone does. 'Religion has her claims, tis true,' they chant, 'Let rites be paid when rites are due.'[17] This orthodox sentiment implies that society *contains* religion. Antigone's innovation, her creative deed, is to reverse this judgement. What I think Sophocles means is that for so long as religion takes precedence over society, there is some scope for tragedy, and the moment it ceases to do so human life becomes circumscribed and fruitless: there is no third way. The *Antigone* was probably performed about 441, at all events before either of the Oedipus plays, and I suggest that it was then, at the earlier date, that Sophocles sounded a 'holy' song 'as a prelude', to borrow Nietzsche's words. But at this stage it is a defiant rather than a triumphant song. The 'holy man's' song of *triumph* is heard in *Oedipus Rex*. Antigone at the last feels herself to be a pious victim, so her creator has evidently not yet learned how to convert such victimisation into a kind of victory.

No doubt the foregoing remark sounds absurd to those who believe, in the contemporary style, that victories other than worldly ones are actually disguised defeats and forms of consolation. The spirit of tragedy, however, rests on the utterly different assumption that the intrinsic value of the individual matters above all.

Commonly, and nearly always in tragic drama, this value is manifested only by defeat. The downfall is not merely destined, but is part and parcel of the ethic (a very exclusive, discriminatory and aristocratic ethic) which the drama – as a quasi-religious act – celebrates. If the Prometheus of Aeschylus were not bound, he would have comparatively little value. Likewise the death of Ajax, far from being a shameful, squalid suicide, completes an heroic career. He recovers his greatness thereby. Antigone does not look for consolation; does not, for instance, believe that her example will help to usher in a 'better world'. She dies for herself alone, preferring her act of will to customs and laws. Thus tragic heroes preserve the individual spirit; a piece of creative individuality tries to pull away from the Dionysian mass and is naturally extinguished. But the vital, writhing mass remains, as it always will.

Before *Oedipus Rex* we can possibly detect Sophocles seeking, with growing confidence, the light of holiness. Antigone constitutes part of his search, but how exactly may she be said to triumph? She preserves her own self intact and that is a sort of triumph, but Sophocles cannot yet appreciate such an achievement to the point of celebrating it. What happens in the Oedipus plays is more miraculous, for the hero gains a kind of radiance as the paradoxical result of looking squarely into the darkness of nature. That is what Nietzsche probably means, or suggests, in a puzzling part of Section 6 of *The Birth of Tragedy*. The interpretation is possibly exaggerated since he attributes to Oedipus a *seemingly* superhuman achievement. Nietzsche implies that Oedipus is not bound by the social code, which softens or quite obscures natural horrors, but stares directly at those horrors. He sees not words, not symbols, not explanations, not myths, but naked reality, in consequence of which he is able to spread light around him. The darkness of extra-human reality gives way to light, *without divine intervention*. Thus Oedipus does not react against reality (and any explanation is a form of reaction) but welcomes it. As I say, this mode of perception is normally inaccessible to human beings; nevertheless if we take Nietzsche to mean (as he properly should) that Oedipus ends his life in a state of Hamlet-like intuition about the truth beyond human perception, then we arrive at a solution of *Oedipus at Colonus*. In this way Oedipus' frame of mind as he takes leave of Antigone and Ismene is perhaps also a faint prelude to the eventual coming of the *Übermensch*. The *Übermensch* will be capable, first of total *amor fati* and secondly, of knowing at every moment that the world with which he plays is other than the 'true' world.

From the beginning of *Oedipus Rex* the hero should be recognised as at least a type of innocent genius. Only genius could have solved the riddle of the Sphinx, since the answer is direct, lacking reference to cultural fashions and social norms. Teiresias rhetorically asks who is so skilled in reading riddles as Oedipus and rightly asserts that this great talent of Oedipus is also his ill fortune. The clumsy innocence of Oedipus is manifest throughout his story. On his way from Corinth to Thebes, in consequence of a petty quarrel, he fought and killed four out of five men, one of whom happened to be Laius, King of Thebes and Oedipus' own father. Yet when Oedipus arrived in Thebes and solved the Sphinx's riddle it did not occur to him that the murders he committed 'at the meeting of three roads' might conceivably be connected with the King's unsolved murder in Phocis. Everyone sees this as somewhat ridiculous, but not everyone notices that it also fits the character of the Oedipus we encounter throughout the play. There are such unguarded people as this, and some of them are in fact geniuses. Nietzsche brings this home to us in a context which is not especially concerned with Greek drama. 'The geniuses', he writes, 'the great human beings, are great because they do not seek their own advantage: the value of a man increases in proportion as he denies himself.'[18] The general interest of this remark is considerable, and it deserves more careful attention than there is space for here. Genius exists whenever someone throws aside the usual safeguards, applying himself radically and, as it were, *ab initio* to whatever has engaged his interest. It exists *because* he so heedlessly tackles the matter. Therefore the genius may be thought to be self-centred, since his preoccupation makes him careless of social forms, brusque, evasive, forgetful, and so forth, though he is not as a rule concerned with himself. He may exceptionally be concerned with his own personality, but in a fresh, creative way, as for example when Freud conducted his self-analysis. However, in doing whatever he does, the genius disregards those fields (health, income, marital stability, career prospects, numerous social transactions) with which the others, the non-geniuses, are largely engaged. In brief the genius looks for some answer which is not, as it happens, connected with his own advantage. It will avail him nothing and might destroy him to find that the planets move around the sun, or to perfect the symphonic form, or to pursue a philosophy that cuts the ground from under everyone's feet. So genius is apt to be destructive of self and others, but in any event unconcerned with survival.

It is helpful and not at all fanciful to see Oedipus in this way. His life, governed by a curse, is a series of mishaps and blunders, lightened by the one deed of defeating the Sphinx and the love of his daughters, Antigone and Ismene. In the course of the first play he makes exactly the moves that will destroy him. In fact he has done so ever since he made enquiries of Apollo in Corinth. Whatever he does it is the 'wrong' thing, and this through a lack not of intelligence but of ordinary social sense. If only he did as everyone else, glancing sideways at his fellows to see what they intend, observing the unuttered rules, believing whatever it is customary or topical to believe, he would experience neither deep misery nor illumination. He would be 'happy'. The Greeks clearly delighted in the multiple ironies and indeed the whole ingenious plan by means of which Oedipus is made to secure his own downfall. And this delight does not lessen the tragical effect but consolidates it. Nothing is fortuitous. This is where the gulf opens between the Greeks and us modern people. For instance, Jan Kott, speaking of tragedy in general and referring to the assertion of Camus in *The Myth of Sisyphus* that 'in a tragic work fate always makes itself felt better in the guise of logic and naturalness', exclaims that however absurd accidental cruelty might be, 'cruelty endowed with the divine rigour of inevitability is unbearable'.[19] No doubt it seems unbearable to a great many of our contemporaries, yet to the Greeks it was not simply bearable but exhilarating. We still need to believe that we can prevent misfortunes and alter destinies, though the Greeks seem to have been pleased to be reminded of their helplessness. They desired to belong to nature with all its terrors, its uncontrollability and its divine fecundity, while our deepest wish is to command nature utterly and to deliver ourselves from it. What a superior sort of delight must have greeted the first performance of *Oedipus Rex*! What an audience to marvel at the sheer neatness of Oedipus' peripeties and discoveries, to take an exquisite *intellectual* pleasure in those reversals of fortune, while at the same time pitying the hero and fearing for him! Above all, what a high quality of spectator not to want consolation, promise of better times ahead (as at the end of Shakespeare's tragedies), joy in heaven or the glow of moral superiority! The Greeks were untouched by philistinism, scarcely thinking, 'we are the morally superior ones'.

Oedipus, like other Sophoclean heroes, stands above average humanity, and the average people gathered in the Theatre of Dionysus must have relished that very fact: the last thing they wanted was to bring Oedipus down to their level. Nevertheless almost everything he does, the very pattern of his career, is misguided. Leaving Corinth, killing Laius, accepting the throne, marrying Jocasta his mother, consulting Teiresias and the Messenger, suspecting his brother-in-law (or uncle) Creon, rushing ahead with a vow and curses: all these are doings from which the majority would know to hold back. Oedipus is neither good nor bad but unwary. He is unwary in his very cleverness, since in terms of 'lateral thinking' his acts are sound enough. And when his self-protective instincts are aroused, as for example in his suspicions about Creon, he is wrong, just because he is not by nature self-protective. B. M. W. Cox has remarked that the hero's search for the killer of Laius 'mirrors the scientific quest of the age'.[20] That Oedipus finds himself to be the goal of the quest would have been especially piquant to the dialectical Greek mentality, for in this celebrated case the dialectical procedure is the *modus operandi* of tragedy. Reasoning things out and making quasi-scientific enquiries have not replaced tragedy but helped to bring it about. That is the haunting fact about this play. For Sophocles tragedy reigns supreme, *governing* both reason and morality.

Oedipus is best regarded as the pioneer, or scout, for Sophocles: the dramatist sends the dramatic figure on ahead testing the possibilities of affirmation. How much can Oedipus affirm and accordingly how much horror and hopelessness can Sophocles tolerate without bringing himself to believe in an unbelievable creed? We must not try to close the gap between author and character, yet the old, blind Oedipus is clearly the fruit of Sophocles' long life of contemplating the pains and joys of existence. To edge nearer to the evident truth, Oedipus is Sophocles' medium for discovering how pains and joys might be harmonised. This suggests that Sophocles (like Aeschylus before him, and like the philosopher Heraclitus) appreciates that we divide into pains and joys what is actually indivisible. Existence in all its forms is not on the one hand joy, on the other hand pain: it is all one, a 'seamless garment', or an onflowing river.

The Oedipus of this late play is cut off from the community, not as a stranger but as an outcast. An integrated member of the community could not produce the same effect and would never suffer in the same productive way. Not being a god or even a Titan like Prometheus, Oedipus needs the guidance of his daughter Antigone, but he is at first bereft of nearly everything else: homeland, friends, reputation, health, means of support and all forms of solace. There is no other-worldly consolation for Oedipus. He is the most wretched person alive, a blind, intolerably filthy beggar who nevertheless still possesses a sense of destiny. Someone might suggest that the goal of Oedipus is itself a solace (certainly a powerful argument against suicide), but, just the same, reaching the goal precludes every sort of wish fulfilment, every tempting diversion and stopping place. Further, Oedipus does not know what his goal is: as he approaches it he will recognise it for the first time.

From a purely social point of view (meaning not only secular attitudes but most religious attitudes as well), Oedipus is certainly not superior to members of the community, but theoretically inferior through his atrocious crimes of incest and parricide. And these are not just social crimes, not deeds against the law alone, but deeds against nature. Oedipus is the criminal of criminals, because no natural creature does such things. The seed does not normally grow to destroy its procreator. For all that, Oedipus calls forth a mixture of horror and great respect. Despite his theoretical inferiority, he is in a yet-to-be-discovered way superior to the common run. He needs to establish his own, unprecedented criterion of value, and finding it will almost coincide with finding his goal.

Oedipus is moreover aware that he is noble. The nobility is apparently fundamental, a 'matter of being', as we say, rather than of doing. To be accurate, we cannot distinguish being from doing, but must collapse the first into the second. Therefore to remark that Oedipus has a noble nature means that his characteristic deeds are relatively independent of social forms: he is not a creature of society. As a corollary his acts are never sinful; they have nothing to do with the social categories of good and bad. Nietzsche's own point in regard to this rare quality of Oedipus is expressed in the following words:

> The noble human being does not sin, the profound poet [Sophocles] wants to tell us: though every law, every natural order, even the moral world may perish through his actions, his actions also produce a higher magical circle of effects which

found a new world on the ruins of the old one that has been
overthrown.[21]

This passage is unusually important for our understanding of
Sophocles, and eventually for our grasp of Nietzsche too. The
remarks amount to saying that noble deeds disturb the natural as
well as the merely social order. Those whom we most admire, the
noblest ones, cannot but do things which, though natural, are in a
sense 'contrary to nature'. The idea here is astonishing, for
Nietzsche has in mind that such people are, first, supremely
creative and secondly that they create by breaking up what is
understood in their day to be the system of nature. In other words a
person of this rare sort apparently turns against the natural world
that gave him birth. As a result of such an horrendous deed not only
does he or she suffer dissolution after the pattern of Dionysus, but
at the same moment the world as a whole changes. A 'higher
magical circle of effects' comes into being. What we see in this
context is Nietzsche's early (and scarcely thought-out) introduction
of the theme of the overman. These are snatches of the overman
prelude, so to speak, which Nietzsche will not develop into a full-
blown theme until *Thus Spoke Zarathustra* (1883–5) about twelve
years later.
   Nietzsche's insight corresponds with our experience of the play:
Oedipus is a sinner without sin, one who commits crimes in such a
way that we feel he has opened up the possibilities of human life –
as the Prometheus of Aeschylus did before him. And yet while
Prometheus is a Titan, Oedipus has for long enough seemed to be
no more than a man. Even he regards himself as at best an exalted
man:

> For I am taught by suffering to endure,
> And the long years that have grown old with me,
> And last, not least, by true nobility.[22]

Over the course of many years Oedipus' virtue has been endurance.
Ever since his self-blinding he has manifested passive endurance.
Until the blinding he was (disastrously) active, but from then on he
has been 'pathetic', a character of *pathos*, a more or less pure sufferer
of experience. He genuinely has had no designs on others, unless
we count the indispensable Antigone. Now as he comes to Colonus
he realises, through the words of the Stranger, that here, in the

grove of the Eumenides, is his destination. Here he will find his purpose and will therefore, fittingly, die. In youth he was told by Apollo that he would prove to be a blessing to the land of his resting-place and a curse to his native town of Thebes. This vicinity is consecrated to Poseidon while nearby is a spot where Prometheus is worshipped. Thus Sophocles has chosen Colonus because it is his birthplace and also because it is extraordinarily sacred. The play is suffused in pious feeling and is a socially challenging work for that very reason. Oedipus is now in the first stage of his self-elevation from the ranks of humanity to the status of Hero, a being between people and gods. (Sophocles himself was accorded the rank of Hero by the Athenians after his death.)

Oedipus' growing awareness of his singular destiny leads him to send for Theseus, King of Athens. For the same reason Oedipus is able to fend off the forceful requests of the Chorus of Citizens of Colonus that he, the defiled one, leave their territory. Soon he is joined by his other daughter, Ismene, who brings him news of the quarrelling twin sons, Eteocles and Polyneices. Ismene also tells him that the citizens of Thebes now want him, alive or dead, since the welfare of Thebes depends upon his presence. Oedipus responds by saying, possibly without bitterness, 'So, when I cease to be, my worth begins.'[23]

When Theseus arrives he quickly, though not immediately, realises that this blind wanderer is a visitant in something of the mystical sense. The ability of Theseus to do this signifies his own higher disposition which befits him, uniquely, to be the recipient of Oedipus' secret knowledge. The true quality of Oedipus is what Creon and Polyneices fail to appreciate: each in turn seeks to exploit Oedipus, because their petty, personal, *active* wills cannot understand the purport of Oedipus' desire to share nature's secrets. I put the matter so because the process of learning those secrets is what Nietzsche – and perhaps he alone – understands as the activity of genius. In this connection, however, 'learning' may not be confined to the scientific and empirical methods we practise in modern times, but should include different varieties of explanation. In broad terms it here refers to every sort of pioneering exposition of nature. Nor is genius seen as exceptional talent, but as a challenge some few people thrown down to nature. Forces of nature are perturbations in nature, and Nietzsche's idea seems to be that when geniuses heroically assert themselves they act as natural forces and thus 'disturb the universe' – to borrow a phrase from T. S.

Eliot's 'The Love Song of J. Alfred Prufrock'. This belief is almost the reverse of modern nihilism which assumes that one's acts are insignificant, essentially undistinguished and, except for their pain-pleasure potential, meaningless. Nietzsche's idea, to the contrary, is that one's deeds are far-reaching, universal rather than personal, never purely social, let alone private. An action reaches out to the universe, so that if someone commandingly calls upon nature to yield up her secrets, then the agent does indeed disturb the universe. This is grand hubris, not mere petty arrogance.

Only towards the end of the play does Oedipus realise what form his goal must assume: he now knows that he has been recognised by the gods for what he is. Kitto writes as follows:

> In taking Oedipus to themselves as Hero the gods are but recognising facts. By his stature as a man Oedipus imposes himself on the gods; it is not forgiveness, for there was no sin. The *Coloneus* is Sophocles' answer to the tragedy of life. He knows he cannot justify God to man, but he can justify man to man.[24]

I wish to expand upon these words, for they do not sufficiently explain the matter. Kitto is right to insist that 'there was no sin'; therefore all our moralistic readings of the Oedipus plays are along the wrong lines. Similarly it is true to say that 'The *Coloneus* is Sophocles' answer to the tragedy of life.' But what, in discursive terms, is this answer? First let us note that the tragedy of life is not an aspect of life but a proper interpretation of the whole. When the Chorus chants the most pessimistic words ever uttered they are, up to a point, speaking for Sophocles:

> Not to be born at all
> Is best, far best that can befall,
> Next best, when born, with least delay
> To trace the backward way.[25]

This is certainly the tragedy of life as seen by the woebegone Chorus, but Sophocles presents an answer which is not a cure so much as a way of transfiguring the undeniable facts. The way turns misery into joy, for it consists, initially, of total, unqualified acceptance, in a word, *amor fati*. The gulf between *amor fati* and resignation is immensely wide. The latter remains doleful and the practitioner, who may be a stoic or a fatalist in the old Eastern style, derives some melancholy pleasure from his submission. Constantly he consoles himself with thoughts of his comparative virtue and, to be candid, with dreams of death: he is 'half in love with easeful Death'. Ease is his watchword, for why rebel against the nature of things?

On the other hand, Oedipus – and therefore Sophocles – finally rejoices in his destiny, recognising that it is intrinsic and vital to the whole. If the career of Oedipus could be altered, if it were aberrant and remediable, then this fact could be detected only by some agency outside the whole. There are signs that Sophocles shared this Heraclitean vision and to that extent looked forward to the vision of Nietzsche. Heraclitus has it that since one is part of the world-process, nothing can be changed because whatever one proposes to change has already flowed on – and one has flowed on also. 'The sun is new every day,' says Heraclitus,[26] and 'You could not step twice into the same river; for other waters are ever flowing on to you.'[27]

The destiny of Oedipus is part of the flow and, since no part is finally distinguishable or dispensable, that fate *is* the flow. However, what Oedipus evidently can do on behalf of Sophocles is *assault* nature: it is his role to kill his father, marry his mother and solve the riddle of the Sphinx. These deeds have proved to be biologically possible, and are therefore to be classed as 'natural', however unnatural they might appear to be. Further, they are natural to Oedipus, since he does them willy-nilly. By commiting the unprecedented crimes and suffering the consequences without any sign of supernatural redemption, Oedipus magically *elevates* nature. The actions of Oedipus 'produce a higher magical circle of effects which found a new world on the ruins of the old one that has been overthrown'.

Plainly this new world (our world) is not remotely that preposterous conception, a different physical universe 'as such'. We may only interpret the universe, so Nietzsche means that the actions of Oedipus constitute a reinterpretation. They form a sublime re-interpretation, not just a fresh idea at the level of what we ordinarily regard as hermeneutics or discoveries in physics. The Sophoclean–Oedipal transformation rests upon an appalling crime and the consequent metaphysical horror. The shock of this change is almost impossible for us to imagine – we who occupy the new world raised up by the deeds of Oedipus. Oedipus comes along in his generation, after all the generations of life hitherto, and does what no creature has done before. He behaves in an 'uncreaturely' way, not a spiritual way, which merely aims to shade human eyes against nature and reality, but in a manner both material and utterly new: the seed can, if it is human, violate its own stock. Therefore the limits of the natural are almost non-existent. But, as we have already learned from Aeschylus, crimes must be paid for, and extending the limits of the natural is a great crime. After Oedipus the world exhibits a 'higher magical circle of effects'; in other words the world is suddenly seen as less clogged, less mud-bound, less *stupid*. Nevertheless these fresh characteristics still form a circle, not parts of a linear or non-tragical progress. It is agreeable, if nothing more, to suppose that in 1872 Nietzsche was already thinking in terms that presage the doctrine of eternal return.

4

Impious Euripides

To an extraordinary degree Nietzsche thinks in terms of millenia, judging centuries and generations as phases of millenial developments. The attitude towards history in the essay 'On the uses and disadvantages of history for life' is likewise unusual, since the argument is that we need history 'for the sake of life and action';[1] that is to say, not as a record, not as a compartment of knowledge, not as a field from which lessons might be learned, and certainly not as an insider's discipline. Nietzsche presumes that history is quite different from the actual character of events (whatever that might have been) and, in any case, should be compiled and respected for its life-giving properties alone. This does not mean that historians are free to invent, but that they should never forget their mission to invigorate, since facts are nothing in themselves.

Few historically decisive events or periods have ever occurred. It is always the underlying flow that matters, not the spectacular and sometimes seemingly catastrophic eruptions. The nationalistic European wars of the nineteenth century, which will certainly continue on a vastly greater scale in the twentieth, *merely* herald the amalgamation of the countries of Europe.[2] Socialism is bred out of the 'Caesarian despotic state of the present century, because . . . it would like to be its heir'.[3] In turn socialism will breed its own rebellious offspring whose cry must be 'as little state as possible'.[4] The Renaissance was a burst of creative energy and a shortlived interruption of the long march towards nihilism. The French Revolution was nothing more than a 'gruesome farce', except that it gave us Mirabeau and Napoleon. The great historical watershed must be located in the ancient world and it inevitably took the form of a person, namely Socrates, and, to be quite specific, Socrates' refutation of tragedy. In this Socrates was abetted by Euripides. The true division lies here, between the tragic and the non-tragic consciousness. Before Socrates and Euripides the human race knew itself to be at one with the animals and the earth; afterwards people

71

began to draw away, to separate human potentiality from its somatic foundations and to align the human spirit with Plato's God, the fount of reality and truth. So Nietzsche sees a great drama being played out, the plot of which begins with the Socratic–Euripidean rejection of tragedy and leads – as the thread of this book will emphasise – to the late nineteenth century when 'nihilism stands at the door'.[5]

Prior to Euripides the heroes of tragedy were so many masks of Dionysus, their names little more than insignia of Dionysian guises. It was always fundamentally the god himself who experienced the elation and agony of individuation and was 'torn to pieces'. This Nietzschean reading of tragedy still requires some elucidation. For instance, do we think of Antigone as an expression of the god, or can we do so? Surely the original spectators of Sophocles imagined a woman behind the tragic mask, a social creature like themselves. However, to raise such an objection is to underestimate Nietzsche's idea.

Tragedy was born 'out of the spirit of music', as the phrase has it in the first title of Nietzsche's book. This means that tragedy arose from a non-dramatic and non-representational form of art in which nothing was expressed except universal oneness; in other words, no single thing. On the other hand, Dionysus was certainly worshipped in the sense that this god of countless forms signified precisely the universal oneness. Before Thespis, or at least before the advent of classical tragedy, the Dionysian myth was changing into a childish sort of history, which means that it was losing its mythic potency, growing almost prosaic. Now it received what Nietzsche calls 'its most profound content, its most expressive form'.[6] Notice that while in Nietzsche's eyes the origin of a force determines its character, that character is not fully realised until a later stage. Soon afterwards the character is perverted. In fact what I have just presented as happening in clearly defined stages must occur in a fluid manner, so that a blight imperceptibly begins to spread when the character is ripe. Thus tragedy is mature in Sophocles and therefore contains the germs of its decline.

Nietzsche has in mind that Antigone, for example, was once perceived as both a person and a mask of Dionysus. Her personhood was relatively unelaborated and her godhood implicit to the spectators of Sophocles. No doubt their conception of her moved easily between what we think of as utterly distinct modes of being.

They were so close to the religious origins of tragedy that they could not fail to see the masked figure of Antigone in a religious light. But 'religious' in this context has no connotations of the purely spiritual and few of the moral. Here a simple analogy will help. When we contemplate flowers in a garden or field we do not normally think of each flower apart from its roots in the soil. The flower is, amongst other things, the roots; it vitally consists of the connection with the earth. In fact the flower is an emanation of the earth *and nothing else*. The Dionysian religion accepted this as the condition of every natural thing; there were no deracinated things any more than there are rootless flowers. That creatures are not rooted to a particular spot does not affect their *substantial* kinship with the soil. When Antigone asserts herself in the face of Creon's law she attempts to preserve that natural bond of kinship. The original spectators chiefly saw Antigone in this way; she was not a distinct and separate individual so much as a shape of Dionysus, since any organism, in so far as it seeks to preserve and increase itself, is a Dionysian shape. So Antigone was a human name and form of the universal god of vegetation and fertility. At the period of Sophocles' Antigone, however, there already existed an unacknowledged and sacrilegious tendency to see the figures of drama as purely social beings. This was the tendency that Euripides accelerated, so ushering in the modern world, our world.

The fatal contribution of Euripides was to transmute myth into fiction to a markedly greater extent than his predecessors had managed or desired. Since Nietzsche this has become generally recognised so that everything now depends upon the commentator's attitude towards Euripidean innovations. Many scholars, finding Euripides' work absorbingly interesting, see no need to reproach him for secularising tragedy: the play's the thing and the world is secular now. Euripides made Electra, Orestes and Iphigenia into pseudo-historical personages whose stories he convincingly retold. Electra is not remotely deified but the counterpart of an unfortunate and hysterically bitter woman watching the play. Electra is no longer a mask of Dionysus, but a psychologically motivated being. In this way Euripides gives the impression that people are distinct and *basically* individualised, while gods and the entire apparatus of religion are dispensable myths. Now of course we might well argue that if Euripides followed such a procedure, then Euripides was right: people are individuals and myths are dispensable. For that matter each specimen of the genus Rosa is an individual rose. But that is not exactly the point, for Euripides, as it were, cuts the ground from under everyone's feet or creates an unnatural gulf between people and nature. Their world is social and manipulable, while the great world itself is now a backcloth and at most a contingent environment. In the course of time we shall imagine it reduced to the status of territory to be annexed.

So Euripides abandoned Dionysus, since in point of fact he regarded Dionysus as a mere belief. But – and, as we observed in the first chapter, this is Nietzsche's devastating contention – when there is no Dionysus there is no Apollo either. Without an overwhelming recognition of the primary oneness of things, the things that we see before us lose their reality. A character in a tragedy, for instance, is real not in virtue of his or her distinctness, but because that distinctness emerges from a blurred background. For all their surface pecularity and angularity, characters must flow away into darkness, not stand against the darkness. To the extent that they are 'characters', separated from the darkness which is the sheer inexplicability of all being, they lose nourishment. There are two orders of reality: first the clear-cut presence of our familiar world, and second the more profound, indeed the bottomless whole out of which we have fashioned our familiar world. In this latter sphere things and people *appear* wholly observable and analysable, though all such clarity is in fact contrived. Thus the characters of even the most realistic fiction (especially of the most realistic fiction) are only, so to speak, 'superficially real'. This clearly perceived sphere is only a painted world and the realism of art is no more than a minute but essentially lifeless correspondence of apparent thing and copy. More than that, one's emotions are subtly histrionic and indeed one's life is all but reduced to a set of subtle devices. Nietzsche contends that Euripides, along with Socrates, produced our human comedy of *involuntary* artifice. Such at any rate seems to be a fair deduction from Nietzsche's scattered remarks. Our theatricality, unlike that of the pre-Socratic Greeks, is largely unrecognised. Euripides was scarcely the first reactive individual in a generally affirmative culture. Perhaps in a strict sense human nature has always been reactive,[7] but Euripides more than all others except Socrates, that epochal genius and 'buffoon who *got himself taken seriously*',[8] pushed us towards a humanised world in reaction against the incomprehensible. He borrowed sophists' techniques and, relying upon his own observations of behaviour, addressed himself to Socrates and to his own questioning intellect: the crowd mattered hardly at all. Nietzsche believes that this attitude was immediately restorative but fundamentally decadent. Socrates recognised that instincts were getting out of hand and growing dangerous, perhaps fatal. Therefore he controlled his own instincts by an inordinate, indeed an absurd use of reason. Only one in desperate need of reason would have relied upon it so completely. Nevertheless healthy insticts are, by definition, at the service of life while domination of the instincts by reason is potentially anti-life, that is to say, decadent. Thus Socrates imparted his decadence to Athens, hence to us.

At this point we must begin to consider matters which are little more than hints in Nietzsche. He addresses Euripides: '. . . rouse all the passions from their resting places and conjure them into your circle, sharpen and whet a sophistical dialectic for the speeches of your heroes – your heroes, too, have only copied, masked passions and speak only copied, masked speeches'.[9] This figure suggests that Euripides displays and controls human passions as a ring-master supervises the beasts. Now we can see the animals clearly, inspect them, note their forms and, it seems, their dispositions also, but in fact we are watching a *performance* which is something quite other than the behaviour of these same animals in the wild. Moreover the heroes of Euripides are sometimes given sophistical arguments to utter, and so their passions are couched and defended in clever speeches. The entire exhibition is now 'realistic', as opposed to real.

For certainly Euripides is comparatively realistic, but if he had chosen to indicate or announce passion, as his predecessors did, he would have better preserved it. Passion also is theatricalised and intellectualised, not by the plain contrivance of Aeschylus but by the relative naturalism and ingenuity of Euripides. There is a striking difference between naïve and sophisticated histrionics. The people of Homer are, after all, constant actors (Achilles is a stirring performer in every sense) but they know that reality lies apart from their gestures and declarations. On the other hand, someone such as Euripides' Electra is so capable an actor that her most sincere feelings are 'copied' and 'masked'.

Euripides can be said to have initiated a society of actors who reproduced the manners of passion more skilfully than their passionate forebears ever did. The latter were actors also, but of a different kind, for they worked up genuine feelings by ritualistic means – as primitive people still do today. Now the spectators of tragedy began to enjoy the comedy of passion. But, as I have suggested, this process does not stop in the theatre, for it moves out into the market-place until the nation is composed of persons consummately acting anger and love, contempt and even pain. Perhaps it is not unknown for people even to die 'realistically'. The wild animals are tamed and in consequence we forget that around us and within us, stretching from the nerves and sinews of human beings to infinity is, so far as we know, only a wilderness.

Nietzsche implies that a naturalistic so-called tragedy is in essentials a comedy; to the extent that actors expertly reproduce the signs of feeling they alienate the audience from everything more occult and indecipherable than mere appearance. Accordingly we are entertained by one another's appearances. Hence the attachment the poets of the New Comedy felt for Euripides. We have to remember that to the older Hellenes nature was conspicuously imperfect. To copy rather than to surpass nature seemed a crude and comic exercise. Before Euripides the poets were evidently aware of unseen regions into which their most glittering figures tailed away, as comets tail off into the darkness. That is Nietzsche's excellent simile. To those older Hellenic singers the blackness into which their comet-characters vanished was not more exalted than the visible environment but quite the reverse, an earthy sphere of substances, demonic influences and tangled mysteries. Consequently their songs emerged from nature and never disowned their source. The poets beautified, aestheticised, *without elevating themselves or mankind in general.* Improving on nature meant cutting neat shapes from the tangled mass. Thus the early tragic poets preserved their sense of the universe as meaningless in both moral and intellectual terms. That indeed was the ultimate point of tragic ritual and drama: the meaning was neither moral nor intellectual, but *tragic.*

As we have remarked, the tendency of Euripides was to concoct a form which he still thought of as 'tragedy' without Dionysus, one of the two vital gods of tragedy. If an author thus attempts to make an exclusively Apollonian tragedy, the best he can hope for, according to Nietzsche, is a species of dramatised epic, from which, as a matter of the highest priority, his sympathetic emotions must be kept apart. In fact Euripides did not stay detached but instead became entangled with his heroes and heroines: he felt agitated on their behalf, or, better, he 'became' them, emotionally speaking, as he worked. Now such emotional self-identification is quite other than the virtually suprapersonal vision with which Aeschylus and Sophocles wrote their plays. Neither cared on his own account but each swept his characters and himself along on a submerged current above which personal feelings remained as minor, disregarded eddies. There is still something impersonal about Clytemnestra and Orestes, Ajax and Oedipus. Perhaps that seems absurd; how can a woman bent on murder, such as Clytemnestra, be described as 'impersonal'? The answer is: more or less as a natural force is so described. Clytemnestra is not much more than the personalisation of a force and is not yet what we think of as a complete person. It seems impossible to comprehend the *Agamemnon* in any other terms. We sense that the plays of Aeschylus and Sophocles are other than tales of individual psychology, and recent attempts to expound them in relation to social conditions are more fashionable than satisfactory. The two older dramatists acknowledged the sovereignty of Dionysus and appreciated without thought or reservation that perceptible things, including the signs of feelings, are worthy of tragic treatment – or indeed belong to a tragic universe – only because they are governed by unknown forces.

Conversely Euripides seems comparatively modern, often raising questions for debate, suggesting that grave matters may be settled by debate. In fact a mere argument never disposes of a genuine affect but only of the feigned and theatricalised feelings that now reign supreme. Alternatively an argument is a trick for arousing some sort of emotion – in oneself or others – but while Euripides clearly recognise such social manoeuvres, he basically believes that emotions may be and preferably should be expressed in dialogue. He *is* modern in that he tends to confuse passion and voluble sentiment. Therefore he is exceptionally interesting to us and scarcely tragical. Yet even in the next generation Aristotle thought of Euripides as 'the most tragic certainly of the dramatists'.[10] Today we admire Euripides because he is the early master of shrewd observation, eloquent feeling, thorough argumentation, clever construction; because in a word, he is interesting. Just the same, I hope to indicate why Nietzsche's estimate of him, though a simplification and in that sense unfair, is accurate.

As I have earlier suggested, there are two principal characteristics of Euripides which set him apart from his predecessors: a love of manipulation and a compulsive tendency to self-identification with his *dramatis personae*. I mean that he identified himself not so much with a series of coherent figures as with the *successive moods* of his characters. Medea, for example, may or may not be a credible personality, yet it is certain that Euripides has given life to all her aspects by throwing himself into each aspect in turn. Further, Euripides composed his plots with remarkable freedom. Such sweeping confidence means that, before *The Bacchae*, he could not see any check upon his procedures except a possible social one, which for the most part he despised. Those plays earlier than *The Bacchae* which express anger and pity still imply that woeful conditions are inessential to life. In other words, Euripides earlier conducted a sort of rebellion which was a far cry from an Aeschylean–Promethean rebellion since it contained nothing of *amor fati*. Tragedy was seen by him as a dramatic representation of dire events, not a universal and inescapable condition. Does this make Euripides more of a pure artist than Aeschylus and Sophocles? I think it makes him more of a conjurer and certainly less of an hierophant.

In the *Alcestis* when Euripides presents his heroine the effect is powerful, so that she is memorable as a figure of the utmost nobility. Alcestis bids farewell to her husband Admetus, in her great speech (11. 280–325). She states that by accepting death so that he might live she honours him above her own soul. It would be still more accurate to say that the deed is the measure of her soul. And then, in a manner surprising to us, though we cannot tell how it would have struck the original spectators, Alcestis remarks that had she let Admetus die in accordance with the agreement reached between Apollo and the Fates she might have married any man in Thessaly. This is not an appreciably bitter observation, for Alcestis has no desire to overburden her husband with thoughts of his unpayable debt to her. That must simply be his burden which, it seems, neither she nor anyone else can lighten. Similarly when the heroine says that she could not have tolerated life without Admetus, she is stating a plain fact. She is an exalted being; therefore she says and does such things, while Admetus, however worthy, is less exalted and so does not. That is the end of the matter, though we must remember that to Euripides exaltation is just a disposition, a humour, and Alcestis is scarcely a model from which the rest of us fall short.

Alcestis simply speaks her mind. She emphasises the scope of her sacrifice without diffidence, humility or what we moderns might regard as decent reticence. Her heart goes out to her children and therefore she insists that Admetus must not remarry, since a stepmother would treat the children badly. So the children will be spared at least one sort of unhappiness and, as for Admetus himself, he will live secure in the knowledge that he was once married to the noblest of women. To my mind this is a believable as well as an impressive speech. It makes a mockery of the disingenuous rubbish that often passes for fine utterance in the modern world. The quality of Alcestis is the consequence of Euripides' having thoroughly thought himself into her nature and present circumstances. Euripides is not suffused with sentimental admiration for her, since he briefly *is* her and knows that she is proud and forthright about her own virtue. To us there is an unexpected mixture of mature self-regard and concern for the children. Alcestis has set herself a high task and now lives up to it. The whole is a noteworthy passage which reflects a lost world of assured, aristocratic self-ideals, but it also reflects the sharp discernment of Euripides.

So far, then, we may say that Euripides has been commendably tragical. But he cannot help thinking of Admetus too: how will he fare without his magnificent wife? Somehow Euripides must contrive to have the magnificence without the pain which alone consolidates the magnificence. Admetus will be desolate and all but robbed of his manhood; accordingly as soon as Euripides puts on the mask of Admetus he feels the need to devise a plot which rescues the king from a wretched life and the queen from Hades. Of course we have no good reason to suppose this to have been Euripides' actual procedure: perhaps he decided beforehand to write something other than an Aeschylean or Sophoclean drama, to demonstrate that neither he nor anyone else must be at the mercy of the tragic ethos. Why should we not *play with* tragedy? But at whatever point Euripides decided to exploit, rather than submit to, tragedy he cannot have believed tragedy to be more than a social form. He did not accept it as a formal mechanism by means of which people come to terms with the all-powerful Fates.

Heracles is introduced into *Alcestis* to change the course of events, to draw the sting of tragedy, or in other words to overcome the Fates. And this helps to illustrate why, since the fifth century, we have grown to believe that the Fates are in our hands, not we in theirs. Euripides is not an 'aesthete', so to speak, but a legislator, and what he legislates for is a humanly controlled environment. Heracles arrives at the palace at Pherae in the course of a typically heroic expedition. There he learns that the court is in mourning, though Admetus, out of courtesy to a guest, does not explain that the mourning is for the queen. Admetus tells the Chorus that he will not have his house called 'Guest-hating Hall'.[11] This is only just plausible, but we tend to accept it, sensing that we have suddenly shifted from serious to comic theatre, or that Euripides' urge to manipulate has taken over. Having been accommodated, Heracles dines and wines too well in ignorance of his host's grief. After the meal the drunken Heracles discovers from the Servant that it is Alcestis for whom the court mourns. He decides to resurrect her, either by physically forcing Death to give her up or by making a demand of Persephone in Hades. This feat will be in part a recompense for Admetus' hospitality. In the event Heracles brings before Admetus a wholly covered and silent Alcestis, offering this mysterious woman as a new wife. The King refuses on the grounds that his wife was irreplaceable. The episode is either an irreverent or, conceivably, a grotesque defiance of the spirit of tragedy, and critics have accordingly classified the play as 'tragicomedy' (Kitto) or 'pro-satyric drama' (A. M. Dale, D. J. Conacher and others).[12] However, we are not concerned with classification for its own sake, since that may be used, and often is used, as a means of not evaluating whatever is before us for evaluation. If we call the *Alcestis* a tragicomedy, we shall not need to say that we think it something less than a tragedy. Comparison is called for in this case, because the character of the heroine demands a tragedy. The contrary, humanistic view is that heroines, even of the stature of Alcestis, are still no more than pieces in a social pattern: Euripides 'wisely' restores such a tragic personage to her rightful position in the human comedy. In a nutshell, this is how Euripides wages war against tragedy: he makes a social pastime out of it as opposed to a religious practice. He seeks to demonstrate how the mind may order matters to its own satisfaction. Nevertheless we should not overlook what Nietzsche keeps in the shadows: that Euripides is the originator of psychological drama even as he is the 'grave-digger of Attic tragedy' – to borrow a phrase from Victor Ehrenberg.[13] Euripides brings the action forward to the human mind, thus making it seem more explicable (however strange the circumstances) and of course more familiar. On the other hand Nietzsche's point is that the convincing is not the true, and that to illuminate a process is a far cry from disclosing its actual nature, which must always be hidden from us and is perhaps strictly *meaningless*.

Nietzsche never discusses a question which will occur to many people today. Is it not possible that the sympathetic or empathetic way of Euripides has more to commend it than the comparatively austere procedures of Aeschylus and Sophocles? We may grant that they are correct in their grasp of the tragic foundation of our lives, but Euripides is surely 'right' in a different sense, to strive to know people as suffering individuals and, wherever possible, to justify their suffering on other than tragic grounds. By using argument so thoroughly Euripides lends a moral element to plots from which morality would otherwise be lacking. Further, in opposition to Plato can we not assert that it is precisely phenomena with which the human spirit must contend. The Forms are nothing to us and neither – so we might say – is Dionysus. Finally, is Euripides not to be congratulated rather than rebuked for dethroning Alcestis, since he sustains her goodness but not her role as a criterion of all our lives? The foregoing is what we could put forward in defence of Euripides. But would we not do so because we are creatures formed by a Euripidean culture of surfaces and arguments?

The contrary position, which is Nietzsche's by implication, is that we 'clever animals' have followed a Socratic–Euripidean course to the circumference of our knowledge and now appreciate that however far we push the circumference away, there will always be an abyss on the other side. As the circle of knowledge grows larger, so does the surrounding area of ignorance. Euripides required clarity at all costs and, for long enough, failed to realise that the clarity he provided was critically misleading.

It may be that we cannot account for Medea in convincing theoretical terms and so fall back on saying that she is, after all, a barbarian, a witch from Colchis. For all that, there seems to be nothing especially obscure about her as one watches or reads the play. That is to say, the contradictions in her make-up are of the sort one encounters in life. Moreover she so fully argues her case that we see matters through her eyes. Therefore, so long as we stay within the confines of the play all appears transparent. But outside those confines the world remains an enigma and that is the overwhelming fact that Euripides, before *The Bacchae*, disguises. Aeschylus and Sophocles continually remind us of mystery, since their plays express uncertainty, darkness, fatedness, the non-human roots of human behaviour. To the contrary Euripides sheds light over his characters so that we are blinded for a while to the sheer artificiality of the proceedings. In the course of time human beings will overlook the artificiality of all divisions of knowledge. Out of modesty they will tend to forget not merely that mathematics is a construct or that history cannot be 'true', but that even physics and biology are likewise human creations.

At the beginning of the *Medea* Euripides, in accordance with his usual practice, ensures that every spectator knows the state of affairs in Creon's Corinth and the important pieces of the earlier story of Medea and Jason. No one will be nudging his neighbour to find out what is going on. The Nurse expounds past and present, and immediately causes us to sympathise with Medea by calling her a 'hapless wife'[14] and Jason a 'traitor to his babes and her'.[15] We are excited also to hear of Medea's homicidal and suicidal tendencies. So far she has not learned that Creon has ordered her and the children to be banished. The Chorus of Corinthian Ladies wholesomely but inadequately argues that Medea should calm down for her own sake. Now when Medea comes from behind the scenes she famously puts, not her case alone, but the case of womankind: a woman may not choose or even reject a suitor; a new husband will be a stranger and may be vile; childbirth is more *certainly* terrible than the man's heroic mode of battle. In addition to these general wrongs of women, Medea is without kinsmen, homeland and possessions. Thus Medea brings the Chorus round to her side – though they will naturally balk at her vengeance.

Now the task Euripides has set himself is extremely bold, for he plans to make even the most orthodox spectator favour this outlandish woman. He will also combine within Medea two impulses, each 'anti-social' in itself and, according to our schematising minds, inconsistent with the other. Medea is at once an alien, an inferior who no doubt worships strange gods, and a clever, sophisticated woman, intellectual as well as amusing. Medea is a sophist *and* a murderer, a cold schemer *and* one enslaved by passion. Here is a list of Medea's characteristics: vulnerable, piteous, friendless, mendacious, bloodthirsty, crafty, reasonable, honourable, passionate, passionately loyal and gloatingly murderous. It doesn't matter whether or not this combination is feasible (I dare say it is), since Euripides, as always, transports himself into each phase or manifestation in turn. Probably there is something of the author himself in Medea's outburst to Creon to the effect that the masses loathe wise and knowledgeable people.[16] Euripides' redoubtable effort is to encourage the crowd to support a sort of person whom the crowd, almost by definition, normally hates and fears. The wrongs of Medea are plain; her reaction to them is, not 'excessive' or 'evil' (for these are simply wrong ideas), but *savagely logical*. The savage is outside society, unsusceptible to social pressures, unconditioned by centuries of harsh training. Medea is such a one and that is why it is audacious and almost impudent of Euripides to present her as heroine.

It is impossible for us to regard the heroic Jason as other than contemptible, and this too is almost a piece of impudence on Euripides' part. Jason finds Medea 'tempestuous' but also 'subtle' and to this extent his view resembles ours. His point is that Medea has already received her due, and more than her due, in coming to Hellas from a less favoured land. As for himself, how could he have prospered better than by marrying the princess? He offers Medea money, but she honourably refuses: 'No profit is there in a villain's gifts'.[17] It goes without saying that Jason's case is sincere as well as squalid.

Medea swiftly plots her revenge after the talk with Aegeus, King of Athens. Here is the chief part that accords badly with our stereotypes. We are liable to assume that passion excludes patient dissimulation, for passion consists in undesigning anger, grief, lust, rapture of some sort. On the other hand Medea should not be likened to a berserker or an hysteric (whose designs are, at any rate, concealed from the ego) but, say, to a Victorian poisoner whose dominant drive was 'passion' in some sense. If Medea is to be thought of as a 'tigress', which Jason famously calls her after the murders of the children, then we must have in mind a tigress carefully stalking its prey. She atavistically looks back to tigerish ancestors (patient, unrelenting hunters), yet also forward to disputatious moralists and the ranks of people with 'causes'.

So Euripides turns a witch of folk tale into the perpetrator of what is possibly the most celebrated *crime passionel*. He also makes this evidoer into a heroine in something more than the technical sense, and not only among women but among all who yearn to sweep expediency aside. Just the same, the *Medea* is a shift away from tragedy proper. However forceful, Medea is not to be regarded as a mere force but as an individual; emphatically not a mask of Dionysus but an extraordinary contemporary woman. We probably cannot diagnose Medea, though she is not felt to be a puzzle *because her creator never saw her as such*. Conversely, Clytemnestra, whose motives seem clear enough, remains mysterious since she was so to Aeschylus. Equally significant is the fact that, in the *Medea*, argument has ceased to be rationalisation and become exposition of genuine grounds of behaviour. Comparatively speaking, the reasons of Clytemnestra in the *Agememnon* are a sort of verbal display clumsily related to her actual motives. They do not truly define the motives which, it is understood, must remain indefinable. Aeschylus realises that his Clytemnestra reaches back into the shadows, into whatever lies behind the verbalising human mind – and 'Clytemnestra' knows that as well. But in the *Medea* even Jason's deplorable contentions are nevertheless his real reasons for casting Medea off, and the heroine's fierce eloquence matches her innermost mental processes. There are no deeper mental processes in Euripides, let alone processes arising in the nervous systems and chemical constitutions of the characters. In other words, Euripides knows of none. For the truth about Medea is that she is a clever Greek's version of a barbarian and a thrilling *stage* figure, nothing else. In contrast, Clytemnestra is a thrilling stage expression of an otherwise inexpressible reality.

Euripides has been called a 'rationalist', though of course he did not disbelieve in the gods as a modern rationalist disbelieves in God. On the contrary he reveals a typical artist's cavalier capacity to make liberal use of deities, while acknowledging their irresistible powers. He took for granted the existence and influence of supernatural agencies, for how else could he have explained abnormal human behaviour? To say that an attitude or a deed has been produced by a god is to shed light upon it, as today one seems to illuminate matters by reference to social factors. It is a question of selecting circumstances that will appeal to people as a cause. Such illumination is at best limited and usually quite misleading. Euripides clearly longed for enlightenment and tidiness, seeking those qualities with much ingenuity. The gods are employed to validate matters that lie beyond Euripides' powers of analysis – and beyond our own as well. There is no disrespect in Euripides' use of, say, Aphrodite and Artemis in the *Hippolytus*: the 'disrespect', if it is proper to call it that, lies rather in his hostility to 'excessive' darkness and loose ends, his disdain for the tragic assumption that reality lies outside culture.

We may divide Euripides' ingenuity into two related aspects. First there is the aspect best illustrated by the close of the *Medea*. Euripides needed, for temperamental reasons, to carry the argument between Jason and Medea as far as it would go. What mattered was the debate and its justificatory–exculpatory qualities; hence Medea's escape in her dragon-drawn chariot. But such an argument does not displace the gods; it simply takes us to a further point where the gods must manifestly resume control. The final judgement on Medea lies in the hands of Zeus. Euripides evidently felt that his predecessors gave up before it was necessary; they consigned too much to the darkness, since a good deal more might have been explained in behavioural terms – to use our modern expression. Euripides did not realise that such 'explanations' are a systematic sort of gossip, not explanatory at all.

The second aspect concerns origins as opposed to consequences. Divinities were used by Euripides to validate happenings about which he fancied a worthy spectator would be sceptical. Such a spectator absolutely needed to be shown a convincing cause. Why does Phaedra, wife of Theseus, fall morbidly in love with her stepson Hippolytus? To this day there is no satisfactory answer to such a question. Gilbert Murray, discussing the *Hippolytus*, is constrained to say that 'There is such a power as Cypris in the world',[18] which means that people do fall obsessively and suicidally in love. Kitto remarks that, to Euripides, Aphrodite was 'one of the elemental powers in nature',[19] but he cannot offer a scientific or social diagnosis any more than the ancient poet. Recently critics have indeed been apt to attribute Phaedra's passion to her role as Queen of Athens and to the patriarchal structure of Athenian society. But how is that an explanation? The problem admits of no solution, for it is not in the proper sense a problem at all; it is merely a phenomenon. To Euripides and his ideal spectators (namely Socrates and himself) the case is solved when one reveals that Aphrodite (or Cypris) has, so to say, 'infected' Phaedra with love for Hippolytus as a means of punishing the young man for his hatred of woman and rejection of carnality. Euripides 'solves' by making visible: he puts Aphrodite in full view to start with, so that we know the reason for Phaedra's fatal condition. If this reason appears to us purely historical and unsatisfactory, ought we not to appreciate that our own socio-political reasons, which are supposed to account for a culture that believes in Aphrodite, themselves need to be accounted for? What of a culture that *requires* socio-political reasons? In truth, what Aeschylus and Sophocles knew and Euripides helps us to forget is that there are no reasons other than those found helpful in a given culture.

Euripides also employs the god Artemis, to round off the *Hippolytus*, because he feels that a power is needed to apportion blame and to soothe that anxious ideal spectator who would otherwise cry out: 'Why has the innocent, if haughty, Hippolytus been destroyed by the bull from the sea? Why has Theseus not been agonisingly reminded of his guilty role in the catastrophe? Why cannot a final reconciliation be arranged between a repentant Theseus and his dead son?' Artemis does what only a god might do, yet he is also Euripides' means of making an *enlightened* tragedy, a tragedy in which everything that may be shown, has been shown, so no one should feel bewildered or aggrieved. That is Euripides' way of defying the Fates, and it must be further contrasted with the way of Aeschylus.

We saw in the second chapter that Aeschylus resisted the Fates knowing they must remain dominant. To do so he needed the aid of Prometheus, or, to put the matter another way, he proudly assumed Promethean powers and incurred Promethean sufferings. Necessity would rule eternally, producing bad and unforeseen consequences alongside good. Now Euripides as a young man set out to change the balance of power between human beings and Necessity. If in youth (or indeed in middle age) he could think of an explanation, then it became *the* explanation. From this it followed that humanity might progressively fashion answers until in the future the only remaining questions would be stimulating as opposed to painful. Apart from Socrates himself and his aristocratic disciple Plato, Euripides was the first progressionist in the world. Nietzsche puts the matter more strikingly, for he regards Socrates as a force that spoke through Euripides. More exactly, the will to power that was Socrates (for every being is a distinctive will to power) found expression not solely in his own remarks and the writings of Plato but in the plays of Euripides as well. The specialised wills to power of Plato and Euripides reinforced the original Socratic stimulus. Here we see the first glimmerings of that dream which is only now in the twentieth century dying away, leaving behind confusion, emptiness and paltry, if regular, pleasures.

For long enough Euripides assumed that man's activities had the potential to reduce the powers of the Fates, gradually and incrementally. Necessity itself could be minimised, its dominions conquered one by one. As he grew older Euripides evidently came to feel that this optimistic assumption was wrong. In Section 12 of *The Birth of Tragedy* Nietzsche writes as though the error of the earlier belief dawned upon Euripides only in the 'evening of his life', when he wrote *The Bacchae*. We shall see that *The Bacchae* is the culmination as well as the unmistakeable announcement of a darker vision.

Long before that, and presumably even in childhood, Euripides took control of the province of observable behaviour. He had little use for stereotypes since he constantly discerned the actual motions of souls. He further observed these motions to be greatly variegated, so that one might convincingly dramatise almost anything, if only the spectators could be persuaded to give up their rigid expectations. This explains Euripides' unpopularity and his crankiness in the eyes of Aristophanes, but it also explains the large proportions of his plays that still spontaneously fascinate us. For example, when we watch a play by a modern master (Ibsen, say) we are hardly more carried away than we are by the development of Phaedra's soul as she passes from sick exhaustion to a yearning for meadows and streams, thence to her anger with the pragmatical Nurse and finally to her suicide, leaving behind a message maliciously accusing Hippolytus of rape. The sequence is so interesting, so 'Dostoevskian', that it substantially moulds the play (which is nevertheless named after the hero) and still leaves critics bristling with chivalrous rage and convinced of its truth to nature.

Nietzsche does not mention those plays such as *The Trojan Women* (425 B.C.) and the *Electra* (c. 413 B.C.) in which Euripides' gift for inventive construction is no longer employed to soften a harsh vision. Here on the contrary the harshness is accentuated, yet it is still an Apollonian harshness and Dionysus is kept at bay. The elementary structure of *The Trojan Women* expresses only grief and hopelessness, a movement (not appreciably a crescendo) leading to the killing of Andromache's son, the despairing irony of Helen's meeting with Menelaus and the lament of Hecuba as Troy goes up in flames. The very manners still exclude Dionysus, since the exchanges between Helen, Hecuba and Menelaus are too familiar in our ears, too reminiscent of our politic society. It is true that this is not remotely a Dionysian drama; Nietzsche is thoroughly vindicated. According to Gilbert Murray, 'The tragedy is perhaps, in European literature, the first great expression of the spirit of pity for mankind exalted into a moving principle . . .'.[20] 'Pity,' Murray continues, 'is a rebel passion'.[21] This is obviously meant in praise of pity, but in less flattering, Nietzschean terms we might say that pity becomes a decadent condition when it passes from a fleeting natural feeling into a generalised affective attitude. In Nietzsche's opinion the most promising people certainly feel pity but sooner or later feel the need to overcome it. Pity is Zarathustra's 'ultimate sin', or the last infirmity of his noble mind, specifically in the form of his compassion for the 'higher men', which he finally discards as he sets out to do his redemptive work.[22] Elsewhere, in *The Anti-Christ*, Nietzsche devotes Section 7 to a denunciation of pity which, he states, 'stands in antithesis to the tonic emotions which enhance the energy of the feeling of life: it has a depressive effect'.[23] Murray is correct; *The Trojan Women* is a great drama of pity, and therefore Nietzsche is also correct to imply that it is far from genuinely, Dionysianly tragic. At this stage Euripides retains his desire (now indeed it is a yearning) to minimise suffering and all severity. For that reason, *The Trojan Women*, which we are accustomed to contemplating as an honourable cry against war, is a cry against life as a whole. Our self-deception, derived from Euripides, is based upon a hidden belief that if we protest loudly and long enough, someone, some god presumably, will hear us and eventually respond.

The mood of the *Electra* is altogether different, though it rests upon the same humanistic base. Albin Lesky points out that at the time of this work tragedy had become a problem: '. . . it is significant that tragedy becomes questionable when the gods of the old faith begin to leave the Attic stage'.[24] But the gods have been positively excluded from the stage just so that tragedy might become questionable. Euripides' theory (it is in the strict sense a hypothesis) maintains that whatever is questionable allows for the possibility of correction. Just the same, Lesky is right to emphasise the godlessness of *Electra*, and perhaps another scholar, G. M. A. Grube, is right to affirm of this play that 'in his own genre this is undoubtedly Euripides' masterpiece'.[25] This possibly means – I think it ought to mean – that in the *Electra* Euripides employs his own special talent without any appreciable borrowings or bowings to tradition and convention. And indeed the play is a story of the degradation of murder, even of an 'honourable' murder committed to avenge a father's killing. Euripides has now brought everything into the light of common day; the gods have departed; a hero (Orestes) and a heroine are left to kill their mother Clytemnestra and her man Aegisthus. It is conceivable that up to now no one in Athens had regarded such a revenge killing in precisely this way; that nobody had excluded the gods and all divine significance and *then* in imagination heard a victim's screams for mercy and smelled the blood? It is more than likely that Euripides is a complete innovator here; that before *Electra* the foul reality of such an 'ethical' murder had lain concealed in its mythic significance. Likewise this is the first play – the first literary work – whose author has asked himself what happens to the personality of one who waits half a lifetime to kill her own mother and finally produces nothing but a reeking mess on a hovel floor.

Euripides' question, answered in terms that prefigure the range of all that might roughly be called 'realism' down to Zola, leaves human beings isolated in the universe and clinging to one another for support. At this late stage in his career it occurs to Euripides that he too has been wrong all his life. He has created marvellously out of his very error. Now he seeks to reunite humanity with the world, for if that can be achieved, the most dreadful things will once again be meaningful; Electra will no more be a squalid killer but a traditional tragic heroine. And this will scarcely be an idealistic way out of the human trap, for it will tie people to the earth again and make all their evildoings significant. It means the return of Dionysus and, incidentally, the end of moral anxiety. Naturally we shall not welcome Dionysus, or at least the excessively proud and clever will not do so, because no such person desires a powerful god who neither reasons nor hopes in the human fashion. Least of all do we proud ones wish for a god who may not be opposed, and Euripides has discovered that Dionysus grows more cruel the more opposition he meets.

Dionysus returns in *The Bacchae*, announcing at the outset that he has come in the shape of a man to walk again in the land of Thebes, where ancient Cadmus, former king of Thebes, still honours the sacred tomb of Semele, where the women have taken to the hills, becoming Bacchants, and where King Pentheus has outlawed Dionysiac practices. The various modern interpretations of this strange play ('strange' in terms of content and feeling as distinct from structure) all encourage a distancing effect. *The Bacchae* is today viewed historically or anthropologically or in terms of stagecraft. We are more or less expected to match *The Trojan Women* or the *Electra* with our own experiences, but to see *The Bacchae* as an exotic product, a sort of terrifying museum-piece. When stagecraft is emphasised there is the familiar implication that we are dealing with an artefact somewhat removed from the feelings, as opposed to the skill, of the artificer. As we noted in Chapter 2, Nietzsche was among the first to stress the gulf between a work of art and the everyday personality of its creator, yet he appreciated that work

comes to life, flourishes and has an enduring effect in proportion to
the force of the original will of its creator.[26] The will essentially *is* the
work, so that this play must be seen not as a grisly entertainment by
Euripides (such a piece would have crumbled to dust long ago) but
as the metaphysical testament of his twilight years.

Much awkwardness, amounting almost to idiocy, accompanies a
refusal to consider *The Bacchae* in relation to its *raison d'être*, namely
Euripides' recognition of the unbreakable power of Dionysus.
Euripides means what he plainly says: Dionysus has seemed to
absent himself from the lands of Greece (specifically in the period of
Euripides' apostasy) and has now returned to bewitch the people
once again. The dialectic of Socrates and the drama of Euripides
have merely veiled the god from the people, especially from the
thinkers and debaters. Now that Dionysus has reappeared he will
bring comfort and joy to those who worship him, hideous torment
to his opponents. Lying behind civilised codes and behind even
such long-cultivated feelings as those of mothers for their children,
Dionysus is the dynamic of life-processes. Zeus is master of all, but
beneath the god of gods – as Teiresias explains in the play – are the
earth itself, or Demeter, and Dionysus who, from the human point
of view, is the intermediary between people and their world. As I
have just suggested, Dionysus is actually far more than that, but to
us he appears only in that role. So far as we are concerned he is the
link between ourselves and other organic forms. The words of
Teiresias (lines 266–326) mean that Demeter is substance,
materiality, everything that concretely exists under the sway of
Zeus. However, for so long as the human race survives materiality
will be represented, recognised, defined, known: such processes
bring material things to fruition, or so we necessarily believe. We
are prohibited from thinking otherwise. The human function
cannot be other than the spiritualisation of what is 'in itself' mere
substance. Since we alone spiritualise things, we have no other
purpose in the world. It is Dionysus who gives us this power. Note:
Dionysus emphatically does not correct existence but completes it.
Zeus encompasses all; Demeter may be said to embrace every
material thing, while Dionysus is the animating principle; or
rather, not a principle at all, but simply animation. He animates all
creatures and plants in the ways of their species, and likewise
enables human beings to do what they alone can do: confer
meaning and value. This is done at every point on our scale, from
the crudest responses of attraction and repulsion to the most
refined cultural forms; all are valuations.

Dionysus is the *genius* of mankind, as of all beings. Naturally therefore he is non-rational, though he may employ rationality as a means. According to the Teiresias of Euripides he also gives us our capacity for ignoring the preponderance of sorrow over joy, and, concomitantly, our talent for prophecy and hope. Human beings, alone of all beings, predict the future – however misguidedly. In a word, Dionysus is *power*. Teiresias advises Pentheus, 'Boast not that naked force hath power over men',[27] or, in Gilbert Murray's translation, 'Dream not that force is power'.[28] This assertion falls like a shaft of sunlight upon the murk and cobwebs of our misconceptions, especially, in modern times, our misconceptions of Nietzsche. Teiresias (in this context Euripides himself) must be taken to mean that power lies in the spirit of the individual and has nothing essentially to do with the brute capacity to crush and flatten. More often than not political and military oppression proceeds not from the personal power of the oppressor (which may be negligible) but from his social or professional role. Power resides in the sparrow as in the eagle. The power of each being, or Dionysus as he assumes the form of each being, is individuated, incomparable, indefinable; the sheer dynamic of that one single being. No wonder, then, that the Dionysus of the old legends took myriad forms and died myriad deaths, always coming to life again.

No wonder also that this in late play of Euripides, Dionysus cannot be defeated by the mere rationality and legalism of Pentheus, King of Thebes. Pentheus' rational mind and his antagonism towards Dionysus are self-evasions and defences against his own Dionysian power, for what else could they be? This is a fine point, since Euripides is not, in the style of a modern liberal, censuring the exercise of authority; rather he is distinguishing between morbid and creative uses of authority. A use is morbid, not when an individual (an Ajax, and Achilles, an Agamemnon) imposes himself on others, but when he denies individuality as such. Bizarre though it may momentarily seem to us, warrior-killing is not at all the same thing as denying individuality. Achilles does not expect Hector to be other than he is, to be a different sort of person, but that is exactly what Creon demands of Antigone. A little thought and this attitude no longer seems bizarre but perfectly natural.

Here we have the explanation of that scene (roughly lines 800–50) in which Pentheus finds himself able to utter only the words, think only the thoughts, that Dionysus puts into his head. The King yields to the god because, like all mortals, he is quickened by none other than the god. Pentheus suddenly discovers and is enslaved by the non-rational base of his excessive rationality. Euripides thus turns his extraordinary gift as a psychologist away from the observation of behaviour to the source of our behaviour, to the interplay between somatic processes and their sublimation in the forms of ideology and spiritual yearning.

So Euripides as an old man declares to his spectators that the notion of human progress is wrong when it assumes (as Socrates and Plato have begun to assume) that mortals may ignore the gods. *The Bacchae* is full of references to the 'divine power', or the 'spirit of God', confirming that Euripides has indeed been converted to the religion which as a youth he denied. Perhaps (and this is plainly a surmise) the extreme cruelty of Pentheus' death, his being torn to pieces by the Maenads, reflects nothing so much as Euripides' frenzy of hatred for his former irreverence. But so far as most of the people were concerned Dionysus had become a stage figure. Euripides had so skilfully represented social reality that Dionysus, the well-spring of their lives – as citizens, as members of the species, as creatures locked into the endless earthly cycles of ripening and decay – had dwindled into a concept, an image, or, at worst, a dead superstition.

5

Nature and Purity in the Renaissance

Once the concept 'nature' had been devised as the concept antithetical to 'God', 'natural' had to be the word for 'reprehensible' – this entire fictional world has its roots in *hatred* of the natural (– actuality! –), it is the expression of a profound discontent with the actual . . .[1]

In these words Nietzsche has Christianity at the forefront of his mind, yet the development he analyses began before Jesus. We would nevertheless be wrong to describe it as a biblical manifestation, since the God of the Old Testament is not antithetical to his own creation. In Genesis the earth is created as a division of God's domain, not God's opposite, and man is the sinful overseer of that division.

Even so, hatred of the natural must have been common before Christ, especially among slaves and others not represented in culture. In the aristocratic Plato it was not a question of hatred but of *caution*. Nietzsche contends in *The Gay Science* that Plato's idealism was 'the caution of an over-rich and dangerous health, the fear of *over-powerful* senses, the prudence of a prudent Socratic'.[2] If Plato was thus dangerously healthy – meaning that his senses were almost too powerful for his reason – such a condition is not at all what we normally think of as life-hatred. Among modern people, at all events, the latter accompanies and develops from an infantile reaction of fear, so that the individual desperately substitutes fantasies or words for sense-impressions in early life. Today people rarely, if ever, have over-powerful senses, and the one who hates life wards off comparatively *weak* stimuli. Therefore his idealism, in whatever form it takes, is distinct from Plato's. The idealism of Plato was not itself morbid, though it has served as a focus for morbid forces.

Elsewhere Plato is considered to have been one of that numerous company of philosophers who make mummies out of actual things. 'All that philosophers have handled for millenia has been conceptual mummies, nothing actual has escaped from their hands alive.'[3] Philosophers *embalm* pieces of reality. At this late stage of Nietzsche's career, in *Twilight of the Idols*, he believed that Plato set himself up as more than a guide to the truth, rather as truth itself. 'I Plato, *am* the truth.'[4] Among the Greeks of the sixth and fifth centuries such overwhelming self-assurance was normal for philosophers; each embodied the truth. In 1889 Nietzsche saw both Socrates and Plato as he had seen them in *The Birth of Tragedy*: they were 'symptoms of decay . . . agents of the dissolution of Greece . . .'.[5] The towering confidence of these two men helped to destroy the Grecian world by giving voice to a widespread but hitherto submerged attitude.

We are still left puzzling over the clues to Plato. What, for example is the root of *The Republic*: the *hauteur* of an aristocrat (as Karl Popper believes[6]); sheer creative exuberance, or, as indeed may well be the case, the need for a shield against the glare of existence? Today our senses are too weak, comparatively speaking, and the blinding radiance of the earth has been dimmed, so that we no longer have the same problem. In *The Republic* the existent is held at arm's length on the grounds that it is constantly a process of becoming, of growing and withering away, and this, the entire visible world, is almost automatically felt to be unsatisfactory. Socrates' arguments for the unsatisfactoriness of the actual consist of saying that it falls short of the ideal. Once the ideal is admitted there is no counter-argument. Only that which has *being*: the Forms, the Good, the immortal soul of man and ultimately God himself – only these suprasensible ideas are finished and immaculate.

Plato, like Socrates, gave precedence to our conceptualising and argumentative capacities. What we call 'nature' doubtless falsifies our concepts, or, to be exact, the notion of truth versus falsehood is a human device and has nothing to do with the extra-human universe, about which our knowledge may well be accurate so far as it goes, but can never be 'true'. Just the same, we are compelled to simplify the natural world and the ancients already did so. Thales supposed either that the world rested upon water, or that water was the 'first principle' of all substances; Anaximander believed that all things developed out of a sort of universal non-stuff which he called the 'infinite', and Anaximenes taught that everything grew from infinite air. The capacity for abstract thinking came a little later and presumably evolved from the earlier need to simplify by tracing the great variety of physical things back to elementary physical, or at any rate, unspiritual sources. For long enough, however, such simplification did not denigrate the physical universe. Something of great significance occurred when the universe came to be seen as intrinsically inferior. In the first place it was inferior to the human soul. Nature as a whole was not yet the world and the flesh in the hostile Christian sense, but it was seen even then as essentially undesirable and alien to the soul. In *The Republic* Socrates argues that the immortal soul is encrusted with worldly things as an object in the sea is covered with rocks and shells.

I am speaking of a development which is still incomplete, though today it is in its closing stages. In Nietzsche's terminology the 'genealogy', not of morals but of monotheistic faith, still works its effects, since (to put the matter utterly irreligiously) the source of God – some combination of fearful discontent, creative zeal and lust to crystallise the changing face of nature – now gives rise to prophetic dreams. God was born out of disgust both with existent beings and the imperfections of the gods. Quite suddenly mankind required non-existent perfection (or purity) by which to measure and judge all the forms of existence. But we too – we more than ever – build the future, not out of sheer delight but to redress the past. For all our fears of the future there is a dominant assumption that every trouble has a solution which may surely be discovered. Some troubles are held to be natural, others man-made, a distinction which points up our inherited tendency to distinguish ourselves from nature. Nature is still the antagonist which may be defeated by spiritual (inventive, thoughtful, co-operative) means. So the spirit of man is imagined as the potential victor over nature. The purer the spirit, the less contaminated by nature, the nearer it will come to total victory. While spirit and nature are plainly involved with each other, we still suppose them to be theoretically and ideally separate. The spirit 'could be' pure, while nature is plainly impure, hence inferior, mongrel, a mixture of flourishing and decaying processes, in need of supervision, an aggregate of things that are born and die. Our crazy logic has it that since things die they cannot be pure enough to survive. That belief is seldom uttered today, but it still influences our thoughts.

It necessarily seems to modern people that unsupervised nature,

nature 'on its own' is hugely or profoundly worthless, so that the function we perform consists of completing nature by giving value to a collection of spiritually barren forces. At least we have to imagine them as barren without us; in other words we find ourselves in the ridiculous position of thinking of a universe from which thought has been excluded. We cause the forces to bear fruit; they bear fruit in us. It is in this sense that it seems virtually impossible not to be a metaphysician, and, as we saw in the first chapter, Nietzsche is no exception.[8] He speaks of nature as needing people, or to be specific, needing the philosopher and the artist 'for the achievement of a metaphysical goal, that of its own self-enlightenment'.[9] So nature is 'redeemed', as Nietzsche calls it, presumably not from its sinfulness but from its nullity and harshness. Nature has thrown up human beings who, being themselves natural and gifted with a sense of purpose, confer purpose upon their purposeless world. The grand irony is that since purpose has been thus conferred, it has somehow been definitely acquired. Now with the advent of the human race, nature has achieved the metaphysical goal of its own enlightenment.

By the time of the Renaissance a screen had fallen, blurring if not quite concealing the realities of pre-Socratic times. To Aeschylus, Sophocles and Euripides the god of gods was Zeus, to whom an antithesis is inconceivable. Therefore, as we have amply seen, people needed to meet the pitiless terrors of nature in quite another fashion: how could they simply 'side with' the arbitrary Zeus or think of him as beneficent? When we now look back on Aeschylus or, say, on the *Nichomachean Ethics* of Aristotle it requires some effort to put aside all Platonic–Christian assumptions. Two-and-a-half thousand years of reference to transcendence in one form or another have made it hard to conceive of a *metaphysical* universe (not mere materiality) lacking teleological justification. Such a universe must be eternally 'impure', since the very notion of purity, except in the humdrum chemical sense, demands purpose and distinctions of value perceived, not invented, by the human mind. (Perhaps we should remind ourselves in passing that the gods of the Greeks were 'merely' superhuman, human beings writ large.)

Here it is necessary to mention once more that ethical point indispensable to the theme of this book. To the Greeks of the tragic period existence in all its varieties, including the divine, was riddled with what we describe as 'faults'. There was no conception of the flawless. For all that, no one, neither god nor man, was personally responsible for a fault in the sense that he might have avoided it. Aeschylus' Xerxes is guilty of awful hubris; Clytemnestra is indisputably wicked, yet morally speaking neither is *to blame*. No one blames another except as an expression of feeling, a desire to hurt, a wish to punish, or some such questionable motive. It is plain, for example, that the bitterness of Hecuba and Andromache in *The Trojan Women* is not truly an appeal to general principles. In a moral sense everyone is childlike by our standards, which means, not that they are inferior to us but simply that they have not yet acquired those bedrock moral standards which we are in the process of relinquishing. No one is a moral being; before Socrates the very idea is absurd. The structure of the tragic world rests upon an absence of significant choice. Conversely the notion of free will is the basis of all post-tragic thought. The reason for this is the invention of the idea of purity. Now purity exists, or, to be precise, lies enticingly beyond existence.

The Renaissance is pervaded with guilt because it is rife with spirit. Sensory perceptions mean nothing without the spirits that inform them, and if a perception provokes conflict, say between chastity and lust, the complete meaning lies in the outcome. The visible earth houses innumerable spirits and is what we still perforce take it to be, a meaningful place, on account of those spirits. A Renaissance scholar writes as follows:

> For by the axiom of knowledge every element in man's experience – all the data of sensation from which he derives both the 'images' and the capacity for drawing inferences from them which constitute natural knowledge – becomes an object of cognition that in its hierarchical sweep upward leads ultimately to God.[10]

Thus the very 'facts of life' are located by Renaissance man somewhere on an 'upward sweep' whose apex is God. Matter is never mere matter, a clod is essentially more than a clod. The fascination with decay, for example in Webster, elevates substance above the biological level. The plain reason for this is that Elizabethan England abounds in good and bad spirits. The vitality of this period (a vitality of contrast and contest) directly depends upon the unquestioned belief in the unseen world. Orthodox religion flows into the beliefs and practices of witchcraft and other occult sciences. From one point of view these seeming opposites (the true faith and the damnable activities of a Faustus) are all one, namely the means by which human life is enhanced, stretched to extremes of good and evil, made vastly interesting, perilous and subtle. From the point of view of the Renaissance the simplicities of pre-Platonic Greece appear crude. In those ancient times sin had few nuances, and the gloom of Hades was as nothing compared with the unending agony of hell. There are greater tensions now: angels and fiends; swaggering health and rotting corpses; meads versus torture chambers; the chalice and the poison cup. The peaks we know as 'Renaissance culture' are clearly composed of such tensions. Here we are in the familiar realm of theoretical, as against full-blooded, imaginative understanding. In theory it must be widely appreciated in the twentieth century that the very morbidity of plague-ridden Florence and the stinks of Elizabethan London were the depths essential to the heights. But, as Nietzsche says, 'One recognises the superiority of the Greek man and the Renaissance man – but one would like to have them without the causes and conditions that made them possible'.[11] Our implicit modern view is that if such social foulness is required for such culture (not to mention the superior Renaissance man himself), then we had better not have the culture; but is there not also a scarcely acknowledged dream that a yet fairer and cleaner society than ours will produce unprecedented artistic glories?

On the other hand, Nietzsche uses a simple metaphor in *Thus Spoke Zarathustra*: the prophet, speaking of a tree on a mountainside, tells a young man, 'The more it wants to rise into the heights and the light, the more determinedly do its roots strive earthwards, downwards, into the darkness, into the depths – into evil.'[12] He means primarily that the greatest creators take nourishment from their own roots in evil (in malice, as it might be, or in cruelty), but, more widely, an historical period may also be seen in the terms of this metaphor. The roots of the Renaissance strove 'earthwards, downwards, into the darkness, into the depths – into evil.'

In contrast to a common modern assumption, Nietzsche holds that life universally requires 'steps', distinctions and conflict.

> Life wants to raise itself on high with pillars and steps; it wants to gaze into the far distance and out upon joyful splendour – *that* is why it needs height!
> And because it needs height, it needs steps and conflict between steps and those who climb them! Life wants to climb and in climbing overcome itself.[13]

This need was generously satisfied in the period of the Renaissance, quite without what we normally regard as 'intention'. And of course the heights of that time were not narrowly cultural in the modern sense, according to which culture is a detachable layer or compartment of social activity. Greek culture constitutes a mighty upward step, but perhaps we are right to call it less a harmony of contrasts than the culture of the Renaissance. The Greeks, for all the starkness of their tragedies, never contrived to make a scene of horror into a thing of beauty, yet that is what the Renaissance *symptomatically* did. The churches of Rome are great caverns of gloom and pain, so that today it is a relief to wander off into the sunlight of the Forum. As for the Greeks, they instinctively excluded ugly scenes – as Aristotle enjoins in the *Poetics*[14] – and no one had yet realised that what is ugly in life may *easily* be rendered beautiful in art. The most important point, which Aristotle already seems to imply, is that tragedy never can approximate to realism; the two modes are utterly distinct, since the second concentrates the mind upon events, the first upon their meaning. The real, in the sense of the apparent, obscures tragic significance. Tragedy is not mimesis, but, insofar as the religious source of tragedy develops into drama, such drama must not draw too far away in spirit from ritual celebration of creative–destructive natural processes. Now in the Renaissance saintliness, agony and beauty are fused; likewise vice is beautified even as it is reviled. So the vital quality of Renaissance art is the union of subjects which *in theory* are separate and opposed.

Such aspects of life and mind had to be forced apart in the first place, which they scarcely were among the Greeks of the tragic period. The priestly cast of mind has intervened, distinguishing not just vice from virtue, but varieties and degrees of each. According to Nietzsche, the priest also makes everything more dangerous; he enhances the danger and hence the interest of daily life.

> For with the priests *everything* becomes more dangerous, not only cures and remedies, but also arrogance, revenge, acuteness, profligacy, love, lust to rule, virtue, disease – but it is only fair to add that it was on the soil of this *essentially dangerous* form of human existence, the priestly form, that man first became *an interesting animal*, that only here did the human soul in a higher sense acquire *depth* and become *evil* – and these are the two basic respects in which man has hitherto been superior to other beasts.[15]

So by the time a mode defined as 'tragic drama' begins to flourish once again in the late sixteenth century, ordinary life has become spiritually hazardous and by the same token profoundly interesting. This period is marked by the fusion of two dissimilar qualities: the priestly psychology of good versus evil (including, as I have mentioned, the divisions and gradations of both) and, on the other hand, the heroic psychology of risk-taking, expermentalism and unpriestly audacity. The point is that these two branches of human activity are first placed in different compartments and then suddenly merged. It was necessary for them to be set apart (for centuries, for an entire millenium) before they should be creatively joined.

To illustrate this let us, by way of contrast, momentarily recall the *Oedipus at Colonus*. No one could have suggested to Sophocles that the agonies of Oedipus somehow belonged in a different sphere from the final nobility of Oedipus' soul; that the latter should be categorised as spirit while the former is no more than corrupt and dying flesh. Therefore the merging by Sophocles of the pain and nobility of Oedipus is not a union of opposites, or even of highly unlike things. Contrariwise, the Renaissance inherits the Platonic–Christian tradition according to which the universe is a duality of being and becoming, or of spirit and flesh. On the one side are visible things high and low, while on the antithetical side are, in ascending order, the immortal soul of man, the minor spirits, the nine orders of angels and the three-personed God. God is truly lord of both the corporeal and the spiritual; he arches over all. This Augustinian system, the basis of Renaissance optimism, still predominated in the sixteenth and seventeenth centuries. For the system gave to human beings, gravely imperfect though they were, a divinely rational faculty, and confirmed them in their ascendancy over the earth. Further, it was possible for an individual to receive the unmerited grace of God, hence to rise to heaven.

Outside this deep-rooted metaphysics art would be impossible, life unbelievable; there is no 'outside'. No one can be a free-thinker in the casual modern sense. Free-thinking is exceedingly hazardous. As the seventeenth century progresses science and philosophy begin to destroy the old world-picture, but they only begin to do so and, from our securely distant perspective, thinkers' procedures seem wary indeed. Descartes undermines the foundations not by the results of his thinking but by its *way*; after him serious thinkers are compelled to think radically. Doing philosophy somewhat as though it were astronomy or mathematics, combining the advantages of logic, geometry and algebra without the limitations of those subjects has been, Descartes says, his whole endeavour. And this endeavour, this quest for certainty is his (tremendous) legacy, while his proofs are proofs of what everyone already knows: that God alone is being or perfection, while all else is subdivisible, contingent and impure. Similarly the mind is utterly irreducible to matter – but only in modern times have some people started to contemplate a coincidence, or even an identity, of mind and body. Today we still have not caught up with Nietzsche who, as early as 1883, has Zarathustra declare that 'your little intelligence, my brother, which you call "spirit", is also an instrument of your body, a little instrument and toy of your great intelligence'.[16] So far as Descartes' contemporaries and immediate posterity are concerned, the new dualism is calculated to augment rather than weaken the new notion of tragedy which depends upon an image of mankind as both free and fallen. In effect (not in intention) Descartes certainly tilts against *classical* tragedy, since he believes in freedom of the will. His own will 'easily goes astray, choosing the bad instead of the good and the false instead of the true'.[17] The plain reason for this is that his will is 'much wider in scope'[18] than his understanding, which amounts to saying that the will is generally wanton, in need of restraint by the intellect.

Spinoza alone of seventeenth-century philosophers (or indeed of all modern philosophers before Nietzsche) logically demonstrates that the will is *not* free – just as the pre-Socratics along with the early tragic dramatists already understood.[19] But we in turn need to understand what Spinoza means by the unfree will: in blunt terms, one wills whatever one wills and is not at liberty to will something else. Here we should elaborate upon an important matter which we considered in Chapter 2 (p. 43ff.). A person is not able to will himself into loving God if in fact he prefers the devil. He who imposes 'love of God' upon his heart acts against his will and so becomes muddled and vengeful. In this way Spinoza points back to a basic insight of ancient tragedy, but now (in 1677) his belief – or, as I prefer to think, his convincing demonstration – is untimely. The new sort of tragedy, despite Corneille, Racine and Dryden, is already under sentence of death, just because humanity is entering upon a period in which this non-tragic freedom of the individual will is seen as all but axiomatic. A sinner is now more than ever (more than in the Middle Ages, for example) thought able to 'correct' his behaviour. I mean that while the will used to be regarded as free to obey or disobey God, it will soon be supposed to be entirely and idiosyncrastically free to choose itself out of a variety of possible wills. Nietzsche's own position on this is straightforward: there is no free will. He refers to 'the boorish simplicity of this celebrated concept of "free will"'. On the other hand, 'the "unfree will" is mythology; in real life it is only a matter of *strong* and *weak* wills'.[20] The will (whatever its nature) is prior to other operations of the personality such as cognition and perception. Only a weak will can be thoroughly conditioned by reasoning or social example, but in any case the will, weak or strong, is determinative and entirely escapes the concept of freedom. One can no more direct or strengthen one's will by taking thought (to use the language of the Sermon on the Mount) than add a cubit to one's stature. We shall pursue this matter later, especially in the last chapter, but it is worth suggesting at this point that the 'free-will period' is coming to an end in the late twentieth century, thus preparing the way for a further (and of course surprising) evolution of tragic thought and art.

What we designate as tragic in the sixteenth and seventeenth centuries, Racine's *Phèdre* as against the *Hippolytus* of Euripides, is an altogether fresh form which usually rests upon Christian–humanist foundations. Mankind is now the illuminated field of thought and contemplation although everyone assumes that man's corporeal frame belongs far from the top of the material ladder and his immortal soul at the foot of the spiritual ladder. For all the contemporary denunciations of pride and the references to the loathsomeness and merely instrumental significance of the earth, individuals advance to the front of the stage as never before. A character in a Renaissance tragedy no longer tails off into the fluid, indivisible world of nature but stands square against everything else – even if he is a mere clown or third murderer. He 'lives', as we say; he 'comes alive', or, in other words, what alone now seems to live is individuality, the temper, manners or objectives of an individual. Macbeth is apparently a complete individual, though of course he is nothing of the kind. If Macbeth is also representative of something, namely vaulting ambition, the representativeness is secondary in every sense. We are interested in this person Macbeth, and our prized interest in the moral lesson of his story is very tame, not to say laborious and self-deceiving. In fact we thrill to the entire poem *Macbeth*, to its interwoven imagery, but this, in one way or another, is a seduction to life and *against* morality.

Shakespeare's play typifies Renaissance tragedy in that it seduces to life and only pretends to preach a moral lesson. The morality of *Macbeth* is no more than an integral part of its dark and bloody fascination. One might say, 'Well and good, but isn't that what Greek tragedy also does in its different fashion?' The difference, however, is very great, for Greek tragedy reconciles spectators to the reality behind appearances. As a rule this reality is inferred, or at most sensed, and would be unbearable, not desirable in human eyes, if a figure did not rise to tragic heights. Aeschylus and Sophocles both managed to hearten people by sounding sombre and ominous notes. No one can have been deceived and yet people enjoyed the tragic festivals; they relished the iterations of doom and the very lack of glittering surface. Elizabethan and Jacobean tragedy, on the other hand, is in the best sense superficial: it brings almost everything on to the stage and leaves nothing mysterious except for the sake of theatrical effect. The audience assumes that Macbeth's guilt alone robs the world of meaning, but even the least blameworthy Greek knew that life has no rational significance – for what else is the point of tragedy? To the Elizabethans anything and everything may manifest itself, and everything, however inhuman or superhuman, is humanised. Conversely, although the Greeks anthropomorphised world forces, they left an all-important gap between their own ideas of right and wrong and the attitudes of superhuman powers. In the *Oresteia* the Eumenides necessarily have the likeness of human beings (hideously masked), yet their slavering lust to kill Orestes, though it is 'rationalised' in argument with Apollo, is not fully accountable in human terms. Everyone watching a play – which is as much as to say every human being, unless it be a madman – justifies Orestes and dreads the Furies. But ghosts in Renaissance plays are 'human' enough and their behaviour varies from the farcical to the majestic. The most decent and honourable ghost, the ghost of Hamlet's father, is thoroughly 'human' in the sense of being more explicable than his brilliant son.

It is time to consider some particular plays of the period from the late sixteenth century to the late seventeenth, but to do so with no object other than to discover (uncover) what then constituted 'tragedy'. The following pages are scarcely literary criticism, though I hope that nothing I say can be falsified by close reference to a text. Nor is what follows literary history in the usual sense, for, apart from other criteria, I shall begin out of order with Corneille and Racine, then go back to Marlowe and his English successors, since our theme is more transparent in the French dramatists than in the English.

Corneille's *Polyeucte* (1642) and Racine's *Phèdre* (1667) afford us a relatively smooth transition from ancient austerity of form to the elaborateness of the Elizabethans. Far more important is the fact that these two playwrights emphasise Platonic and Christian assumptions which are veiled in English plays. The Frenchmen plainly illustrate how the Renaisssance contrived to make its own sort of tragedy out of what we have come to recognise as essentially untragical material.

Polyeucte has encountered a varied critical reception over the centuries, but the consensus today is that it is a flawed masterpiece – flawed because of its hurried final scenes and, so it is often argued, the nature of the hero himself. The latter would seem to be a sizeable flaw, although Polyeucte in exactly his existing form, with no alteration or improvement *is* the meaning of the play: his behaviour is in no respect a technical oversight. For Corneille has built his work upon a faith that was seen even by some contemporaries as misguided. Nowadays it seems intrinsically ridiculous and yet we cannot gloss over it on the usual grounds that an author is entitled, above all, to his vision. I am referring not to Christianity as a way, but to that strand of Christianity which proclaims death preferable to life. I do not know how important the strand now is, though historically it has at times been indispensable. The third century, with which *Polyeucte* deals, was such a time. Needless to say, the preference in question is quite other than the stark preference of the Chorus of *Oedipus at Colonus* quoted earlier in Chapter 3.

> Not to be born at all
> Is best, far best that can befall,
> Next best, when born, with least delay
> To trace the backward way.[21]

Here the Chorus is emphasising the pains and calamities of life, not the sins of human beings. In *Polyeucte* sin and misery are Christianly compounded: the world is the sphere from which the good man escapes to heaven.

This play inverts all love stories, since the hero is eager to forsake his wife Pauline, a noble and loving woman (not to mention the prospect of a good life in Roman-occupied Armenia), for the infinitely greater joys of heaven. Pauline is also loved by Severus, a gallant Roman knight who has recently secured golden prospects for himself by saving the life of the Emperor Decius. Pauline's father, Felix, Governor of Armenia, loathes and eagerly executes Christians, while Pauline herself regards the Christians as an 'impious' crowd. Finally Pauline and Felix embrace death as converts to Christianity, having been overwhelmed ('enlightened') by the example of Polyeucte and his friend Néarque, who have joyously led the way through martyrdom to heaven.

Corneille has set himself the most intractable problem for an artist, since he seems not to have exploited religion in the usual artist's fashion, but subordinated his art to his faith. Can this actually be done? Not only does the art suffer in such a case but the nature of any ideology (*any*, from early Christianity to Marxism) must be distorted and eventually destroyed by works of art above the level of the mediocre. Nevertheless, Corneille is so able an artist that he still makes a formidable play out of a belief which must, when taken seriously, crush all plays, all culture indeed. Remember we are not talking about weak and liberalised Christianity, but the invincibly resolute faith of the early Church. Tragedy is about the going-down of the hero, not through moral error and certainly not as a result of moral excellence, but somewhat as the fruits of the earth fall when ripe. If the hero chooses death (Sophocles' Ajax, for instance) he does so in such a way as to encourage the audience to welcome, not detest, natural processes. The hero's death brings a sense of loss because of his former power, but paradoxically it also brings a sense of gain because life-processes are generally enhanced. Even Clytemnestra's death has this dual effect, for she too, in spite of her wickedness – or not to be mealy-mouthed, as a result of her wickedness – provides a stimulus for us all. *Polyeucte* reduces life to ashes; it has no meaning other than as a succession of points of departure for heaven. Towards the end of the play Polyeucte declares that he regards Pauline (whom the audience certainly love) as an 'obstacle' to him, one who would detain him from the 'holy sweets' (*saintes douceurs*) of heaven (Act IV, Scene 2, lines 1144–5).

In what sense can this hero be esteemed as heroic? Heroism involves struggle, but Polyeucte appears to exert himself no more than Christ, for his progress to death is effortless and more or less joyful. He never doubts for a moment, unless he does so at the outset over his wife's nightmare and her consequent worries. Thinking of Jesus, Nietzsche remarks, 'But if anything is unevangelic it is the concept hero. Precisely the opposite of all contending, of all feeling oneself in struggle has here [in the psychology of the redeemer] become instinct . . .'.[22] Nietzsche's implication should be teased out. He intends us to realise that Christ's lack of contention was a mode of *self*-assertion. Christ continually asserted his gospel – which was, and has remained, utterly co-existent with himself – by his exemplary forbearance. Thus a unique form of life, Jesus, set itself against other life forms. He either dominated or stood firm against other forms through his inner certainty and not by dispute of any kind. Christ did not argue; he was neither a dialectician nor a politician. It is true that Polyeucte argues his case, but only in a pleasant, well-disposed style. However the point is that such a way of life is meaningless except as a preparation for death; it indicates a yearning for death. Jesus is not a stimulant to life but the reverse; his teaching is a rejection of life in favour of eternal life. Eternal life is not life infinitely extended but something entirely different, without development or suffering. In fact, of course, the example and the words of Jesus have provided countless suffering people with precisely a means of living. The important question, which we should not pursue here, concerns the value of a life sustained only by the supposition of eternal life in Christ.

Corneille's extraordinary play is wholly Christian, as Christian as a play could possibly be, which makes it a piece of culture whose object must logically be taken to be the elimination of culture. It tells us that natural life is impure while eternal life is pure. We need to understand some variant of the same notion behind much Renaissance drama. Even when the dramatist is audacious enough to oppose the idea, the idea has formed the basis of his play. I hope to show that Shakespeare alone discounts purity, but authors generally accept other-worldly perfection as the fundamental fact upon which their words, however vigorous and 'true to life', must rest.

This is so with Racine. He makes tragedy out of irrational behaviour set within a tight neo-classical framework. In this way a play by Racine is *formally* intelligible, while the real measure of the action, of all its passion and despair, is 'celestial' rather than worldly. So there is a sense in which Racine, masterly playwright and exquisite poet that he was, had the best of all worlds: first, of the 'classical world', as that was understood in the seventeenth century; secondly, of the sphere of psychopathology; thirdly of the aesthetic sphere, and then, in the final analysis, of the pure moral world as the criterion of corrupt human nature.

Phèdre (1677) illustrates this Racinian combination perfectly. Racine claims in his preface that the conception of the character of the heroine has been taken straight from Euripides, but, as we noted in the last chapter, the Phaedra of the *Hippolytus* is sufficiently explained in terms of Aphrodite's revenge; that ancient heroine is an irrational instrument of Aphrodite. To Euripides, Phaedra is the pathetic means by which the goddess of love punishes Hippolytus for spurning sexual love. Having thus given us the cause of Phaedra's behaviour, Euripides is free to concentrate upon that behaviour as it unfolds: it is highly abnormal but acceptable in its abnormality. Racine's procedure is similar up to a point, but then subtly different. He states: 'Elle est engagée, par sa destinée et par la colère des dieux, dans une passion illégitime, dont elle a horreur toute la première' (Preface). So far, then, Racine is perfectly 'neoclassical', but he also wishes to minimise Phèdre's guilt. Euripides' Phaedra is justified in the sense that she has no free will (or has been robbed of choice by Aphrodite). On the other hand, Racine's Phèdre, though nominally a pagan, is seen in terms of Christian psychology and so possesses free will and must be justified by moral means.

Racine causes Oenone, nurse and confidante of Phèdre, to be so crude as to accuse Hippolyte of raping her mistress. This accusation does not even occur as a fantasy to Phèdre herself. The heroine is noble (obsessional and self-destructive, but noble) and therefore incapable of lying slander, while Oenone makes what Racine regards as a typically servile assumption. This is that one is, of course, honourable, but not to the extent of allowing oneself to be falsely vilified. To counter such an unfairness a sensible person might be expected to vilify someone else. Racine cannot have a Phèdre who deliberately destroys the man she loves, or indeed any man. The heroine is 'guilty' of her monstrous passion, that is to say, guilty through no fault of her own, but over and above that her will is free and relatively innocent. In a moment of floundering desperation she tarnishes her honour by crying to Oenone, 'Do what you will' (Act III, Scene IV, line 911), but she barely knows what she is saying and in the marvellous final scene, having taken poison, owns up to Thésée. Her honour is more than a set of malleable rules, since it pervades her personality.

Racine's portrait of events is masterly in a strange way, for he has no need to present a fully comprehensible sequence (such as we usually find in Shakespeare). Behaviour in Racine's play has the opacity of life rather than the transparency of literature, but because of its strict form the drama seems clearer than it is and does not strike us as questionable. However, there is another reason why we do not question the behaviour. Phèdre's world is manifestly 'the world'; it would make rational sense only if it were purer, more influenced by decent persons such as Hippolyte and his beloved, Aricia. Racine rightly gives the motive-power to Thésée (the adventurous and lustful Theseus) and to the worldly Oenone. Hippolyte, Aricia and Phèdre herself are victims of the action, not its dynamic causes. So Racine preserves the Platonic–Christian contrast of evil (active) versus good (reactive) inevitably making the former the cause of the action of his drama: no evil, no action. The good in Racine is negative, but so long as purity is the ideal can we find an author of whom that may not be said?

If there is such a one it might be Marlowe, who at first makes an ideal of non-moral energy. No doubt this ideal is progressively qualified as Marlowe matures and is perhaps quite destroyed in *Edward II*, but most will agree that it seems to provide the main thrust for this reckless and defiant poet. I am suggesting that since Marlowe's nature was reckless, his poetry suffered as (for whatever reason) he grew more circumspect. 'Circumspect' here means not cautious but watchful, prone to observe actual circumstances. *Edward II* is plainly more 'circumspect' than *Tamburlaine*, and, I maintain, is less of a poem for that reason. It was not in Marlowe's temperament and certainly not part of his genius to be much concerned with social reality – or even the realities of nature.

Both parts of *Tamburlaine* are perfectly reckless. Marlowe celebrates his hero's pride, and the counter-movements to Tamburlaine's progress are mild variations in the triumphal music of the plays. Calyphas exasperates his father but is not in the least a threat to the latter's self-esteem. Tamburlaine's killing of his unwarlike son is too easily accomplished even – or especially – by epic standards, for who can imagine a Homer or a Virgil including such a scene? The death of Zenocrate is magnificent, not appreciably sad, or to be exact, Tamburlaine takes possession of the sadness on behalf of Marlowe and is not diminished or modified by it. A hero such as this would be diminished if he felt defeated even for a moment; if he took Zenocrate's death to be a rebuke by the gods or an occasion for the reform of his own character. On the contrary, Tamburlaine's reaction is to wish to overwhelm the very Fates, 'to hale the Fatal Sisters by the hair / And throw them in the triple moat of hell' (Act II, Scene IV). The attitude here reverses the classical attitude, since no ancient hero could dream of over-throwing the Fates. At the same time Tamburlaine's response is neither mad nor infantile: it is merely Marlovian. But what does 'Marlovian' mean in this context? It would be wrong to see Marlowe as just making the scornful, perverse gestures of youth. He is indeed scornful and perverse, but for the uncommon reason that he aims to overthrow the entire sphere of the priests, the sphere of morality. He is trying to exhibit a kind of innocence, and of course great merit, in 'badness'. He assumes that heroism alone has value, by which I mean the heroism of self-aggrandizement as opposed, specifically, to saintly self-sacrifice and self-immolation. One announces a high ambition and then goes after it. Nothing else is worthwhile; the rest is just the backdrop to heroism, or the material that heroes use. There is a definite ethic here which for most of us would be harder than altruism and would certainly give rise to a different culture. Nor would it reproduce an ancient tragic culture, but something quite distinct.

Marlowe is so contemptuous of the long generations of moral lawgivers that he sees not only kings and emperors but even the *Moirai* as his victims. This is a deluded notion, though the exact nature of the delusion is not easy to define. We need first to distinguish morality from fate, hence the moral God from the God of fate. One might overthrow morality, as Tamburlaine does, and thus strive to create new values. That is indeed Marlowe's own endeavour. Nevertheless, at all times the 'Fates' (to speak appro-priately) may not be evaded, let alone thrown in the moat of hell. When Tamburlaine dies, within six lines of the end of the play, he is still urging his son Amyras, to put honour before love (which does not mean to reject love) and, still evaluating himself as the 'scourge of God'. This would be intellectually acceptable if Tamburlaine meant simply the moral God, but not when he means God as the inescapable commander of all things. God in this absolute sense, unconfined to religions, epochs and moralities, reigns alongside the Fatal Sisters and may not be finally and satisfactorily distin-guished from them. At the close of the sixteenth century, Marlowe cannot escape the tradition according to which morality is of a piece with eternal truth; to defy one is to defy both.

The weakness of the *Tamburlaine* plays is that Marlowe has not

seen this distinction; he is so busy tilting at the moral God that he
cannot, in his time, make the clean break he longs for between
acknowledgement of one's destiny, the affirmative response, and,
on the other hand, mere moral defiance. Consequently reality is
held at arm's length, replaced by glorious language. Here again the
attempt is praiseworthy but the hero's achievements are gained
without a corresponding sense of depths, of abysses. Such correspondence is a good part of what we mean by the 'Fates'. Marlowe
has not grasped as yet that historical 'great men' – Alexander,
Caesar, the real Timurlane – must inevitably have experienced both
giddy heights *and* depths, in their souls as well as their
circumstances.

Perhaps few people have ever wanted more works of the
Tamburlaine kind, and yet the service Marlowe does for us by
providing the rich language of the plays is only one aspect of his
accomplishment. In addition he thrusts against the Renaissance
ideal of purity; that is to say he substitutes his own notion of purity.
In his untimely way he tries to get beyond good and evil, for what
he plainly desires is another sort of glory than the glory of Christ.
He is little concerned with everyday reality. Certainly the
'signified', in the Saussurean sense, is too completely in Marlowe's
own head, or, to express the point another way, is insufficiently
related to its 'referents' in the outside world. Thus the Virgins of
Damascus, Bajazeth, Zabina and all the numerous victims are
entirely viewed from the perspective of one whose self-definition
implies that he will not actually *observe* them. You cannot comprehensively conquer someone without first subtly knowing him, for
otherwise you are conquering something vulnerable in your own
make-up. It is in this fashion that Marlowe has substituted an anti-
moral, anti-rational kind of spirit for the spirit of Plato and
Christianity. Instead of remaining faithful to the earth, he too has
soared into the empyrean. That the plays are only a pseudo-
conquest and Tamburlaine a pseudo-overman is not in the least
a matter for satisfaction, since Marlowe, at this early stage,
recognised (in his exultant Renaissance way) what *sooner or later*
needs to be done. Thus he leapt so far ahead of his own time as to be
still ahead of ours. After *Tamburlaine* Marlowe's supposed access of
at least some ethical considerations and his slow 'coming to terms
with reality' are symptoms of decline.

I mean they are symptoms of his personal decline as a poet,
representing the loss of some of his potency and special excellence,

his *virtù* in the old sense. In *Doctor Faustus* he pits two imaginary spheres against each other, the Good Angel versus the Bad Angel, the living Christ and Lucifer. He has the genius to appreciate that hell is now (in 1604) comprehensible only as a frame of mind, but, for all that, his desire as an artist combines with his ancestral fear to conceive of hell as an everlasting location. Marlowe makes poetry out of his spiritual ambiguities. He also recognises the sheer poverty of humdrum social life. He knows that such life must be transcended, although there is only one hazardous way to do so: it is vital to 'try one's brains to gain a deity'. This suggests that human beings are on the road to replacing God, not with mundane considerations but with the sort of endless creativity that Marlowe represents (or, to be accurate, misrepresents) through the medium of Faustus.

Marlowe sets on one side of the scales the might of the Church, St Jerome's Bible, the study of theology, and on the other side the 'metaphysics of magicians'. He has no understanding of any sin but pride; the rest are all-too-human frailties so far as he is concerned. How can anyone dignify such activities as adultery and covetousness with the name of sin? Marlowe assumes that destruction of the prevailing pattern (whatever pattern prevails in any age) is both proud, which is to say 'sinful', and vital for creation. Therefore the great speech of Faustus as he awaits his doom in the last hour of his life refers to what Marlowe evidently thought of as the only purpose of humanity, namely reinterpretation and recreation, taking life upwards to ever-greater heights. Such aspiration alone could foster such terror. I speak of 'terror' but must presume that whatever fear Marlow might originally have felt would have been swept aside by the energy and loveliness of his language. This particular kind of beauty, dependent upon the despair of Faustus, is unattainable today. And Marlowe was able to express or imitate this feeling only by ignoring so much of concrete reality – the actual qualities of things, fair or foul. In *Doctor Faustus* he again reached out for purity, not nature. We have still not discovered how to incorporate actuality into radiant vision, since we are now preoccupied with actuality 'for its own sake'.

When Marlowe descends to the actual, as he does to some extent in *The Jew of Malta*, the radiance fades. Those fine and famous phrases – 'I count religion but a childish toy'; 'And fram'd of finer mould than common men'; 'Infinite riches in a little room'; 'And besides the wench is dead'; 'Shalt live with me and be my love' – are flashes of colour in a comparatively drab landscape. It is as if Marlowe is saying to himself and us: this Machiavellian world of Barabas and the deceitful Christians is what is left when you exclude 'spirit'. That is, when you exclude beauty and aspiration (or pride), for to Marlowe spirit is composed of those elements and has no orthodox ethical dimension. From such a point of view Barabas is one who aims too low, a crude, imperfect aspirant; yet he is at least superior to the muddled and spiteful Christians. In *The Jew of Malta* one little value remains: that extra self-awareness which always in literature and sometimes in life lends esteem to a scoundrel.

At the time of *The Jew of Malta* Marlowe is beginning to *sink* into social reality, which tendency is increased in *Edward II*. We are usually advised not to oppose Marlowe as poet to Marlowe as playwright, since he was in the process of adapting poetry to the flexible requirements of drama. Even so, Marlowe's failure to make much good poetry out of the twists and turns of socio-political life is instructive. It goes without saying that Marlow was no mere aesthete and no mere Gaveston. What he sought is intrinsically desirable: a justification of *the total quality of life* by aesthetic means (to adapt Nietzsche's phrase in *The Birth of Tragedy*).[23] That implies anything but evasion, for high culture should not be employed to paint over displeasing facts. On the contrary, the facts must be grasped as both 'displeasing' (to put it mildly) and in some remarkable way beautiful. Aeschylus and Sophocles shielded their spectators from the intolerable waste and ferocity of nature by beauty and selection, not by essential falsification. We for our part have settled for ordinariness: as between beauty and the everyday world we move so far towards the latter as is consistent with a minimal degree of the former – minimal beauty and absolutely no grandeur. We do this without realising that ordinariness may itself be a form of camouflage. It is not a question of Marlovian splendour versus reality, but of two kinds of protective vision.

Edward II remains a protest against prosaic conditions; that is the *raison d'être* of the work, for Marlowe still wishes to rise above the earth. On the other hand, Shakespeare's supremely efficient powers of perception were somehow connected with what, for want of a better word, I will call his 'pluralism'. He remained faithful to the earth, offering no solace in the form of ideas which contradict or otherwise modify worldly events. He regarded each perceptible thing as having intrinsic significance, contextual significance and, moreover, general significance (consider the vast number of sentiments expressed and the sheer sententiousness of the most unlikely characters), but no *higher* significance. In brief, things mean whatever they mean inside worldly limits. However, Shakespeare was faithful to the *surface* of life, by which I obviously do not mean that he was in the ordinary sense superficial, but that he scarcely qualified his observations – more particularly his psychological observations – by reference to unseen worlds. To us he is the complete aesthetical psychologist. In this extraordinary fashion Shakespeare is at once the most universal and the least universal of artists, the opposite of a Dante to whom everything is what it is in virtue of its place in the Divine Comedy. Shakespeare's 'unruliness' applies as much to values as to form and structure; consequently the moral point of an action in Shakespeare is confined to its pattern and has no divine connotation. If someone calls upon God (say Richard III cries out. 'Have mercy, Jesu!') then that is solely a human or dramatic utterance. The moral significa- tions in Shakespeare are aesthetic and psychological before they are moral. Further it looks as though Shakespeare had comparatively little interest in ensuring that matters should turn out in one way rather than another. Everything comes, everything goes away; nothing endures. As for 'purity', we shall return to that before long, but for the moment I wish to suggest that Shakespeare thought of it, correctly, as an impossible ideal having no place *within* a work of art. When the ideal of purity is seriously considered, as it is in *Measure for Measure*, it is dismissed as a worldly possibility. Nor is it even held to be a sensible criterion of conduct.

Shakespeare's vision was comprehensive in the special sense that he excluded nothing out of fear alone. He was not noticeably self-protective in his work. He adopted masks, a thousand masks, but each enabled him to see without fear or favour. The other sort of artist, the usual sort, the one whose vision is rigidly insistent, is vulnerable because much of the accessible truth has been sacrificed to sustain the vision. For instance, the modern artist who thinks of himself as starkly realistic, exposing brutality and squalor, merely ignores every qualifying factor: to try to see a wider design would expose his constricted and, in the final analysis, *defensive* personality. He shelters behind the squalor, of which he is in the process of making himself master. Conversely, it is as if Shakespeare lacked ego-defences of the ordinary kind.[24] Thus he used poetry as his means of embracing every experience, the 'world' as a whole. I repeat, the specialised ways of most artists (including 'great' artists) shield them from whatever knowledge they are loath to take into account. Such knowledge would cripple them as artists. Michelangelo presumably could not contemplate the mean or crudely lethargic; even the statue 'The Dying Slave' exhibits elegance and a reposeful sort of beauty that strictly belongs to health rather than disease. But Shakespeare could utilise everything under the sun. That is what his negative capability amounted to: he exploited the malicious, the sinister, the base and the weak, by taking them into himself. This was Shakespeare's way of knowing people and his aim, I believe, was the relief not of others' suffering but of his own. He relieved his sorrow by knowing it, by acting it out, by mimicking it. But this sorrow was entangled with all that be observed or contemplated. Nietzsche makes an observation which might, in the end, be connected with Keats's well-known remarks about negative capability. Nietzsche writes: 'I know no more heart-rending reading than Shakespeare: what must a man have suffered to have need of being such a buffoon!'[25] Now a buffoon in Nietzsche is sometimes a fool but commonly, as here, one who 'gets up to tricks', specifically in order to camouflage his rapid mind and exquisite sensibilities. Socrates was thus a buffoon and, to take an apt literary example, we might say that Hamlet's antic disposition is a piece of buffoonery. (Some of Nietzsche's friends who visited him in his insanity wondered if his condition might be a colossal and sustained performance of exactly this kind.) Shakespeare possessed extraordinary powers of empathy and this is what Keats means when he declares that the 'poetical character . . . has as much delight in conceiving an Iago as an Imogen'.[26] But Keats's unelaborated remark is only part of the truth. Let us venture a little further into this problem. Shakespeare's emotions were excessively, not to say appallingly keen. Is that not obvious to us? He kept his emotions from destroying him simply by verbalising them. In other words, he did not thereby falsify them. Contrariwise, most people misconceive, ignore or falsify their feelings as a matter of course. Shakespeare was 'pleased with his own passions and volitions' – to borrow that expression of Wordsworth, used with reference to all poets, to poets as such.[27] The question remains: how could Shakespeare have been pleased with, say, the feeling of humiliation we find in the sonnets? Initally he was devastated, then, perhaps with astonishing speed, he acknowledged the emotion. He did not deflect it into an idea (for example, 'I am a sinner and deserve this wretchedness') or assign a blameworthy cause to it, even though there was such a cause in the form of the faithless one. Next he lighted upon some entirely accurate words, such as 'The expense of spirit in a waste of shame', and at that point, but perhaps not a moment sooner, found a source of delight in his feelings of distress. Not the original emotion but the representation of it gave him the delight. But now the original emotion was pushed aside by the words in which it was nevertheless precisely formulated. Thus pain was translated into pleasure without the least make-believe. This was Shakespeare's regular 'buffoonish' manner of dealing with emotion. No ideology was required and no consolation in the usual sense of the word. So Shakespeare did not turn his despair into a source of melancholy satisfaction; that is a different and altogether inferior procedure. His identity (or as Keats would have it, his lack of identity) lay in the constant preference for creation. I mean *creation*, not wish-fulfilment. Thus Shakespeare never, or perhaps one should say, rarely, used a feeling to teach himself a higher, more spiritual lesson. There was no contemplation in the way of a Wordsworth or a Coleridge, which must inevitably involve some self-deceit – one sees oneself as a sadder and a wiser man.

In a similar fashion both Iago and Imogen were not so much observed or copied as *incorporated*. Shakespeare merely needed to experience Iago's malice, not to note or analyse it, least of all to criticise it, but to share it with complete self-abandon. He briefly filled himself with Iago-feelings and to that extent became Iago. Being incorporated, Iago was conquered. Shakespeare exercised the best form of will to power in this fashion. This means that he had few, if any, moral objections to Iago. It means also that Shakespeare's famously Protean nature consisted not of being all things to all men ('buffoons' are never that) but of assimilating others to himself – at will, and likewise wilfully discarding them. This is the sign of great health and is so even when it includes – as it must – imaginative experience of disease. Such a man can treasure even disease as knowledge, ultimately as another source of power. We would all behave in such a way if we had the nerve. We would seize hold of our various proclivities, not trample so many of them into oblivion. At the same time it would be absurd of us, here and now, to revere the character of such a multifarious man as Shakespeare. Which character should we revere? It is also worth recalling here that according to Yeats, the soul of Shakespeare lingered 'on the storm-beaten threshold of sanctity', a 'terrible and crime-haunted' place, so the dramatist was intimately acquainted with all sorts of ghastly behaviour.[28]

The Shakespearean procedure, then, differs from the common procedure in that most of us stop at the stage of hating Iago; indeed we loathe him to the extent that we cannot assimilate him. We construct an ethic out of our thwarted feelings, or, rather, we assign Iago to the sphere of a traditional ethic. Since it is wrong to be Iago, we scarcely notice our own leanings in that direction. So we oppose such leanings and fail to dominate them. Shakespeare did not grow narrow even as he aged. In the end he acknowledged Caliban, a creature to be mastered, certainly, but not placed at a remote distance in place or time. When in his last phase he felt a glow of enthusiasm for the excellent Imogen, he did not thereby yearn to eliminate Iachimo – meaning the Iachimos of this world. Shakespeare clearly recognised that without Iachimo there could be no Imogen. And, as I have already implied, he did not long to reform Iachimo, to change him either by Socratic questioning or by dogmatic instruction, let alone to eliminate him altogether. For Shakespeare Iachimo was neither feared nor classed, correlatively, as bad.

Shakespeare carries the Euripidean tendency to its highest point – in poetry and drama, though perhaps that peak is reached by others in the novel. Let us remind ourselves of the Euripidean tendency. It is, first, the 'dramatised epos',[29] in other words a story of varied action in which the author puts himself in the position of each character in turn.

> The character must no longer be expanded into an eternal type, but, on the contrary, must develop individually through artistic subordinate traits and shadings, through the nicest precision of all lines, in such a manner that the spectator is in general no longer conscious of the myth, but of the vigorous truth to nature and the artist's imitative power. Here also we observe the victory of the phenomenon over the universal, and the delight in a unique, almost anatomical preparation; we are already in the atmosphere of a theoretical world, where scientific knowledge is valued more highly than the artistic reflections of a universal law.[30]

What Nietzsche here describes (in Section 17 of *The Birth of Tragedy*) is what Shakespeare does superlatively among poet-dramatists. It is also what the philosopher assures us is consummately non-tragical. It cannot be tragic because it is too individualised, non-mythic, and in an odd way even *scientific*. Watching or reading Shakespeare we encounter not a myth but specific people doing specific things: Richard III behaves 'unnaturally' because he is himself 'unnatural', a crookback; Coriolanus is forced to sacrifice either his family or his prized honour; Romeo and Juliet die in defiance of their milieu; Timon is presumably 'too good' to survive; Brutus kills his friend Caesar and must eventually kill himself *because* he is the noblest Roman of them all; Macbeth's nature is foreign to the murders he commits; Hamlet needs to act though he knows *all* action to be fundamentally pointless; Lear begins by demanding pretence and ends by denying life itself; Othello takes a high romantic view of his nature but behaves as a calamitous fool; Antony and Cleopatra make a heroism of their sensuality as against the needs, as well as the mediocrity, of nations. We could continue in this vein, roughly summing up other tragedies and, for that matter, non-tragedies which betray the same interest in persons mismatched with their circumstances.

This is a regular interest in the theatre, almost the stuff of drama, but Shakespeare exploits such discord to the full in his tragedies. Now the exploitation enabled Shakespeare to use his combination of talents – the talent for human observation and the talent for language – so that the sheer scope of the discord was surely his reason for welcoming it. However, we are for the moment concerned with psychology in the old pre-systematic sense. As we have noted, an accurate (if simplified) study of behaviour cannot, of itself, be deemed tragic, no matter how grim or self-engendered the hero's fate might be. For tragedy is in a special way metaphysical, surpassing human psychology and mere social arrangements in the direction of a universal 'law'. Tragedy cannot be primarily concerned with this person Lear, or even, more generally, with kingship and kinship, but with a natural condition which *King Lear* should, in so far as it is a true tragedy, bear out. According to our Nietzschean reading, tragedy points towards the very condition of being. An anatomy of callousness, treachery and countervailing love, such as *King Lear*, is not necessarily tragic unless it is more than a bounded story and has mythic possibilities.

Shakespeare, the supreme poetical anatomist, seems to have regarded the visible world as *finally* inconsequential and unreal. It is not certain that he positively believed in a spirit world behind or above our familiar sphere, though it is usual to suppose that he shared the sceptical and unfailingly open-minded attitude of Montaigne. On the other hand he understood the universe as an immensity of appearances. We recognise that Shakespeare is the most frequent exploiter of the notion that a play is merely a play, an entertaining illusion, but he also adapted this conventional idea to a far more remarkable vision, namely that the world outside the theatre is an illusion in the sense that there is no solid ground.

In his own voice, and I think not just conventionally, Shakespeare writes:

> When I consider everything that grows
> Holds in perfection but a little moment,
> That this huge stage presenteth naught but shows,
> Whereon the stars in secret influence comment . . .
> (Sonnet XV)

The two ideas in these lines are both noteworthy: first, all that is presented to us, natural or artificial, consists of 'shows', and secondly, every growing thing has its own tiny moment of perfection, the moment it 'lives for', so that the rest of its life is either preparation or falling off. The latter idea suggests that for every creature there can be no greater meaning than is contained in, or expressed by, its one little moment of perfection. This is not a universally valid meaning, but merely a perfect meaning for that creature. Now as we know, the ancient Dionysian understanding saw the creature, the phenomenon, shading off into an indivisible universe, but Shakespeare's belief seems to have been that each thing, and indeed the multiplicity of forces we call the universe, rests upon no firm base whatever. Thus the creature's or the plant's moment of perfect self-realisation is likewise illusory, but it is the best anyone can hope for. Apart from that moment 'life's but a walking shadow'. Macbeth's despair accounts for that remark but does not invalidate it. I suspect that Shakespeare himself found it irrefutable in the terms both of argument and everyday observation. Nevertheless the one who sees his life as a preparation for an unrepeatable instant will at least fend off such desolation, since his life has its own, *organic* meaning and purpose. The rest is no more than a walking shadow, and this is what one realises when one goes badly astray. Today many will regard this view as odd, fanciful, certainly obsolete, but I believe it can be shown to be mistaken only by reference to Nietzsche's understanding of tragedy. This subject will be pursued in the final chapter – indeed, we cannot begin to master it before then. For now let us just appreciate that the centuries of belief in spirit have caused Shakespeare, in a sense the 'master' of actuality, to find actuality unreal. It is unreal because it is ungrounded: Shakespeare cannot conceive of actuality as self-grounded. To him only the spirit world might support the visible world, and, conceivably, there may be no spirit world.

Macbeth is not necessarily misguided so far as thought could reach in Shakespeare's time. When he concludes that life is a tale told by an idiot, he is not, as we suppose, categorically wrong, 'pathological' because guilty of evil. Rather, having discarded the filter of morality, he sees clearly and nakedly. That is to say, morality and a decent life, which provide the connection with one's fellow men, conceal life's utter meaninglessness. If the tale is told by a moral person it bears a moral meaning and individuals seem to acquire substance, become more than shadows and poor players. Remove the moral tale and only the idiot's tale remains. *But in our day this may no longer be an argument for preserving the moral tale at all costs.* The idiot's tale is not thereby invalidated; on the contrary the moral interpretation is now seen to be circumscribed and purely conditional.

Somewhat similarly, Hamlet, as a person of genius in what is, for him, the most confining set of circumstances, a perfect maze or spiritual cage, sees the world in a particular way:

> How weary, stale, flat and unprofitable,
> Seem to me all the uses of this world:
> Fie on't! Ah, fie! 'tis an unweeded garden,
> That grows to seed; things rank and gross in nature
> Possess it merely.
>
> > (*Hamlet* Act I, Scene 2)

But the world might reasonably be described as an unweeded garden growing to seed, possessed by things that appear to the delicate senses of human beings to be rank and gross in nature. The morbid Hamlet is right about that, and he is right also to observe that the uses of the world are unprofitable. That they further seem to him weary, stale and flat reflects his melancholia, but he is the penetrating philosopher to note that the mere notion of profit (in all senses) is a human notion. The universe is 'useless', unless we give it use. Thus as Nietzsche points out, Hamlet sees into the 'essence of things':

> In this sense the Dionysian man resembles Hamlet: both have once looked truly into the essence of things, they have *gained knowledge*, and nausea inhibits action; for their action could not change anything in the eternal nature of things; they feel it to be ridiculous or humiliating that they should be asked to set right a world that is out of joint. Knowledge kills action; action requires the veils of illusion: that is the doctrine of Hamlet, not that cheap wisdom of Jack the Dreamer who reflects too much and, as it were, from an excess of possibilities does not get around to action. Not reflection, no – true knowledge, an insight into the horrible truth, outweighs any motive for action both in Hamlet and in the Dionysian man.[31]

Hamlet, then, has insight into the horrible truth. Shakespeare *as thinker* is scarcely greater than Hamlet, but for once has created a character whose mental capacity rivals his own. In comparison Prospero is not a very remarkable creation, but he too is not a trivial fragment of his creator, and he, like Hamlet, knows the world *as human beings see it* to be a vision, that is to say, something other than the so-called 'truth'. Here we are faced with one of Shakespeare's conventional utterances, but we can sense the merging of convention with personal conviction. Rather we can detect the adaptation of convention to conviction. I think I had better, with apologies, reproduce the familiar words so that they are at the forefront of our minds:

> Our revels now are ended. These our actors,
> As I foretold you, were all spirits, and
> Are melted into air, into thin air;
> And, like the baseless fabric of this vision,
> The cloud-capp'd towers, the gorgeous palaces,
> The solemn temples, the great globe itself,
> Yea, all which it inherit, shall dissolve,
> And, like this insubstantial pageant faded,
> Leave not a rack behind.
>   (*The Tempest*, Act IV, Scene 1)

The lines are a clear statement that just as 'this insubstantial pageant', *The Tempest*, has ended, so will the world, and 'leave not a rack behind'. The play, as part of the great globe, has faded, but the globe itself is finite. Now the word 'globe', must be taken to serve for the visible universe, the stars in their courses as well as the planet earth. We can translate this into our own terms by reminding ourselves of the belief of some modern astronomers that there was once a void, and that, after countless ages, the void will return. But such is not exactly what Shakespeare means: to him the universe emerges from something or it is of no final consequence. To Shakespeare substance itself is 'insubstantial' unless it is supported by something else. When he imagines an unsupported universe, he thinks of essential nothingness, since visible things are simply parts of the existential pageant. Substance equals meaning and, in Shakespeare's eyes, radically changing substance is not properly substance at all. *Thus there is no true meaning so far as we are concerned.* Our human meanings are variable, temporary, no more than stories, visions and codes. In this way Shakespeare sensed an interminable nothingness against which his productions were mounted, and knew the productions themselves to be as nothing.

We must see Shakespeare's socio-moral injunctions in this way: they are not God-given regulations but devices, varying from simple expediencies to desperate techniques for keeping anarchy at bay. 'Anarchy' has become an inadequate word, since what I mean is nothing less than a universal crack-up, or better, a universal meltdown. Even if the universe does not itself melt into a fluid mess and ultimately (at the 'end of time') into a vacuum, our perceptions of it will soon do so, if we abandon rules: that is Shakespeare's nightmare. In nature the normal pattern is for the lesser to subordinate itself to the greater, though at certain appalling times the planets 'in evil mixture and disorder wander', presaging a like disorder in human affairs. Thus Ulysses in *Troilus and Cressida* (Act I, Scene 3) advocates 'degree' so that people shall follow the regular (though not absolutely invariable) way of heavenly bodies. Just as the earth depends upon the sun, so ought a subject to depend upon his king. Now this quasi-philosophic doctrine is false – by which I mean historical – but Shakespeare did not know it to be so. What keeps the planets from wandering in disorder is the play of forces which constitutes the solar system. The planets themselves are force; all is force, but today we no longer need to believe that force requires some kind of unseen design. No doubt we cannot tell what force is, but at least we have little reason to give it a spiritual explanation. We assume, to the contrary, that whatever spirit is, it arises after force, and gives force some doubtless temporary meaning, for example the meaning according to the quantum theory. We absolutely do not require a belief in spirit as that which *precedes* force.

Shakespeare naturally required such a belief, or, as I have said, the world was nought. As compared with his great Greek predecessors Shakespeare, in his optimistic and increasingly scientific age, is overwhelmingly Apollonian; he reproduces Apollonian images. But what lies behind the images, into what do their roots penetrate? The pre-Socratics knew that the roots go back into an immense tangle, the Dionysian. They cheerfully accepted the utter discord which Shakespeare feared above all. For him, as heir to generations of Platonism, the roots go back to spirit or to nothing. How can we place our trust in phenomena, in shadows, in things that change and die? The play of universal forces might at any moment be changed into 'mere oppugnancy'. Either, then, we rest upon spirit or have no resting place, which is to say, no *being*. Shakespeare could accept the primitive with comparative ease: Caliban, though he endures, may be controlled. Contrariwise, as Euripides demonstrates in *The Bacchae*, Dionysus grows less controllable the more one tries to control him. Caliban is not to be thought of in this way, and, in truth, Shakespeare had no sense of the Dionysian.

What happens, however, when a poet does not keep nihilism at bay but on the contrary takes his creative substance from the condition? This sounds a desperate or even hopeless procedure, since one needs a positive standard, expressed or implied, in order to make a work of literature. There must be discrimination of values even in reference to a world from which values are in theory excluded. I am thinking now, finally, of Webster: it is fitting to end not with Shakespeare's teeming variety of perspectives but with Webster's single perspective. The value-distinction Webster nevertheless manages to draw (the only possible one, given his 'premise') is between the conscious, deliberate nihilist and a merely wicked society. The former is not entirely dishonourable and may indeed, *through sheer stubbornness and self-determination*, practise, at times, more honour than society demands.

Webster appears to be one of the most complete sceptics about moral values within the Platonic tradition. He is within that tradition, in the sense that its shadow lies over him. This is so thoroughly the case that critics have sometimes found it hard to reconcile Webster with their own rock-bottom assumptions. He seems to be the only artist before the modern period who cannot find either a cure or a comfort for the evils of life. Our tendency is to assume that the very savagery of Webster's vision – the contempt, the hopelessness and the barely mitigated recital of forms of corruption – implies that he was on the side of the angels. Plainly Webster does not justify the degeneracy he so consistently displays; he is the reverse of a tempter, but why does he not show us more virtue? I mean, of course, more impressive virtue. And why does he not speak more often and more enthusiastically of heaven? In the length and breadth of Webster there is only one 'positive' recommendation, namely Delio's praise of 'integrity of life' at the end of *The Duchess of Malfi*. Certainly there are other utterances we may admire ('I am Duchess of Malfi still') but no other affirmative teaching: integrity of life seems to be the only ethic – if indeed it can be called an 'ethic'.

Now Delio's injunction is no Polonius-like urging to be true to one's own self so that 'thou canst not then be false to any man'. Webster is not concerned with social integrity, and falsehood to others is not exactly the fault he chiefly has in mind. The world as a whole is rotten in Webster's eyes. It is (and Nietzscheans will agree) a monstrous, senseless play of forces, having no justification and no purpose. Above all, the natural world is the sphere of decay and death, of writhing creatures endlessly feeding upon one another. According to Ralph Berry, Webster's irony attacks precisely the absurdity of the universe.

> Finally, the artistic validity of irony still requires justification ... if its constant deployment is not merely a set of nihilistic tricks. Irony is in great part an awareness of time; and time is an expression of death. The ironic technique is especially well adapted to a philosophy that disdains final knowledge, and depicts man as a unit of consciousness in an 'absurd' universe.[32]

These remarks, shrewd though they are, overlook another interpretation of Websterian irony. It is not, indeed, a set of 'nihilistic tricks', for to believe that it is implies a Webster who held back some genuine inner creed and 'deployed' the tricks for theatrical effect. No critic is likely to have thought that, because the devices in question are so much more than devices; they are, rather, expressions of a total cast of mind. At the same time there was *logically* (or, in a broader sense, philosophically) no need for Webster to see the universe as positively absurd unless – and this applies to modern 'absurdists' also – he had some dominant reason for wishing it to be otherwise. I have tried to show that Shakespeare was already pretty sure that the universe makes no sense, and yet it is not usual to think of him as an early absurdist. In other words, Webster's irony is a gesture of defiance, a sardonic rejection of what he is inescapably part of. He refused to accept the absurdity and that refusal constituted his identity. Once absurdity is *fully* accepted it ceases to be a problem. Why should the universe make sense in its very constitution? The whole business of 'making sense' is, so far as we can tell, exclusively human.

On the other hand Webster 'chose' (to put the matter in an existentialist fashion) to see the entire world as degenerative, cancerous, treacherous, suppurative and irredeemably evil. This means that Delio's 'integrity for life' is not a panacea but simply a salve for the noble individual. He, or preferably she, seeks posthumous honour by striving to live *against* the conditions of life. I think Webster must be taken to mean not only that human societies are perforce corrupt but that it is, as it were, a natural law of human behaviour that people band together in arbitrarily regulated societies. More than that, it is presumably a law of all classes of organic things that the members of each class join forces in certain nonrational ways. The point about Vittoria Corombona in *The White Devil* and the Duchess of Malfi is that each is aware of the radical imperfection of things and lives defiantly accordingly to that awareness. Neither has much use for virtue in the conventional sense; indeed they regard virtue as no more than an accident and, anyhow, of no particular use – or even value. All true value lies in the resolute and contemptuous opposition of one who neither pretends nor wishes to be virtuous. Really the creed is heroic as opposed to moralistic, since the heroine is sooner or later set apart from the milieu in a fatal way and therefore from the natural 'law' which fixes human beings within such milieux. Webster simply favours those few who see things for what they are: theirs are the only significant deaths. Webster's 'argument' is against society both in itself and as part of the polluted entirety of nature. Vittoria and Flamineo, the Duchess and Bosola are the persons of the two plays who in their different ways partake of this Websterian vision.

The heroism, then, such as it is, works against that which all moralists in the Platonic tradition hold to be immoral. The heroism is against *actuality* (a word with which I recall Nietzsche's remarks

quoted at the beginning of this chapter). Vittoria's scornful behaviour at her arraignment and the Duchess's demeanour when
Bosola comes for her with the executioners are, I imagine, Webster's
best reasons for writing the plays, his *justification*. But such dignity
and defiance require what is seen as oppression by nature, albeit in
the form of rapacious society. The people behave like extraordinarily cunning and painted animals. Now what alone sets
people apart from other animals? To Webster it seems that this
exclusively human quality is the urge to define oneself. This is an
uncommon as well as a purely human practice. Webster understands a society to be a naturally corrupt collection of people who
make up little (by no means always formalised) rules for themselves
and turn on the tiny number who break these rules. Such 'free
spirits' define themselves as renegades and their superiority lies in
setting themselves apart from the arbitrariness of social systems.
The value consists of an assessment of oneself as relatively free –
free of society, not of nature. Webster's heroines scarcely take
refuge in society as the rest of us do. But along with every other
fragment of the natural order they are also, in Webster's judgment,
diseased.

Webster scarcely mentions purity any more than he dwells on
images of heaven. Purity is not even expressly contrasted with
nature, yet it is certain that Webster could not see nature as he does
unless he tacitly juxtaposed it with purity. Strictly speaking it is the
Websterian perspective, not the universe, which is absurd. For all
his ferocious brilliance, Webster judges in relation to – in subservience to – the age-old Platonic dream. That is why his plays
should rightly be viewed as satires rather than tragedies.

Tragedy proper accepts and even welcomes the conditions of
life which Webster finds intolerable. In this book, following
Nietzsche, we have come to see tragedy as an aesthetic means of
helping the uniquely clever, courageous and sensitive human race
come to terms with the cycles of creation and destruction, of birth
and death. Nothing else is sensitive; we alone need an artificial
form such as tragedy in order to survive. Webster's plays are a
protest against natural cycles, against fundamental impurity, and
therefore he dwells upon human animalism as though it strictly
ought not to be. The truth is that Webster's tainted heroines,
Vittoria and the Duchess, are, by our normal standards, not at all
excessively tainted. Vittoria's worst act is to exult in what she
supposes to be the death-agonies of Flamineo, her brother (who has

of course asked her to shoot him), yet we hardly reproach her as we watch the play. As for the Duchess, she is no more than sensual (and of necessity deceitful), yet so powerful is Webster's persuasion that we come near to faulting her for what we do not usually regard as serious faults. Webster's judgments are themselves decadent: he is a piece of life that moves to reject its own well-springs. More than anyone else Webster reveals the Renaissance quandary; indeed it is his theme. This creative quandary consists in finding life fascinating while pronouncing it evil. It is not fascinating *because* it is evil in the late nineteenth-century fashion (people are not *fleurs du mal*), but rather because the sheer upsurge of culture and experiment is interlinked with belief in sin and, overwhelmingly, with consciousness of death. Everything dies, therefore everything deserves to die. But how vigorous is even one's sense of the omnipresence of death! From now on the growth of science begins to whisper to human beings that they may, in the distant future, virtually remove themselves from the natural order. Exactly this assurance, this modern misconception in other words, is assailed by the next phase of engagement with the tragic.

6

Ibsen and Hardy, Nature's Lost Sons

In earlier chapters we suggested, but did not emphasise, that original tragedy should be taken to provide the criterion for future varieties of the tragic – the criterion of tragic spirit, not of artistic excellence. To whatever extent later forms differ from an obscure first form, they ought not to have a manifestly different purpose. It is the purpose which is tragic, and at the birth of tragedy that purpose was to celebrate the reconciliation of nature with her 'lost son, man'.[1]

Already there are indications of a shift away from nature in Aeschylus and Sophocles, but these faint signs have nothing to do with the formality of the dramas; indeed the formal structures are calculated to remind spectators of their natural home. The hero, as opposed to the chorus, knows his vital connection to be with the earth rather than society. The hero, however, is precisely the individualised one; his affects and volitions are distinct from whatever the chorus expects of the community. We are impressed by the hero's individuality, but why are we so impressed, since he lacks the memorable personality of a character in Shakespeare? The reason lies in the very tension between *emergent* personality and the conventional words of the chorus. From one point of view this tension is the subject of the play. Thus the drama is ambivalent at its roots, being a tacit encouragement to the 'crime' of personality that it castigates. Such encouragement was implicit in the addition by Thespis of an actor's part to the age-old choral proceedings. In this way, although Greek tragedy exhibits a link between individuality and hubris, it cannot fail to illuminate the individuality of each spectator, or to coax that quality of selfhood into being. This link gave tragedy its peculiar power and at the same time foreshadowed its transformation into Euripidean drama, thence into the New Comedy.

Now, to recapitulate: the dialectic of Socrates, followed by Christian belief in the intrinsic wrongness of the world, eventually replaced tragedy proper with a Renaissance mode in which personal catastrophes are the consequences of errors of free will. At least that is the apparent intention of the dramatist and more or less what audiences imagine they have learned; for example, we think we have been warned against the ambition of Macbeth and the heroic pride of Coriolanus. Corneille's *Polyeucte* is a grand oddity whose catastrophe is a triumph and 'error of will' a supremely admirable choice. This play at least is 'anti-tragic', but even here our pleasure is in the conditions which foster Polyeucte's sacrifice, the conditions of the sinful world. Now in the sixteenth and seventeenth centuries tragic deeds are held to be aberrant in a purely ethical sense, no longer challenges to nature itself. And these ethical tragedies ultimately depend upon the world's evil. In theory the natural has been quite devalued, though whatever of tragedy gleams through the ethical screen is a piece of richly recalcitrant nature, and the hero's quality, at best, *transcends* ethical considerations.

Before we proceed to the next phase – namely a glimpse in the nineteenth century both of ancient times and of times to come – it is necessary to say something about the growth of science after the Renaissance. For long enough science appears to shift everything into the foreground. People come to favour scientific and political solutions: 'problems can be worked out'. The individual, who only began to emerge (so daringly) in the Greek tragic dramatists is now paramount. Human beings are presumed to be more than flesh and blood. We imagine ourselves able to surpass worldly conditions; the earth is our home but not our prison. Now it is axiomatic that sufferings should be vanquished rather than endured. All this optimism rests upon the most untragic and purely Apollonian of assumptions, the belief that science consists of the accumulation of knowledge about reality and is thus independent of human perspectives and desires. But, as we noted near the beginning of the book, Nietzsche argues in *Beyond Good and Evil* (1886) that

It is perhaps just dawning on five or six minds that physics, too, is only an interpretation and exegesis of the world (to suit us, if I may say so!) and *not* a world-explanation; but insofar as it is based on belief in the senses, it is regarded as more, and for a long time to come must be regarded as more – namely, as an explanation.[2]

Our post-Einstein minds are beginning to see the truth of this: physics is an exegesis, and if that is the nature of physics it is clearly the nature of other, non-empirical forms of knowledge. Therefore, to pursue the story of tragedy we need to look for modern authors (authors emphatically of the age of science) who see the inadequacy of the scientific world-picture. I do not mean people who mistrust science on the grounds that it rides roughshod over emotions, moral conditions and fine perceptions, but quite the reverse: those who are only too well aware how much of human nature is already expressed by science. To such people science is creative, having the disadvantages as well as the advantages of all creative activities: it must destroy as well as create. Above all it brings certain natural things forward, thrusting others into the shadows. Thus it is Apollonian, since it pretends that the things brought forward actually possess the prominence and independence we have conferred upon them. On the other hand the sort of writers we seek recognise the power and durability of Dionysus. But in modern times what can Dionysus be taken to mean; what is now 'Dionysian' according to Nietzsche?

> The word *'Dionysian'* means: an urge to unity, a reaching out beyond personality, the everyday, society, reality, across the abyss of transitoriness: a passionate – painful overflowing into darker, fuller, more floating states; an ecstatic affirmation of the total character of life as that which remains the same, just as powerful, just as blissful, through all change; the great pantheistic sharing of joy and sorrow that sanctifies and calls good even the most terrible and questionable qualities of life; the eternal will to procreation, to fruitfulness, to recurrence; the feeling of the necessary unity of creation and destruction.[3]

It will at once be clear that many a contemporary author who depicts a world of crumbling morality is not in the least what we require but virtually the reverse. The great majority of such satirists are reformers, however bitter, desperate or simply facetious they might seem. But a few writers who may be said to fall into this class sound anticipatory notes of a Promethean to come. Prometheus, as we saw in the second chapter, aims for godlike powers, knowing such powers to be accompanied by appropriate pains.[4] Even when Prometheus is free he will not be free according to our childish dreams: he will have shaken off his bonds, but not escaped the hardships of creative existence. A Titan or a god also *exists*; Zeus himself is not 'happy' in a painless fashion. To replace the gods means to assume their problems instead of merely human ones. It would be better to say that replacing the gods means taking into our own souls what we once allocated to Olympus.

In any case, 'Dionysian' authors can be no more than those who acknowledge the god and are therefore alive to the gulf between their interpretations and the reality beyond interpretation. They will instinctively understand, as Nietzsche's words suggest, that life has a 'total character' but may only be grasped piecemeal. Therefore they will appreciate that creation and destruction are a unity, and that joy and sorrow must fruitfully co-exist. Their strongest urge (even if they sometimes betray themselves) will be to sanctify and call good 'the most terrible and questionable qualities of life'. Such authors are rare and will not normally be seen in a true light even long after death, because too often in their careers they need to accommodate their Dionysian awareness to social requirements. They mask themselves as social persons and bow to uncomprehending applause.

Nearly a century after his last play *When We Dead Awaken*, Ibsen should be a clear case of such masking, yet, if I am not mistaken, he is still taken to be a basically 'realistic' dramatist with an exceedingly keen eye for the deceptions of social life (the life-lies by which many of us survive); in other words, he is for the most part identified with the guise in which, for a while, he chose to appear. In 1891 the quality of 'Ibsenism' was seen by Shaw along such lines; that is, as candid and searching radicalism. Our contemporary procedure is, inevitably, to place a pattern over Ibsen's works, obscuring if not quite concealing everything that does not fit. By this means we, for our part, diminish exactly Ibsen's tragical aspirations, substituting a figure bound far more to domestic psychology than to ice and high mountains. Ibsen is thus 'domesticated', turned into a subject for scholarly study and agreeable theatregoing.

The modern pattern either excludes or emasculates the bulk of the work. Someone might object that, on the contrary, Ibsen's power is widely acknowledged, but in fact that power is more often mentioned than felt. People are not impelled by Ibsen towards his own tragic grasp of life and he remains a dramatist whom it is common to think of as 'disturbing', at most, rather than as one who changes the very basis of our values. The supposedly disturbing quality is easily enough contained and, besides, we are now face to face with the vastly greater challenges of the twentieth century. But it seems to me that Ibsen at his most advanced runs ahead of the twentieth century, anticipating a future that will alter man's relations with the non-human.

At present the first eight of the twelve early dramas are a little too readily ignored as prentice stuff, while the seven major plays of the final phase from *Rosmersholm* to *When We Dead Awaken* are indeed highly esteemed and much analysed but in terms that betray the critic's reluctance to advance much beyond his understanding of the preceding phase. So the plays of the fifties and sixties and likewise the plays from the late eighties onwards are excessively coloured by the output of the intermediate period. Even *Brand* becomes a massive oddity, while the last stage tends to be judged somewhat as photography leavened by flights of imagination. In fact it is a flight *from* the real in the sense of the photographic. Ibsen regularly reveals his dissatisfaction with what we define as the Apollonian. At the end he knows, as he knew in the beginning, that people are enhanced, not lessened, when they are restored to nature. Anyone who spoke of 'Ibsenism' today might have in mind a set of darkly accurate portraits, a Rembrandt quality. But the dominant impulse of Ibsen's life was, to borrow Nietzsche's phrase, a 'revaluation of values'. At this point a digression is required.

Some still think of truth as a lofty realm intermittently revealed by phenomena. Events are thus supposed to signify *something* of the truth, as though truth transcended all mere events. This style of thought is a remnant of full-blooded Platonism according to which each manifest thing is an approximation to a suprasensible Form. So Plato speaks of justice and beauty, meaning Forms from which all instances of justice and all beautiful things fall significantly short. In this Platonic sense the truth of something, meaning its Form, is exactly what cannot be conveyed in a work of art. Conversely there is now a widespread notion that the word 'truth', simply refers to the correspondence between an event or a being and its representation in some medium or other. According to Plato, then, whatever belongs to the realm of truth is above and beyond appearance, while according to the contrary idea the sensuous, the apparent, is itself the simplest criterion of truth.

Heidegger conducts an interesting discussion of the key difference between Plato and Nietzsche in his *Nietzsche, Volume 1 – The Will to Power as Art*, especially in Chapters 10 to 25.[5] For our purpose what emerges may be summarised as follows. To Plato and Socrates mimesis can never produce an adequate version of a thing, since the thing, a table for instance, may be shown by the artist in but one perspective, or at most (when the artist is an author) from a limited number of perspectives. The table itself must elude him. An artist's representation of a table is therefore something *less* than an actual table, no matter how skilful his copy might be. However, even an actual table is necessarily less than the Form of 'table', because that Form is singular, unified, immovable: it has *being*. There can be only one truth of 'tableness', which must be superior to all mere tables. In Plato, then, the supersensuous stands above the sensuous. For Nietzsche, on the other hand, the sensuous takes precedence over the supersensuous since the latter is only an abstraction.

If we look at things in this Nietzschean fashion (and so far we are only fitfully *inclined* to do so in the modern world) we must accept, as Heidegger shows, that every thing nominated as 'true' is but a perspective. Now this is no trivial logical point, because we are here (specifically in certain fragments of *The Will to Power* but generally and tacitly in Nietzsche and, for that matter, in a good deal of recent thought) beginning to overthrow two-and-a-half thousand years of Platonism. Now we realise that life is made up of perspectives and semblances; there is nothing else. But what does this mean? Among other things it means that life is not finally and importantly distinct from art. This is not simply because art is part of life, but rather because both life and its constituent art consist of will to power. Everything proceeds and in one manner or another 'apprehends' according to the perspective most favourable to it. In other words, according to the perspective most apt to augment it. How may a thing be said to 'apprehend'? It is easy to see that plants as well as animals make use of their environment; therefore we are scarcely abusing language to remark that both classes take hold of their environments exploitatively. Such is the normal, the inescapable life-procedure. The growing plant exploits the soil so that it is probably strict, not lax, to remark that every organic thing, by definition, has some rudimentary capacity for response and assimilation which may be, and in the last analysis probably should be, located on the same scale as human power of apprehension. At least it is hard to see why our grasp of the environment must be functionally different from the crude capacities of simple organisms. Do not all things arrange the world to their own advantage, whether by simply nourishing themselves upon it or by means of mathematics and philosophy? Nor may the inorganic be permitted to block our progress towards defining a universal condition. Modern chemists no longer draw a distinction between the organic and the inorganic. Likewise physicists follow Einstein who maintained (in an account of relativity given in 1909) that 'we were driven to the conclusion that inert mass was nothing other than latent energy'.[6] So what used to be thought of as the inorganic is 'nothing other' than something waiting to be vitalised. It follows that we are right to assert that the world is exclusively made up of perspectives, semblances, tricks, dodges, devices: this is how the universe works.

This longish but nevertheless still inadequate digression will help us to see Ibsen in a proper light. He often indeed imitates real life, for example in the conversation between the heroine and Judge Brack in Act II of *Hedda Gabler*, but he does not do so for the sake of showing some truth or other. What kind of truth might that be? Ibsen already knows that nothing is true in the old sense and that the phrase 'true to life' refers only to a modern artist's mode of presentation – or trickery. His purpose in creating the conversation between Hedda and Brack is to place a value upon these characters, notably upon Hedda. Another and actually better way of putting the matter is to say that the will to power of Hedda is thus measured against that of Brack. Hedda's will to power is not a force within her as a component of her personality but a force which comprises her personality: it *is* her personality as force. Now the quality of each character in *Hedda Gabler* is necessarily shown in relation to other characters. The proceedings, then, are existential, since Hedda, for example, exists in, and only in her dealings with others. These are inescapably moments of *becoming*, moments in which Hedda as an organism waxes and wanes. The value which Ibsen gives Hedda is unavoidably a perspectival value, but this is not because she is 'only' a literary creation, for we are obliged to rate one another in everyday life in the same perspectival way.

Here is an appropriate place to emphasise something about the objective of this chapter. Some literary criticism is involved, but not as an end in itself. Rather I interpret Ibsen and Hardy for a purpose which lies beyond interpretation. The thread should lead us towards an understanding of modern responses to *life as tragedy*. Ibsen and Hardy are therefore tackled as portents; by implication they are seen as directing us to the final chapter of this book which is concerned with how tragedy might be resurrected. A tiny number of other authors could also be considered here: Lawrence and Hemingway are clear candidates. But Ibsen and Hardy place the question of tragedy at the forefront of their minds as no one else does. Most others indeed, if they are made wretched by the drift of modern life, or if they are in any way deeply impressed by that drift, fall back on satire: they are comic nihilists. Alternatively Ibsen and Hardy are 'neo-tragic', each to his own degree.

Curiously enough, Ibsen is the more value-conscious, the more concerned with values. The virtue that Ibsen cherishes is the independent will opposed to, or at least distinct from, conventional patterns of thought. He esteems the moral outlaw who, it should immediately be observed, is quite other than our latter-day favourite, the nonconformist. For there are, absurdly, leagues and multitudes of 'nonconformists' while Ibsen's admired ones are singular creatures. All are flawed in relation both to their own aspirations and to social requirements, but what they plainly desire is a 'higher' sort of life.

Ibsen referred to what he sought as 'aristocracy' or 'nobility', meaning not a social class but a quality. In a rather well-known speech to the Workers' Association at Trondheim on 14 June 1885 (that is, between *The Wild Duck* and *Rosmersholm*) he spoke as follows:

> There is still much to be done in this country before we can be said to have achieved full freedom. But our present democracy scarcely has the strength to accomplish that task. An element of aristocracy must enter our political life, our government, our members of parliament and our press. I am of course not thinking of aristocracy of wealth, of learning, or even of ability or talent. I am thinking of aristocracy of character, of mind and of will. That alone can make us free.[7]

These remarks indicate Ibsen's scheme of values and, as we shall see, are very roughly on the same lines as Nietzsche's searching thoughts. A more elaborate and accurate notion of Ibsen's desideratum is given in the character and opinions of Dr Stockmann in *An Enemy of the People*. The title is a pointer: the Ibsen hero is always (not just in this instance) an *enemy* of 'the people', meaning the group or the mass. Stockmann takes it for granted that every social creed, every fashionable attitude, every widely agreed ethic is corrupt, a pool of stagnant water. Stagnation is more than simple inactivity, for it breeds foulness and poisons. In the same way received ideas pollute the spiritual life of a nation. Stockmann's ideas are abusively anti-democratic yet are often quoted with approval in our time. The reason is plain enough: this hero instantly spots any discrepancy between a set of circumstances and a formula for it, with the result that modern observers who merely feel victimised identify themselves with him. The difference, however, is important to our entire consideration of Ibsen as one of 'nature's lost sons'. Stockmann is ebullient, somewhat insensitive, a happy warrior; he never feels himself to be a victim. The more common sort of reactive person looks for kindred spirits from the outset and supposes himself hostile to power as such: power is evil. On the other hand Stockmann dislikes collectives and gangs, and presumably would be critical even of a group of downtrodden workers. It is the loss of identity within a group that he deplores, the exchange of one's own vision for some crowd-idea. He readily sees through that seductive dream of a mass of individuals with a common purpose, for it is precisely one's self-defining purpose that distinguishes one from the mass – any mass, no matter how righteous. There can be no such thing as a collective of individuals; to join such a body as a means of self-enhancement (say, to join the 'women's movement') is to diminish oneself. That is Stockmann's view, as unfashionable now as in the 1880s. Stockmann is not opposed to power, but against inertia. Further, he desires and exercises strength as an end in itself: 'the strongest man in the world is the man who stands alone' (Act V).[8] There is no pretence of virtue here, for I do not think that Stockmann or his creator believes that strength may itself be a virtue. Nevertheless it is the quality that Ibsen admires, though he explores its contradictions and treacheries. Ibsen sees most of society as made up of persons only trivially and technically differentiated from one another, but this mass is creatively disturbed and given whatever value it possesses by a few strong individuals, or aristocrats of character, mind and will. In brief, Ibsen's preference is anything but democratic, or is democratic only in the sense that the strong are by no means confined to the ranks of the well-born. Neither is there anything progressionist in Ibsen's vision. At all stages since the Romans (to restrict ourselves to Ibsen's range of reference) the same fundamental circumstances have prevailed; the mass against the few who stand alone. To this limited extent there is a similarity between Ibsen's views and Nietzsche's, and it is worth noting in passing that to Nietzsche, such spiritual innovators as Ibsen admires have historically been obliged to be self-torturers and madmen.[9]

In this way Ibsen had uneasy relations with both tragedy and morality. He tended towards the tragic in an age which had difficulty in divorcing tragedy from Christianity, or, in the widest sense, from goodness and notions of waste – of 'promise unfulfilled'. But Ibsen was drawn to the pre-Christian and pre-Platonic belief that tragedy is the art form which most accurately points to the conditions of all life. It is true that Ibsen strove to do something entirely new: he aimed to indicate those conditions by more or less realistic means; that is, to present a vision marginally closer to that of Aeschylus and Sophocles than to that of Euripides, but to do so by ultra-Euripidean techniques. As for morality, that must be largely conventional. A morality which consists of an original – which is to say, a creative – response to every fresh situation, the reverse of a morality of custom, must always seem to be precisely a lack of morality. Morality is a code, rigid or comparatively lenient, and choices are never quite left to the individual and his personal perceptions. Is that not why Christ was seen by the Jews of Jerusalem as immoral? He *was* 'immoral'. Ibsen's admired characters (anything but Christ-like) are marked by originality, perversity, singularity and contempt for rules. They are irredeemably at odds with their fellows. More than that, their stories constitute a reaching-out by Ibsen for a 'wild' form of life, since such people tend to ally themselves with nature rather than society. Plainly this is itself an artificial distinction, but it is the one Ibsen regularly makes.

The chief recurrent matter of Ibsen's early plays is not exactly the 'Norwegian Myth', as the editor of the Oxford editions calls it.[10] That myth is at best Ibsen's raw material, which is worked for a peculiar purpose, namely to define *new* values. We cannot guess how far at this stage Ibsen appreciated his own originality. Most likely the youthful author 'found' his standards in the sagas and fairy tales, by which I mean he projected his preferences and insights into the mythical and historical material. Thus Ibsen first appeared before the public in the guise of one seeking to restore the old Norwegian spirit which had flourished before the 'four-hundred-year night' of the subjection of Norway to Denmark. But this was not his true interest, and while he certainly wished to arouse his fellow-countrymen from their nineteenth-century slumbers, he was critical of Norway in a far more defiant and less hopeful sense. Even as a very young man Ibsen was busy implying that the received ideas of his compatriots were third rate. Nor was this in general a kind of inconoclasm that contrives to please a self-satisfied audience, the inconoclasm of a Shaw for instance, since it included signs of a quite desolating assault. In contrast Shaw intensified and blazoned forth the chief notion of the preceding two centuries, the notion of progress. In his *Everybody's Political What's What* (1944) Shaw maintains that so far the human race has not 'progressed' in the usual sense of the word, and then proceeds to argue that 'if this book is to be worth writing or reading' real progress, meaning a change in human nature itself, must be presumed possible.[11] This sort of faith is usually considered brave, or at least necessary but would it not be less cowardly to presume the contrary: that 'real progress' is the post-Renaissance delusion? And the young Ibsen, though superficially and sporadically a progressionist, was so far advanced as to have seen through the whole idea of progress. Naturally he was not a conservative; not a great deal should be preserved except as a seed of new adventures. But the liberals' idea that such adventures must lead to a better life for all was dubious notion. Now and again Ibsen wanted positive political results, but in the main he was aristocratically concerned with behaviour for its own sake. The value of Catiline in Ibsen's first play obviously has nothing to do with success and indeed Catiline's merit, as against that of such as Cicero, lies in his recognition that success means either bowing to contemporary idols or being misconstrued by the public. You need to join the group which Ibsen, like his Catiline, was loath to do. Catiline is too noble as well as too complex to play a consistently shrewd political game – and it will be remembered that nobility is a far cry from goodness. Ibsen himself was already looking for heroism of a more paradoxical and spiritual variety than can honestly be discerned in either the sagas or the history of Rome, and was, he thought, conspicuously absent from nineteenth-century Norway.

Catiline (1850) is almost ludicrous if we look at it with the eyes of literary critics, but if we judge it as psychologists and students of tragedy it is illuminating. Catiline wishes to overthrow the Senate in order to rid Rome of corruption and restore the warrior virtues that flourished up to the time of Sulla. In the course of his conspiracy Catiline enters into a deadly pact with the vestal Furia, who leads him to kill his loyal wife Aurelia, and finally, at his bidding, stabs him to death. The striking fact is that Ibsen at twenty-two grasped what was obscure in the mid-nineteenth century and, despite Nietzsche, is still considered mysterious today: that life in the basic biological sense is best served by conflict, especially internal conflict. Our logic sees this fact as paradoxical, but logic is a mere human tool. An organism is vigorous according to the vigour of its constitutional strife, while absence of strife is death, the inert. Just before Furia plunges the dagger into Catiline's breast he realises and declares what he has sensed all along, namely that life for human beings is 'an unabating struggle / between the hostile forces in the soul' (Act III).[12] So Catiline learns that to be at peace with oneself is not desirable but morbid. As Nietzsche puts much the same point, ' "peace of soul" [is] as a chronic disease.'[13] In a different context Nietzsche remarks that 'life itself is *essentially* appropriation, injury, overpowering of what is alien and weaker; suppression, hardness, imposition of one's own forms, incorporation and at least, at its mildest, exploitation . . . '.[14] Ibsen's hero is tempted and finally destroyed by Furia (presumably an image from the depths of Ibsen's mind) because he believes, obscurely for most of the play, that liveliness is superior to and inconsistent with peace of soul. Actual death is regularly presented in Ibsen as preferable to living death, or apathy.

Most of Ibsen's early heroes – or, correctly, heroines – are variations upon this theme. The second version of *The Burial Mound* (1853) extols the Vikings over the Christians. (The first version, designed, I suspect, to placate church-going sentiments, is Ibsens's solitary expression of preference for the gentle virtues and was a failure anyway.) *St John's Night*, a fairy-tale comedy of 1853, may be summarised as declaring that orthodox Norwegian ways of the time constitute a sort of ennervating over-garment beneath which the true spirit of Norway, a spirit of magical self-surrender to nature, lies unwholesomely concealed. *Lady Inger* (1855) is a tortuous but far from dull tragedy concerning a passionate, middle-aged noble-woman caught in the toils of a patriotic vow made in youth. Ibsen's chief point is that Inger Gyldenløve is 'great' as opposed to good. She is admired by her creator for her uncompromising tempera-ment, her noble imprudence. (I am obviously omitting the compli-cations of this and other plays. For instance Lady Inger tries to be cunning but lacks the talent for it; she especially lacks the *commanding* instinct for self-preservation which Ibsen attributes to mediocre persons).

The Feast of Solhoug (1856) presents us with a heroine, Margit Gauteson, who tries to poison her weak and ageing husband. There is no doubt about Ibsen's sympathy for this would-be murderess, and if the sympathy is at all qualified, it is so in obedience to the dictates of psychology, not morality. *Olaf Liljekrans,* a comedy of the following year, is memorable for the character of Aelfhild, a rather simple-minded, potentially homicidal young woman who ends by marrying the 'troll-struck' hero Olaf. After Catiline and Lady Inger the most remarkable of these youthful creations is Hjordis, the heroine of *The Vikings of Helgeland* (1858), since she is positively savage, which is to say atavistic, not just in relation to the nineteenth century but to her own tenth-century period also. She holds that 'happiness is his who is strong enough to do battle with the Fates' (Act III).[15] At first sight this is not a tragic attitude, for, as we grasped in Chapters 2 to 4, no protagonist of Aeschylus, Sophocles and Euripides could conceivably say such a thing. Not even Oedipus sets out to do battle with the Fates, though his destiny is to transform nature itself. I mean of course that Oedipus transforms nature in men's eyes, but the qualification is unnecessary since there are no other eyes capable of anything worth calling interpretation. Then, Orestes rouses the Eumenides to vengeful fury, but that is emphatically not his intention and they are pacified at last by Athena. Just the same, I think the statement of Hjordis is Ibsen's attempt at a genuinely tragic motto, since, as we shall see, he echoes it in *The Master Builder.* He means that one's creative deed must always be nothing less than the 'impossible', for what else is creative? That is to say, the means of doing the deed must be bravely *invented.* In fact the wicked Hjordis is raised to superhuman heights. She aspires not to goodness but to creativity. Finally, after her warrior-suicide, Hjordis is seen riding through the air with the man she has just killed, her virtuous sister's gallant husband. The suggestion is that Hjordis is worthy to join the Valkyries themselves in Valhalla.

This resumé of most of Ibsen's early plays would be far too brief for any purpose but my present one, specifically to present an idea of his outlook as a young man. The outlook was never discarded or lopped off as dead, for it is evidently the stem of his later plays. *Brand,* that stark work of Ibsen's period as a poet-dramatist, is from one point of view a confrontation of the teaching of Christ with the heroic code; from another, equally valid point of view a strange reconciliation of the two ways. Brand's very hardness and resolution takes him *higher* than other men, nearer to God, yet at the same time leave him pitifully stranded on the earthly side of the great metaphysical divide. Those who think of Christianity as a heroism (in the manner of Bunyan, for example) should reflect that Nietzsche is probably right to maintain that Christ himself was the reverse of a hero and signally did not offer us either suffering or any sort of worldly merit, but simply peace and 'eternal life'.[16] However, no one can struggle towards the way of Christ without self-sacrifice and regular toughness, at least with himself if not with others. So one might 'imitate Christ' by behaving as Bunyan's Christian in the fight with Apollyon, yet his brave procedure is not the style of Jesus. 'The word "Christianity" is already a misunderstanding – in reality there has been only one Christian, and he died on the Cross.'[17] What Nietzsche means by these words is perfectly clear: the teaching of Jesus has never been suitable for anyone else because it demands not perfection but a constitution which one man alone has possessed – a singular, not a flawless make-up. Christ managed to live what Christians regard as the pure life *unheroically*. Now the hero Brand follows Jesus, as he supposes, and in so doing produces suffering for his family and others. Nevertheless, Brand is admirable: 'myself,' wrote Ibsen, 'in my best moments'.[18] In this fashion the play expresses Ibsen's usual attitude, for he respected aspirations, not results – in his art if not always in his life. He (like Thomas Hardy) saw results as either partially or wholly confounding expectations. Just the same, one strives, as do all living things, even if the striving takes a decadent and self-wounding form. Did Jesus aim for the Cross? Possibly he wanted to die, but surely not by that hideous means. It is more important to ask (though the question has been asked before) if Jesus hoped to found a Church in any of its historical forms.

Ibsen valued failure, not sentimentally, not out of humility and not quite romantically, but Prometheanly; that is, when the failure is at once inescapable and the mark of a loftier spirit than can be found on the winning side. So in *Emperor and Galilean* (1873) he goes some way towards reversing the judgment of the ages. In the conflict between fourth-century Christians and Julian the Apostate the Christians won, but they did so, we imagine, because their teaching was an advance, an elevation, while Julian merely wished to maintain the old Roman ways. Nevertheless Ibsen thinks that Christianity triumphed as a degenerate force. Degeneration commonly triumphs over health and may predominate for centuries. It is part of Ibsen's originality and kinship with Nietzsche that his play favours Julian. The drama (in two parts) amounts to an intuitive psychological explanation of why Julian failed to rid the empire of Christianity. He failed, in a word, because his opponents thrived on persecution. Let us see what is involved here. Suppose one wants to be persecuted, not for political reasons but as the royal road to heaven; is that not at once a guarantee of victory and a sign of profound degeneration? The Christians won by renouncing worldly goods, beauty, health and even zest for life. They were happy to be sick unto death; conquering Rome and all paganism was infinitely more important than living. The discovery of this route to victory was a stroke of great genius. Thus the early Christians conquered by means of *biological* decadence.

Julian is certainly a *tragic* hero and in Ibsen's scarcely-disguised opinion the Emperor was right about a fundamental question: life itself with all its pains and even its injustices is preferable not only to death but to Christ's 'eternal life'. Eternal life was Christ's phrase for his personal conquest of death, his solution which he passed on to others. But this immortality is strikingly different from the immortality of Dionysus, since the latter is earthly, being composed of constant growth and decay. Dionysus lives and dies, repeating that sequence endlessly. But Christ's way was to regard life as a brief interruption of the peace of death, the peace of not-feeling.

Ibsen believed that Julian's efforts were based partly on a correct assessment of the decadent nature of Christianity, but also on a 'world-historic' underestimate of the relentless Christian spirit. The more believers he slaughtered the more rose up in a sickly parody of the Dionysian religion. So Julian, like Cain and Judas Iscariot, aided Christianity by his hostility to it. But, encompassing the struggle of Julian and the Christians, Ibsen offers us a glimpse of a yet larger and healthier sphere, a 'third empire' as he calls it. This is an Hegelian synthesis of the thesis of Rome and the antithesis of Jesus. In the distant future there will be a world of learning and *creative* knowledge resting upon an acknowledged Dionysian-Heraclitean foundation. In other words the ultimate reality of all things is not the Christian God but a universe of endless change and creation. Within this universe monotheism will come to be seen as an historical phase, like the polytheism it replaced.

Ibsen more than once referred to *Emperor and Galilean* as his masterpiece,[19] and we should not wish to waste time contesting (or supporting) this judgment. For Ibsen probably meant, not that the two connected plays, 'Caesar's Apostasy' and 'The Emperor Julian', necessarily formed an aesthetic master-work, but that they said what he wished to say more clearly and perhaps more forcefully than his other writings. Certainly much of Ibsen's career makes sense when – and only when – one regards this drama as the centrepiece of his vision.

Following the publication of *Emperor and Galilean* (in book form in 1871) he began his period of 'social dramas', as we may as well call them, and thus won great renown in Europe and America. Today he is still most highly regarded for *A Doll's House, Ghosts, The Wild Duck* and *Hedda Gabler*. But such plays are not the kind he personally favoured and, interestingly enough, *Hedda Gabler* already hints at this fact. The hint, however, is not very explicit and the point I am making is best represented in the first dialogue between Solness and Hilde Wangel in *The Master Builder* (1892). This play does more than reveal something of Ibsen's personality (his aims, idiosyncrasies and anxieties), for it also expresses what he then felt about his entire career. Hilde reminds Solness of his feat, ten years earlier to the day, when he climbed the church tower at Lysanger and triumphantly placed a wreath on the top. Afterwards he passionately kissed the twelve-year-old Hilde, announcing that she would become his princess in ten years' time. Now Hilde has come to claim her title and her kingdom, but it turns out that Solness no longer builds churches, just 'homes for people' (Act I).[20] It has been recognised often enough that something similar may be said of Ibsen himself, for he had given up his youthful aspiration to write sublime works. Now he writes the social dramas which may be likened to homes for people. Prose plays of ordinary life are indeed 'homely', democratic, realistic and modern; perfect bourgeois models, however radical they might once have seemed to bourgeois audiences. The proof is that we have thoroughly assimilated Ibsen's shocking dramas, even *Ghosts*, yet we cannot face and will not see what this new tragedian fundamentally intended.

Solness is now afraid of heights but finally, to Hilde's delight (or better, her ecstasy), climbs the tower of the house he has just built and falls to his death. The death, however, is a consummation for Hilde, since it is heroic. Ibsen's own position is roughly analogous – or it would be, if he still attempted the heights. At this point in his career he is edging his way out of the phase of realism yet lacks the reckless courage simply to climb up to poetry and grandeur.

Perhaps indeed he is climbing a tower, or contemplating such an act, in writing this play, but doing so without the final heedlessness of Solness – and, to be fair, without a Hilde to inspire or tempt him. (Ibsen had learned, as long before as *The Pretenders* in 1863, to make art out of his own weaknesses; now in the nineties he seems to know this very ability to be another and subtler sort of weakness.)

When all is said and done, (and despite the bravura of Wagner) this is the bourgeois century and Ibsen greatly – if guiltily, for *The Master Builder* makes that clear – enjoys his worldwide success. But notice how he has been stealthily moving back towards the mountain tops. In 1885 he produced *Rosmersholm* at the close of which Rosmer and Rebecca West commit suicide, because Rosmer's dream of making 'all my countrymen noble' (Act I)[21] has disintegrated. Rebecca herself is noble (though immoral and deadly) and therefore dies with Rosmer, declaring in effect that such a death is superior to a meaningless life. Now this is already a patrician sort of choice, and the ignobility which the pair elect to avoid is the essential spirit of the twentieth century. But the question is not simply one of honour and aspiration versus accommodating ways, for Ibsen's posture is profoundly anti-nihilistic. He senses that 'nihilism stands at the door'[22] because we are attempting – in a manner now panicky, now complacent – to distinguish ourselves from nature, *though without the countervailing belief that we truly belong to God.* Today there is nothing – *nihil* –since we turn aside from both nature and God. For that reason *The Lady from the Sea* (1888) (which incidently introduces the young Hilde Wangel and presumably takes place in Lysanger) has for its heroine Ellida Wangel whose mind, whose very being ebbs and flows like the sea. She has comparatively little human control but seems to resemble a complete creature of nature, belonging to a pagan, magical and actually Dionysian world. The implication of *The Lady from the Sea* is that we merely appear to have hard Apollonian shapes, though those shapes are unreal.

We are accustomed to thinking of *Hedda Gabler* as the portrait of a lady – unpleasant, destructive and neurotic – and so up to a point it is. But Hedda too is a fairly transparent reflection of her creator. The conflict of her cowardice with her high, contemptuous standards, also the gap between her nervous fastidiousness and the disposition to violence: these traits must remind us of the author. It is Ibsen as much as Hedda who despises Jorgen Tesman's academic scrupulosity and Thea Elvsted's anxious decency. (Ibsen had a generally low opinion of university people. He once wrote to Georg Brandes saying in effect that a worthwhile thinker must find himself opposed by academic philosophers.)[23] Hedda is yet another atavistic heroine, requiring pride and savagery in the world around her to match her own: she kills herself because the world has grown too gentle and well-meaning, therefore, to her, *meaningless*. What Ibsen is doing here and, with the exception of *Little Eyolf*, in all the plays from *Rosmersholm* onwards, is drawing ever nearer, in his self-masking and basically nervous way, to his life-long goal. He now makes plays about such people as Hedda and Solness who hang back, who are afraid, and finally commit themselves – to death itself. At this point the goal should be defined: it is, in a word, to 'translate man back into nature'. That is Nietzsche's phrase, though he was not speaking of Isben, (whom he in fact despised[24]) but of what 'we free spirits' must attempt in the modern age.

> To translate man back into nature; to become master over the many vain and overly enthusiastic interpretations and connotations that have so far been scrawled and painted over that eternal basic text of *homo natura*; to see to it that man henceforth stands before man as even today, hardened in the discipline of science, he stands before the *rest* of nature, with intrepid Oedipus eyes, and sealed Odysseus ears, deaf to the siren songs of old metaphysical bird catchers who have been piping at him all too long, 'you are more, you are higher, you are of a different origin!' – that may be a strange and insane task, but it is a *task* – who would deny that?[25]

I do not see how we can judge Ibsen, of all modern artists, to be attempting anything less than this task. Like his Julian the Apostate he wanted to close the ears of as many as possible to the songs of old metaphysical bird catchers and restore the text of *homo natura*. He desired this all along, beginning with – or, one supposes, before – *Catiline* and *St John's Night*.

The last two plays make this fact still plainer and form a remarkably fitting close to a career that, for the most part, we have still not interpreted properly. *John Gabriel Borkman* (1896) is the study of a man of Napoleonic ambition who has been ruined by a conviction for fraud and a five-year term in prison, but the play is nevertheless more than such a study: it is moreover a (Euripidean) tragedy partly because it reflects and magnifies the author's own feelings of guilt. Ibsen is Borkman in very roughly the sense that Aeschylus personally defies Zeus through the medium of Prometheus. Doubtless it will at first sound ridiculous to assert that the criminal Borkman is an 'enhancement' of his esteemed creator, but something of the sort is nevertheless true: Borkman takes Ibsen's tendencies to gloomy heights and lacks whatever is petty in Ibsen. Borkman once sought to harness the earth itself, specifically the minerals in his mines, and to devise a network of communications for his own creative purposes. This is Ibsen's distorted, in a way his *magnified*, reflection of himself as the world artist maimed by guilt. The guilt in question cannot be precisely defined, but to judge by several plays, not this play alone, it was comprised of a certain coldness and preponderant tendency to use others. Concomitantly Ibsen reproached himself, so it would seem, for turning his back on love. I do not suggest that an opportunity for romantic love necessarily presented itself when he was young, but simply that he chose his excellent wife Suzannah, with an unheroic eye to his own safety; safety, that is, from penury, turbulence and despair, the old hazards of genius. He had been too prudently ambitious. So by a bitter irony Ibsen comes to feel that his ambition has led him to great prestige but held him back from the peaks of achievement, not to mention the peaks of honour and merit. Further, it has robbed him of love; Ibsen's marriage has grown increasingly cold and desolate. He who celebrates reckless heroism has been so much less than a hero.

Borkman's sister-in-law, Ella Rentheim, leads him up the mountain behind his house where he declares, looking over the land to distant fjords, that the kingdom of the earth is his and still awaits him. Ella rightly tells him that he will never be able to take possession of his 'cold dark kingdom' because years earlier, he murdered his love for her.[26] The biographical evidence suggests that Ibsen did not love peple, did not 'give himself' and this is a bleak self-assessment. He fell short of his own standards – so he evidently believed – through cowardice, like Hedda; through over-eagerness for reputation, as Borkman has been too eager for riches and power.

Ibsen desired something altogether tremendous; no wonder it scared him. In the century of progress when all the advanced nations of the world assume that people have, as it were, extracted themselves from nature, in short when 'tragedy' is no longer tragedy, Ibsen wishes to remind everyone that they can never be more than this-wordly as opposed to other-wordly. To Ibsen this ambition is not melancholy but exhilarating and audacious, but how will the public react? To try to stamp out the ideal of progress is to be almost as Julian trying to stamp out Christianity.

How may we explain the resonance of the comparatively short final play, *When We Dead Awaken* (1899)? Rubek, the master sculptor, made his name with the statue of a naked woman, which he called 'The Day of Resurrection'. The woman's beauty was obviously sensual but spiritual also; that is to say, it was 'ideal' in the classical sense and far from animal. It completed the *animal*, neither denied nor falsified it. Later Rubek added ordinary animal figures to this beautiful piece and so obscured his early accomplishment. Thus Rubek came down to earth in the sense of realism as opposed to tragedy. He grew preoccupied with the ordinary, with the crude flesh, and lost sight of his destiny to *exalt* the flesh. But Irene, the model for the statue, appears at the sanatorium where Rubek and his wife are staying, and at the close Rubek and Irene set off up the mountain together, away from the lowlands, the valleys and the unadventurous slopes to death near the summit.

I expect that, Freudianly speaking, there is plenty of evidence here for 'Thanatos', a death wish. The important point remains that by death Ibsen did not understand purity, the dream of heaven, a longed-for absence of pain and the dissolution *only* of corrupt and corrupting flesh. To him death was 'purity' in the sense that one no longer compromised oneself, for example in the very direction of Christianity or for the sake of professional acclaim. Death meant re-affiliation with the earth, the sheerly physical, anti-Platonic, material reality. But this reunion was also, as I have suggested, an exaltation and the reverse of vulgarity. According to Nietzsche tragedy was in the beginning a religious celebration of the recovery of humankind into the physical universe: man was 'nature's lost son'. Ibsen believed the same in an age when the great majority thought they were in the process of liberating themselves from such crude entanglements. By this means Ibsen looked forwards as well as far back, establishing deeper roots and so aspiring higher than his merely progressive contemporaries.

Hardy also looks forwards and back – back to Aeschylus and

further, to the prehistoric past of Egdon Heath in *The Return of the Native*. But he looks ahead gloomily, not, I fancy, to the distant future but to what he takes to be imminent. That near future, perhaps the next two centuries, will be increasingly anxious and strained: there can only be a widening gulf between man and the rest of the universe. Thus Hardy, often enough thought of as 'tragic', is quite other than tragic in the Aeschylean or Sophoclean senses. He cannot contemplate blessing the earth as Sophocles' Oedipus blesses the earth of Colonus. Nevertheless, like Ibsen and unlike other modern artists, he is aware that *sooner or later* 'nescience' (as he correctly and characterstically calls it) must be reaffirmed.

> But the disease of feeling germed,
> And primal rightness took the tint of wrong;
> Ere nescience shall be reaffirmed
> How long, how long?

This is the closing verse of the poem, 'Before Life and After', from the 1909 collection *Time's Laughingstocks and Other Verses*. The poem as a whole declares that before human consciousness all was well, since no creature perceived a discrepancy between what is and what might be. Hardy accepts that no other animal suffers in anything much resembling our sense. Man's consciousness alone finds *error* in the fact of suffering. But the point of 'Before Life and After' is that 'primal rightness' is absolute rightness, rightness *per se*. At some stage, therefore, man must come to accept that his knowledge is a series of Apollonian codes, his getting to know things a creative activity and, at its least valuable, mere tinkering on the surface of life. So Hardy all but says with the ancients that reality is Dionysian, beyond our comprehension or control. Like the Euripides of *The Bacchae* he acknowledges the invincibility of Dionysus. Unlike Nietzsche, however, he is deeply, even desperately reluctant to note that man also is Dionysian in his concealed and most fruitful nature.

In the late novels Hardy places the highest value upon those whose feelings exceed their intellectual grasp. This is no mere matter of their being more emotional than other, 'lesser' people but rather that they cannot make a harmony of the world: the strength of their feelings is a measure of the distance between what they perceive and what they can formulate. I imagine that Hardy might have been able to agree with these words of Nietzsche:

> The entire apparatus of knowledge is an apparatus for abstraction and simplification – directed not at knowledge but at taking possession of things: 'end' and 'means' are as remote from its essential nature as are 'concepts'. With 'end' and 'means' one takes possession of the process (one invents a process that can be grasped); with 'concepts' however, of the 'things' that constitute the process.[27]

Bearing this passage in mind, let us now recall that to Hardy feeling 'germed' and is a disease, literally an absence or destruction of ease. I suggest, however, that what Hardy thinks of as dis-ease is really the sign of our attempts to close the gap between our knowledge, namely our simplified interpretation of processes, and more immediate perceptions. Now here is the start of a profitable insight into Hardy, for it means that he wishes to explore the superiority, not of those who feel most acutely but of those whose acuteness of feeling is the result, or better, the *symptom* of their heightened awareness of ignorance. In terms of certain knowledge we know next to nothing; that is what the valued figures in Hardy appreciate. They feel so much because they peer about uncertainly in what is for others a luminous landscape. Most fail to notice the shadows, the fudging, the merging and the sheer obscurity of things.

A Hardy novel is such a concatenation of varied factors that F. R. Southerington is certainly right to argue that Hardy sees 'nature as an organism which includes man, society, and animate and inanimate states of existence.'[28] Further, 'Hardy reads in everything the absence of Providence, a complete lack of design.'[29] The universe is thus an undesigned and purposeless 'organism', a vast if finite play of forces. Therefore the tiniest event, say a fatal accident to the Durbeyfields' horse, is ultimately connected with an incalculable diversity of universal happenings. So far this may be called a tragic vision, though what Hardy regards as the absence of Providence is more or less what the Presocratics saw as the omnipresence of the Fates. Human beings respond to this all-inclusive condition by means of their specific (species-bound) feelings. In Hardy's novels value is retrieved from the universal valuelessness by means of human sensitivity. People are sensitive;

therefore they possess value. It is after *Far From the Madding Crowd* that what we have said of late Hardy is plainly expressed; beforehand he was perhaps scarcely aware of it himself. Feeling now becomes the standard of value. But, it should be noted, this capacity for feeling, so prominent in Jude Fawley and Sue Bridehead, so relatively lacking in Arabella Donn, must itself be fortuitous. No one has given these characters their qualities except the author and we misjudge him if we think he holds his people to account. Thus he implies that in life no one is accountable. No man is given qualities, for they simply arise in him; they *are* him. In addition, nothing outside mankind gives the prize, so to speak, to Jude rather than Arabella. These remarks apply equally to literature and life.

We have long recognised that Hardy's view of human destiny darkened between *Far From the Madding Crowd* in 1874 and *The Return of the Native* in 1878. Possibly this change – or this movement of a force that had long been preparing within him – was a consequence, as Robert Gittings maintains, of the suicide of Horace Moule in September 1873.[30] To be precise, Gittings suggests that the character of Boldwood in *Far From the Madding Crowd* already evinces a darkened mood which, however, permeates *The Return of the Native*. *Far From the Madding Crowd* still 'makes sense' in ordinary social terms, being on the whole a serious comedy. One needs some luck, but, given that, a Gabriel Oak may be skilful, shrewd, loyal and self-controlled – and may prosper. Such is the normal human expectation which Hardy at this stage appears to share. Many will also agree with Hardy that a man like Oak, who keeps his intellect and his emotions apart, is 'mature' and not at all liable to suffer a tragic fate. What neither Hardy at this point in his career nor popular sentiment brings into the reckoning is that Gabriel Oak's temperament is itself a piece of fate, neither greatly to his credit nor the result of his contrivance. After this novel Hardy seems more aware of that kind of consideration.

At the time of *The Return of the Native* Hardy is convinced that the most nescient people, or those most willing to affirm their nescience, a man such as Clym Yeobright for instance, cannot but be sufferers. These same people are also the vanguard of our race; more and more will come to resemble Clym in the future. Therefore by the standards of *The Return of the Native* even a decent Gabriel Oak must be held to be in some sort 'unfeeling' and by no means in the van, for if he were a pioneer he could not fail to be saddened by his understanding that nature is wholly unsympathetic to man. In *The Return of the Native* some characters are doomed (Wildeve and Eustace Vye are drowned, Mrs Yeobright dies from a snake-bite), but Clym who survives as a preacher is the essential sufferer, the sufferer by temperament, who foreshadows the human pattern of the coming times. On the other hand, Eustacia merely demands a life somehow approximating to her dream on the night she first hears Clym's voice in the darkness of the heath. Hardy observes: 'Such an elaborately developed, perplexing, exciting dream was certainly never dreamed by a girl in Eustacia's situation before.'[31] He means that the dream is exotic and complex in itself but, more significantly, is outlandish in relation to Eustacia's situation as a resident on the sombre heath. Egdon Heath is unremittingly fecund but subfuse except in high summer. Scheherazade might have had such a dream, but for a modern girl and a commoner it represents mere foolish wish-fulfilment. Eustacia's passion for Clym, whom she has not even seen at this stage, 'lowered her as an intellect, raised her as a soul'.[32] This discrepancy between soul and intellect is worth a brief discussion, since Hardy implies that the two should be harmonised by checking the soul so that it no longer soars away from the intellect. Eustacia fails to harmonise them, Clym succeeds in doing so, and Clym, not Eustacia is the hero. For all the elevation of Eustacia as a soul, therefore, Hardy advocates that the soul should be maintained not far above the intellect. The intellect is the ballast and the criterion. This judgment is distinctively modern; imagine telling a biblical figure that he should subordinate his immortal soul to the teachings of his mind! The judgment is also pretty well the opposite of Ibsen's; Hardy will not entertain the possibility that Eutacia's intellect might profitably be brought to serve her soul – not childishly, not by specious rationalisations but by setting the intellect a challenge and a goal. Anyone who approaches that task must clearly abandon such adolescent dreams as Eustacia's and must, above all, try to perceive the actual character of things (of the heath, of Paris, of Wildeve and of Clym), but Hardy is fairly specific here, suggesting, on the contrary, a sort of crippling of the soul. A crippled soul is still a soul and may even be impressive. Thus the scale of the novel is as follows: the maimed soul of Clym, the unbridled, immature soul of Eustacia and then the relative soullessness of other characters. Hardy is actually advocating that one should give up high aspirations, as Clym gives them up. The modern age cannot accommodate high aspirations. This is

an ethical judgment on Hardy's part masquerading as an intellectual one. Perhaps indeed it is only an inferior intellectual
judgement, because Hardy will not conclude that there need be
virtually no limit to human aspiration as such, only to man's
willingness to pay the price. Not only the Titan Prometheus, but the
mere mortal Oedipus, journeys beyond the limits of 'possibility'.
Nevertheless Hardy's supposition here is the general supposition
of the late twentieth century, and he is excellently predictive in that
way, far more discerning than the scientific zealots of his time.

Clym, the object of Eustacia's fantasy, is a man of the future. His
face 'already showed that thought is a disease of the flesh, and
indirectly bore evidence that ideal physical beauty is incompatible
with emotional development and a full recognition of the coil of
things'.[23] This is a common assumption of our day, so that one
hears praise of the countenance, for example, of an anguished poet
or a political prisoner. The implication is that the sorrowing face is
itself *enticing*, of all things, while the face of a pampered and
beautiful actress is not. Beautiful people are thought to be insensitive to the pain around them, narcissistic and morally
infantile. But Hardy's belief and this latter-day notion are alike
dubious, since, to judge from Roman busts, there were as many
apprehensive and tortured faces then as now. Hardy, however,
intends to ram home his belief that the suffering of sensitive souls is
predominantly modern:

> The truth seems to be that a long line of disillusive centuries has
> permanently displaced the Hellenic idea of life, or whatever it
> may be called. What the Greeks only suspected we know well;
> what their Aeschylus imagined our nursery children feel.[34]

We are entitled to discuss these well-known remarks as philosophy
or history; at any rate as something other than context-bound art,
since Hardy openly inserts them by way of a general observation.
The matter is more complex than Hardy suggests, for we have
somehow to distinguish between suffering and sensitivity to
suffering. First it is necessary to discard absolutely that Victorian
notion of the Greeks, which Hardy possibly shares, as 'silver
figures' (Goethe) or, more insidiously, as a people 'Who saw life
steadily and saw it whole' (Matthew Arnold). The Greeks were
indeed a beautiful race, but they were not so because they lived by
illusions which we (to our credit) have abandoned. Aeschylus was

more aware of misery than the vast majority of modern men and women, let alone our 'nursery children'. He imagined the terror of Orestes and the proud agony of Prometheus. The disillusive centuries have now started to rob us of exactly that illusion fostered by Socrates to the effect that man might solve problems and thus become happy. But this illusion never crossed the mind of Aeschylus, as it never occurred to the pre-Socratic thinkers. The 'Hellenic idea of life', in so far as it was zestful (and we may take it to have been remarkably zestful by our standards), was not so because the Hellenes endured comparatively little pain, but rather because they were comparatively unaware of the pain they endured. Much of the time they cannot have recognised their suffering *as suffering*, for it was no more than the nature of things. Hardy does not distinguish between pain and consciousness of pain; thus he gives the impression that the Greeks, relatively speaking, enjoyed a sort of physical and emotional wellbeing in the way of healthy young animals. But in fact such robust and undivided creatures would scarcely have produced tragedy or bothered to philosophise. Hardy also fails to stress that our prized sensitivity is itself but a phase and not the entire future of humanity.

Indeed the sensitivity to pain of modern people is not primary in our make-up, for it rests upon certain ideas. The first of these ideas is that the universe has an apex, namely ourselves. Secondly we view pain as an error or evil from which we at least, as the superlative beings of the universe, should be relieved. Clym Yeobright, as a type of suffering modern man, is not more sensitive than his forebears; rather his sensitivity is focused through an idea – a post-Socratic and especially a modern idea – that the world is askew, a monstrous malformation, since living amounts to suffering and does so in direct ratio to one's perceptiveness. Thus suffering is no longer simply experienced as it was by the Greeks, but consciously and bitterly experienced. The factor of consciousness is all-important and it is certainly true that we are more intricately conscious than the Greeks in their tragic age. In comparison with us the Greeks wholeheartedly belonged to the natural world, regarding their membership as deeper and truer than the dialectic which Socrates in due course made fashionable. Now we are beginning to be disillusioned with what Hardy nicely calls the 'coil of things'. But we still overlook the fact that the dialectic has coiled back upon itself, become self-defeating.

In interpreting Hardy it is important to reckon with the contrast between his near-Hellenic sense of fate and his non-Hellenic response to fate. Time's laughingstocks are not tragic changes of fortune. Neither does Hardy offer much moral alleviation in the way of most Victorian novelists. He cannot, in his age, dwell on sheer 'absurdity'. Moreover there is almost no engaging heroism; however much one sympathises with a Hardy hero, one does not have the pleasure of enthusing over him. There is no 'greatness' in the novels, as there is – acceptably, I believe – in the plays of Ibsen. What consolatory possibilities are left? There is only one: it is now necessary to prize and relish one's own melancholy. Melancholy is precisely the quality that raises one above all the joyful and uncomplaining beings. Hardy recognises that nescience must sooner or later be reaffirmed. That in turn means that moral interpretations too are an assumption, a code, a preference, a fantasy – anything but valid knowledge. Thus when Hardy asks, 'how long, how long?' he is wondering when we shall at last be able to acknowledge the arbitrariness of our own meanings and explanations. In the end Hardy falls back on sadness and puzzlement; he makes these mental states into virtues and so foreshadows the second half of the twentieth century.

One important step Hardy takes, I suggest, is that of disposing of free will. That is to say he hammers another nail in the coffin of free will and thus sets himself apart from Tolstoy, Dickens, George Eliot and, of course, many another. For that reason any study of *The Mayor of Casterbridge*, for instance, or of Michael Henchard in particular which even faintly suggests that the latter might have behaved differently is on the wrong lines. Hardy believes in choices in the sense that no one and nothing obliges Henchard to sell his wife, Susan, at Weydon fair. This characteristic and fateful decision – less a decision than an impulse – is part and parcel of the coil of things. But then so is Henchard's entire nature and the nature of all creatures – not to mention what Southerington calls 'inanimate states of existence'. So if we amuse ourselves by thinking of alternative courses for Henchard (ways of escape from his destiny) we are, so to speak, 'sinning' against not only the canons of literary criticism but against a common-sense rule of life. People in the world have no more choice than people in books; that is to say, we make our choices *characteristically*, therefore necessarily, and they are choices purely in the sense that we are not automatons. An automaton does what it has been externally devised to do, but people and indeed all living things are driven by *internal* will to power, no matter what the external compulsions might be. That is to say, when we yield to a compulsion we have not become automatic, since it is *we* who yield as living creatures, which is as much as to say, creatures of will. Our wills yield.

In this way Henchard cannot but make the choices he makes, for it is only in theory that he has alternatives. Truly there are no alternatives *for him*, not simply because he is a 'man of character' – or one who persists in his own inclinations – but simply because he is an individual. Even the sensible choices of a Donald Farfrae (clearly not a 'man of character') come naturally and unbidden to Farfrae. The latter is not free to behave as Henchard; everyone is what he is and not someone else. In Hardy there is no suggestion that a person might conceivably be, so to speak, 'someone else'. That is why Hardy is not much of a moralist; he complains but does not give moral instruction. So far, then, Hardy seems to be properly tragic and the causes in a Hardy novel are arbitrary because character is arbitrary. When someone in a Hardy novel might be called a villain (say, Alec D'Urberville) Hardy does little more than incline our sympathy towards his victim. The picture I am drawing of Hardy suggests that he might have been prepared to agree with these words of Nietzsche:

> *Unaccountability and innocence* – The complete unaccountability of man for his actions and his nature is the bitterest draught the man of knowledge has to swallow if he has been accustomed to seeing in accountability and duty the patent of his humanity.[35]

But though Hardy may be so far Nietzschean, he stops short before the abyss of tragic awareness. For that further leap, or descent, he would need to know what he knows about fate (that what has happened must necessarily have happened, or that the President of the Immortals has indeed sported with Tess) and then, in 'Aeschylean phrase', wholeheartedly accept the fated conditions of life. As it is, Hardy, unlike the great majority of his cultivated contemporaries, acknowledged what we may as well persist in calling 'the Fates'. The Fates sometimes sleep (consider the *Eumenides*) but never depart and must determine even the consequences of modern science and technology, as Hardy insists in the poem, 'The Convergence of the Twain'. Now while Hardy amply illustrates that so much of life hurts a sensitive modern being, he cannot accept that the ancients were hurt *far more profoundly and* pervasively than we. That is why they were also, not infrequently, ravished with delight.

Tess of the D'Urbervilles is a chapter of accidents, a sorrowful story and, so far as Angel Clare is concerned, a penetrating psychological study. Angel deserts Tess, not through emotional revulsion, nor yet exactly because he is 'less Byronic than Shelleyan',[36] but because there lies hidden within him 'a hard logical deposit, like a vein of metal in a soft loam, which turned the edge of everything that attempted to traverse it'.[37] This vein of logic, of principle, is a modern version of an old quality; it often transmits itself today in politics, and is now the one way people have of 'conquering nature'. The root desire of Angel's kind is to overcome the natural, and he falls in love with one whose mode of response is precisely nonresistance. This does not mean that Tess is somehow 'more natural' than other people, since nature is anything but pliable and nonresistant. Natural things assert themselves at all costs, within the limits of their species. Tess is a construct on Hardy's part; he has fashioned a figure of modern purity, but in order to do this he needed to deprive his heroine of every angular and assertive quality, therefore of *tragic significance*.

The spirit of *Tess of the D'Urbervilles* is contrary to the spirit of Greece, and the celebrated concluding reference to Aeschylus is misleading. The pathos of Greece sometimes included radiant beauty: one suffered – or experienced – both pain and joy. The Greeks also knew ecstasy, by which I mean *ekstasis*, 'standing away' from oneself, and this is what people in Hardy never know. It is possibly what Eustacia Vye longs for, while Tess is scarcely aware of it even at her happiest at Talbothays. From the rich and varied tones of the novel Hardy excludes radiance, since he believed, and has Tess announce to her little brother, that we live on a blighted star. The minor characters of this novel – Car Darch at Trantridge, old Mr Clare, Angel's evangelical father, Joan Durbeyfield with 'the intelligence of a happy child' – all partake of the blight. They lack the élan of Shakespearean rustics. Even Alec D'Urberville goes through a period of setting himself up as a preacher but, in character, ends more or less as he began. Though Alec is a traditional scoundrel, Hardy does not labour to make us see him in that light. In fact it is hard, not easy, to view this novel as a moral tale, for it is merely a story of great pathos, in the modern English sense of that word. Tess is a victim as a creature may be a victim of its own kind. She is wonderfully appealing, sad and sensuous, though what Hardy discloses is not just a pure woman but a 'pure', which is to say an *unanswerable* humanity. I suggest, however, that he could not come to terms with his artist's awareness of our blameless condition.

It seems that Hardy continued to be in two minds: on the one hand he recognised man's nescience, even or especially about moral matters, while on the other hand he felt keen indignation. We are not to blame, and yet cannot usually help blaming people and institutions. *Jude the Obscure* is not a tragedy proper, for its fascinatingly sombre notes exclude nothing so much as a tragic response. Hardy, the one whose intellect and powers of observation cause him to note the worm-eaten roots of indignation, is now massively indignant. Here is the reverse of *amor fati*. The best *must* suffer, as indeed they did among the Greeks, but there is no Greek joy in this fact. It is an honour for Oedipus that he suffers, though of course the honour cannot console him. Sophocles rejoices for Oedipus and so do we. But we do not rejoice for Jude, far from it. In Hardy's novel Jude and Sue Bridehead are 'the best', followed a good way behind by Phillotson, because they, in contrast to Arabella Donn, set themselves against natural and cultural conditions alike. *Jude* is not just a critique of society but of human life on earth. It is illuminating to ask why the *Antigone* of Sophocles is not a similar critique. The answer is that Sophocles expected and prized the suffering of the best. In what way might human life have value unless an Antigone is sacrificed? If Sophocles had contemplated an alternative culture he would have seen his Antigone reduced to the status of a figure in comedy. Without her, that is, without the tragic hero as a mask of Dionysus, there could be no redemption of the world. Hardy also is aware of this nihilistic possibility, but with another part of his mind cannot tolerate the tragic, which he sees as the unjust alternative. As between nihilism and injustice he is completely modern in failing to make up his mind – or, if anything, in tending towards the former. Sophocles, to the contrary, simply accepts 'injustice'; nihilism is no answer at all but a low, comic posture of helplessness.

I have said that *Jude the Obscure* finds grave fault with human life on earth. Barbara Hardy in *The Appropriate Form* refers to 'conditions in nature and society which, in the absence of Providence, work together to frustrate energy and intelligence'.[38] The question however is: why did Hardy – and perhaps Professor Hardy also – imagine that human energy and intelligence might

operate without frustrations? Whence comes this dream of un-
impeded human energy? Plainly energy has to be exerted *against*
something and when the greatest energy is employed human
beings are at their best. Obstacles are vitally necessary, for, lacking
them, we lack both value and force. Naturally it is the best people, or
some of them, such as Jude and Sue (an exceedingly rare couple of
course), who *creatively* criticise both nature and society. Arabella
merely adapts herelf to whatever is going on, to whatever beliefs are
current, as the countless Arabellas always do. Arabella is incapable
of critique, and Phillotson is but barely and timorously capable of it.
Hardy will not see that this is how human life must proceed;
creation means chiselling away at hard rock. A Jude or a Sue
questions the cultural pattern and what they understand of its
history. 'Can this be the girl,' asks Jude, 'who brought the pagan
deities into this most Christian city – who . . . quoted Gibbon, and
Shelley, and Mill? Where are dear Apollo, and dear Venus now!'[39]
The tone and the references are revealing errors here – on Hardy's
part. Gibbon might be allowed, but neither Shelley nor John Stuart
Mill is sufficiently radical. Both the poet and the philosopher 'play
at' radicalism in relation to what is required in order to resurrect
Apollo and Venus (Aphrodite). And 'dear Apollo' is quite silly,
though Jude means it for a mournful sarcasm. Likewise Sue
Bridehead has never understood that her questions – the questions
that gratified her 'in the day when her intellect scintillated like a
star'[40] and now torment her – are inadequate. No wonder she
manages to equate God and 'senseless circumstances', seeing both
as awful powers: she cannot continue to deny God, as Jude still
does, and grant that all circumstances are intrinsically senseless.
Sue has done nothing other than put up her own civilised and
progressive notions against the old Christminster ways, failing to
realise that civilisation and progress are themselves among the
concepts which serious questioners are increasingly obliged to
question. The other beliefs, those that Sue at first effortlessly
rejects, are moving away from us at the speed of light. Truly they are
not even questions any longer. And Jude himself, the most
wretched of heroes, lacks an adviser. He would have the necessary
relentless power of interrogation, yet cannot find a starting point.
He may not begin to unravel what he knows should be unravelled.
Jude remains no more than a decent scholar requiring a guide.
Given such a guide (I mean merely someone to point the way to the
wicket gate), he would outstrip Sue and move ahead of his own

volition. But he takes Sue for a pioneer and does not see until it is too late that she is not even a companion. She is an early member of that now so numerous company which has discarded God and expects the world to behave as though God were still in command; in other words as though there were inherent value in things.

We have seen Hardy as one who recognises yet cannot tolerate a tragic reality – or a reality to which man's most appropriate response is some sort of tragic art and philosophy. In a notebook comment, discussing an idea of von Hartmann, Hardy declares that our human drive should be 'to make the ends of the Unconscious ends of our own consciousness'.[41] These words illustrate Hardy's quandary. On the one hand he is far ahead of his time in realising that our consciousness and genius cannot actually command the world. We can, indeed we must impose our designs upon the world, for how else could we endure? Yet these impositions are both 'false' in some sense and also painful. To aim at universal human comfort is to will human extinction. On the other hand Hardy is perfectly of his time to regard the unconscious as a unified collection of forces with ends in view. In fact the unconscious (let us avoid capitalisation) is simply a term by means of which we apparently unify all world-forces lying outside our own conscious processes. In reality 'the unconscious' is as manifold as Dionysus and, correctly, *is* Dionysus. It has no 'ends' as we understand the term, no goal, but merely exercises and fulfils itself at every moment. It is simply power or force; we alone provide ends which are themselves conscious formulations of uncomprehended and incomprehensible movements within and around us. Thus the ends are strictly speaking misunderstandings and certainly not the 'ends' of the force itself. Nonetheless it is our task and indeed our glory that we propose ends. These are naturally also values.

Ibsen, on the other hand, was held back from thoroughgoing tragedy (both in his art and his general attitude towards life) only for so long as he craved public recognition. Once he had received the recognition he began to slip away from the social realism upon which it was based. He returned in the nineties towards the tragic vision which had been his from youth. After 1895 Ibsen was openly tragical. No one ever says what the words, 'when we dead awaken', mean and indeed the meaning is far from obvious. Ibsen intends to indicate that human beings will come to realise they are things of nature, not essentially superior to the mountain which Rubek and Irene climb, nothing 'higher' than the mist into which the hero and heroine vanish. No doubt man is also the 'redeemer' of mountains and mists, but he cannot perform his task of redemption for so long as he gives himself a different and actually celestial origin. We grant ourselves such an origin not necessarily by speaking of heaven, but simply by distinguishing the soul, or even the mind, from the world. The uniqueness of man's task does not raise him above nature and indeed his task is impossible until he can say, 'The mist is part of me and I am part of it.' That is, until he discovers, or rediscovers, 'the basic text of *homo natura*'. In the end Rubek and Irene accomplish this and so awaken from the dream of Platonism – which is what Ibsen means by death.

7

Zarathustra and
the Rebirth of Tragedy

Behind the verve of Nietzsche's prose and his rejection of the usual processes of reasoning lies a perfectly reasonable belief about the coming of a new tragic age. The matter is not developed as an argument anywhere in the writings: Nietzsche merely asserts that 'at present . . . we are experiencing a *rebirth of tragedy* and are in danger alike of not knowing whence it comes and of being unable to make clear to ourselves whither it tends'.[1] The later Nietzsche, if not the earlier, is in no doubt about the whence and the whither. By now we have probably given enough consideration to the former; as for the latter, the human race is moving towards experiencing what the pre-Socratic Greeks already experienced. For them 'even the immediate present had to appear right away . . . *sub specie aeterni* and in a certain sense as timeless'.[2] Needless to say, when we come to grasp the immediate present as timeless our manner of doing so will differ strikingly from that of the early Greeks, but we shall thus recover the *pathos* of tragedy; that is, we shall altogether lose the notion of 'progress'. For our purposes we had better at this stage, summarise Nietzsche's belief.

From *The Birth of Tragedy* in 1872 to *Thus Spoke Zarathustra*, published between 1883 and 1885, a cycle of thought is completed. The beginning of that cycle can be expressed as follows: Greek optimism after the tragic period manifested itself in the production of the theoretical man who believed he could 'guide life by science and actually confine the individual within a limited sphere of solvable problems . . . '.[3] From Socrates onwards we have been in the grip of one variety or another of 'Alexandrian' culture which promises, so to speak, a *deus ex machina* for every problem. There is always a way out, if only we can find it.

We long ago came to regard anyone other than a theoretical man as undesirable, if indispensable at times, for example in time of

160

war. Such a person is immoral or crude (undeveloped), quite commonly a criminal type, sometimes a fearsome prodigy. Solutions normally present themselves as ideas or pieces of knowledge, so that a Napoleon who settles things by means of force is certainly bad. We Alexandrians place our faith in learning, analysis and sympathetic discussion, for such procedures are good as opposed to the wickedness of sheer Napoleonic force.

This great proliferation of Alexandrianism has grown from a single root, namely the urge to universal happiness. For a considerable time the happiness of all has been regarded as a real, though elusive, possibility. The suffering of anyone on earth is no longer acceptable, unless we can say with complete confidence that he has 'deserved' it. The purest accident might in theory have been prevented.

However a great, indeed an insuperable twofold problem confronts us. First, according to Nietzsche an Alexandrian culture depends upon the existence of a slave class, while the optimism of the culture denies any such requirement. Nietzsche does not support his assertion and initially we may be strongly inclined to reject it. Why do we need slaves or why must we be slaves? It should be clear that Nietzsche does not mean slaves on the model of the ancient world, nor is he predicting totalitarian forced labour. I doubt if he quite anticipated Brave-New-Worldian menials, conditioned and happy, though that prediction seems nearer the mark. He uses the word 'slavery' to refer to the essence of unfreedom, not to any one of its forms and once we grasp that, the idea seems more worthy of consideration. In *Beyond Good and Evil* Nietzsche maintains that the enhancement of our race has always been achieved by an aristocratic society, and will be so achieved 'again and again'. Such a society believes in 'order of rank' and 'needs slavery in some sense or other'.[4] The last phrase implies that we should banish images of slavery from our minds, for who knows what forms slavery might take in the future?

The essential difference between masters and slaves is expressed elsewhere in *Beyond Good and Evil* and much illuminated in *On the Genealogy of Morals*. Masters create values for themselves, while slaves simply are whatever they are considered to be. In practice, it is true, many people (though not all) exhibit both masterly and slavish behaviour in their lives. The slave, however, predominantly judges himself as others judge him. Such a person may be socially quite exalted but nevertheless his being has been formed and is manipulated by the community. He believes others are in the same boat, although some, so it seems to him, are too stupid or arrogant to know it. If you tell him that an aristocrat, 'in some sense or other', posits his own values and unresentfully passes judgment on the community, he replies that the aristocrat is deluded. But where is the standard of reality by which this delusion may be recognised? Precisely in the community; it is a communal standard and nothing more. Masters, in contrast to slaves, are spiritually aloof from the community, discerning, judging and constantly creating values. Now we can see why an Alexandrian culture depends upon slavery, since its problem-solving nature entails numbers of functionaries operating well below the creative level. Note: an Alexandrian culture may be either aristocratic or democratic. There is nothing automatically democratic about it, as a momentary recollection of Plato's *Republic* will testify.

The second aspect of our problem is less political and more purely intellectual. In every department of knowledge the cleverest people quickly reach the boundary. In his early twenties a physicist may know as much as anyone else about his field. The foremost practitioner of a subject then pushes beyond the boundary, establishing a new boundary. But of course this means either that the subject becomes exhausted or there is a succession of boundaries. When the latter happens a suspicion grows that we are dealing not with knowledge in the old-fashioned, reliable sense ('permanent', if evolving, knowledge), but with human creativity; one might almost say, with ingenuity. At any rate, people must grow less and less sure that the field of learning called 'physics' will still exist in, say, another two hundred years, or that man's way of apprehending the universe will then be in line of descent from present-day physics. Our cosmology may have altered out of all recognition and our so-called laws of matter and energy become confined to museums and quaint histories. Even the law of gravity is no longer safe. Thus the possibility lurks in our minds that knowledge is neither more nor less than a strategy. The activity of knowing already stands in need of revaluation.

If we now combine these two aspects of Alexandrianism, the slavery it entails and the brand of scepticism it promotes, we glimpse the limits of the Socratic way. Conversely tragedy celebrates the flow of life, for it is understood that the hero's death, his personal finitude, is life-enhancing. Since tragedy, as either art or thought, is the formal delineation of an ever-flowing reality, it can have only formal limits for the artist or thinker. And these limits are designed to suggest limitlessness, or in other words the Dionysian actuality of all things.

Thus tragedy, however stark and challenging, cannot bring us to despairing nihilism; indeed it is our antidote to such nihilism. On the other hand it can and will bring us to nihilism of another and invigorating kind. But the Alexandrian way *guarantees* the nihilism of despair, and this condition has now come upon us as a result of two-and-a-half thousand years of attempting to denaturalise human nature. Nietzsche commonly speaks of nihilism and indeed he more or less appropriates the term. Book One of *The Will to Power* is entitled (by Nietzsche's editors) 'European Nihilism' and over a hundred observations on the subject are gathered there. The word is most comprehensively defined as 'the radical repudiation of value, meaning and desirability'.[5] So nihilism means to Nietzsche that nothing commands either general esteem or a single unchallenged interpretation. To be precise, one who has the will to create a value certainly does so *commandingly*, but this new value has two striking characteristics: first, it is for the creator – it 'belongs' to him, it *is* him – and second, no one doubts that it has been individually created, not received from on high.

To be such a creator of values is of course rare, but more than a negligible number of people already recognise that whatever meaning they ascribe to specific things or to the cosmos is provisional, therefore in some sense false, and whatever value they place upon anything is likewise precarious. Perhaps the word 'recognise', is incorrect, for we are speaking not of a recognition but of a slow dawning. And for the great majority of people such a dawn has not yet broken, since they still assume that value and meaning lie outside themselves, in or behind the world-process or, at the very least, in the twists and turns of 'public opinion'. So nihilism is not one simple thing, but two; on the one hand it is a dim and vacant activity like the shifting of a herd of cows, while on the other hand it can be revealed, if rarely, in an original, purposeful movement towards an individual's essence.

Nihilism is the net result of the process begun by Socrates. Perhaps he saved civilisation by his argumentative questioning, more especially by the example it set, but in doing so he pointed the way to our present predicament. Now there is nothing left but argument and while this is (rightly) esteemed as a potentially useful and constructive procedure, we do not grasp its almost ridiculous limitations: how can one argue with Dionysus? Argument can only be deemed 'tragic' or 'tragicomic' when set against the larger reality. Nietzsche writes:

> Once upon a time, in some out of the way corner of that universe which is dispersed into numberless twinkling solar systems, there was a star upon which clever beasts invented knowing. That was the most arrogant and mendacious minute of 'world history', but nevertheless it was only a minute. After nature had drawn a few breaths, the star cooled and congealed, and the clever beasts had to die. – One might invent such a fable, and yet he still would not have adequately illustrated how miserable, how shadowy and transient, how aimless and arbitrary the human intellect looks within nature.[6]

This is the truly tragic world-picture to which, so Nietzsche supposes, we are slowly and with varying degrees of reluctance, returning. At this point, then, we can summarise Nietzsche's prophecy as follows: tragedy must come back, as art, philosophy and in the very texture of language, when we accept that the alternatives to it absolutely cannot sustain us. So settled are we in a dialectical groove that the belief I have just ascribed to Nietzsche sounds like a dogma. It is certainly an opinion, but an opinion to which no counterthrust is forthcoming. Or rather, human history since the Greeks has consisted of trying all the alternatives. Thus Nietzsche's opinion is not a hypothesis, since it has been devised after the experimentation is over. This would normally give it the status of a law but we dare not call it a law, and, in any case, tragic thought alters the status of all laws. The point is that we are so wedded to experimentalism that we refuse to acknowledge the end of experiment so far as this particular thought is concerned. Nietszche himself speaks of viewing life as an 'experiment of the seeker for knowledge'.[7] Yes indeed (and one can see the marvellous effect of this liberation in Nietzsche's writings), but Nietzsche has in mind endless experimental seeking as an entire way of life conducted on the assumption that beyond one's tests and trials, one's probes into space or the depths of the mind, one's whole Faustian enterprise, there is nothing but the universe which is itself both the arena of man's adventures *and* an ever-expanding play of forces. It is a *play*, a manifold of activities without a dominating purpose. So the one experiment mankind may no longer carry out (since it has been carried out *ad nauseam*) is the experiment of 'being'. There is no being in the traditional sense of the word, as something apart from becoming. In fact the only conceivable form of being for a modern thinker is being as Heraclitus saw it, specifically the 'being' of constant activity. Thus the world (the cosmos) simply *is* in the following saying of Heraclitus:

> This world, which is the same for all, was made neither by a god nor by a man, but it ever was, and is, and shall be, ever-living Fire, in measures being kindled and in measures going out.[8]

I do not think we should be distracted by the celebrated Heraclitean notion of 'Fire' (which is interestingly explained by Nietzsche in his *Philosophy in the Tragic Age of the Greeks*[9]), but may apprehend simply the vision of a permanency of process, of 'flames' (to speak metaphorically) flaring up, dying down, then flaring up again – for ever. Since the only being is the being of becoming; that is to say, since everything in existence endlessly develops, the only comprehensive and accurate form of aesthetic representation must be *finally* tragic. It need not be blatantly tragical but it must be understood to rest upon a tragic base, namely a base of living and dying *pointlessly*, lacking justice according to the Christian-moral version of justice. We should stop calling this sort of vision 'absurdist', because there can never be a non-absurd alternative. The very idea of non-absurdity is a modern remnant of what Nietzsche, by way of a summary of the history of philosophy since Plato, calls the 'history of an error':

How the 'Real World' at last Became a Myth

HISTORY OF AN ERROR

1 The real world, attainable to the wise, the pious, the virtuous man – he dwells in it, *he is it*.

(Oldest form of the idea, relatively sensible, simple, convincing. Transcription of the proposition 'I, Plato, *am* the truth.')

2 The real world, unattainable for the moment, but promised to the wise, the pious, the virtuous man ('to the sinner who repents').

(Progress of the idea: it grows more refined, more enticing, more incomprehensible – *it becomes a woman*, it becomes Christian . . .)

3 The real world, unattainable, undemonstrable, cannot be promised, but even when merely thought of a consolation, a duty, an imperative.

(Fundamentally the same old sun, but shining through mist and scepticism; the idea grown sublime, pale, northerly, Königsbergian.)

4 The real world – unattainable? Unattained, at any rate. And if unattained also *unknown*. Consequently also no consolation, no redemption, no duty: how could we have a duty towards something unknown?

(The grey of dawn. First yawnings of reason. Cockcrow of positivism.)

5 The 'real world' – an idea no longer of any use, not even a duty any longer – an idea grown useless, superfluous, *consequently* a refuted idea: let us abolish it!

(Broad daylight; breakfast; return of cheerfulness and *bon sens*. Plato blushes for shame; all free spirits run riot.)

6 We have abolished the real world: what world is left? the apparent world perhaps? . . . But no! *With the real world we have also abolished the apparent world!*

(Mid-day; moment of the shortest shadow; end of the longest error; zenith of mankind; INCIPIT ZARATHUSTRA.)[10]

From the range of this nice, sardonic summary I want to concentrate on the sixth item, which I take to characterise the phase we are now approaching; we are perhaps somewhere between phases five and six. This is Heidegger's focus in his *Nietzsche* Volume III and we shall certainly need to refer to Heidegger, though our purpose is different from his. At present, then (in 1988), Plato has already blushed for shame and until recently (that is to say in the period which positively ended with the First World War) everything seemed to promise a return of cheerfulness and *bon sens*. That was the fine fresh morning, then we moved, and are still moving towards noon and the shortest shadow. We are also nearing the zenith of mankind. Now plainly the zenith means not so much the period of the greatest felicity (though it will be felicitous for some) but rather the time when mankind 'comes into its own', having shaken off the 'real world'. But this time of man's assuming his proper place in the visible, sensible world is enormously dangerous and frightening. It is physically dangerous, since human beings might destroy themselves, but that material risk is accompanied by a great metaphysical anxiety – perhaps it is even a terror. The terror lies in the possibility that behind the apparent world, meaning everything we *know*, there is no other reality. There is no 'real world', because we have cheerfully abolished it. But – and this is Nietzsche's greatest irony – the apparent world, which took its very meaning from the real world, now has no meaning and therefore no tolerable existence. It visibly exists – though our senses might be playing tricks on us – but what is tolerable about 'mere' existence? Can we tolerate space and galaxies and stellar nebulae and black holes 'as such'? Further, the evidence of our senses is mediated through ideas, which are clearly dubious, at any rate manufactured, and 'have no basis', as we say, 'in reality'.

At this desperate point in man's history '*Incipit Zarathustra*'. Now who is this Zarathustra and why does he, *as his defining quality*, come just now? He is anything but a messiah and when we try to see him as a prophet we must change our notions of prophecy. He is certainly the precursor of the *Übermensch*, but not as the Baptist was the precursor of Christ. As a precursor is he not simply a role adopted by Nietzsche? According to a lecture of 1953 by Heidegger entitled 'Who is Nietzsche's Zarathustra?' this remarkable figure (scarcely a 'character') is best defined as an advocate.[11] But he is an advocate whose advocacy is also the means of his own self-recovery, his own convalescence. As for Nietzsche himself, he declares in the preface to *Ecce Homo* that Zarathustra should be seen as a seducer, one who will only be found, truly found, after he has been denied, opposed by every means in one's power. Later in *Ecce Homo* Nietzsche comments that Zarathustra is the 'annihilator of morality' in whose mouth the word ' "overman", as the designation of a type of supreme achievement . . . becomes a very pensive word'.[12] (It is notable, by the way, that 'overman' is a pensive word;

even Nietzsche does not know exactly what it means.) Later still in
Ecce Homo, in the part called 'Why I am a Destiny', Nietzsche
remarks that Zarathustra, the Persian prophet, was the first man on
earth to make a meaning of human life by dividing it into good and
evil: Zarathustra invented good and evil as warring categories.
However the invention was a calamitous error and since
Zarathustra has thought longer and more carefully about this self-
generated error than anyone else, he must be the first to reveal it as
error. Strictly speaking, of course, Neitzsche is the philosopher who
first calls attention to the fallacy of good-and-evil, but Nietzsche's
viewpoint becomes more convincing the more it is allocated to a
Zarathustra who has left his home in the mountains and gone back
into society. Nietzsche always speaks and thinks of Zarathustra as a
being other and more wondrous than himself. A suitable analogy
might be the relation of Milton to the Satan of *Paradise Lost*.
Whether or not we see Satan as the hero of Milton's poem, we are
expected to find Satan a more astonishing and awful figure by far
than his creator Milton, yet at the same time he makes psychological
observations which Milton alone had the genius to make. Milton is
the Satanic analyst who exposes, approvingly or otherwise, what
Satanic pride consists of. Likewise Nietzsche is the one who thinks
of Zarathustra's utterances, who knows Zarathustra's wisdom, his
trials and temptations, yet can express all such matters only through
the mouth of Zarathustra. At least when he expresses similar or
ancillary thoughts in his own voice in the works after *Zarathustra*,
these later versions are in his judgment less impressive, less
durable. Zarathustra is the necessary guise of Nietzsche, a
heightening and 'idealising' guise for one who explicitly sets out to
hasten the demise of ideals.

For Zarathustra, by whom I mean (for once) Zarathustra–
Zoroaster rather than Nietzsche, also proclaimed truth to be the
highest virtue. In the scheme of Zoroaster truth takes precedence
over good and evil; it is 'beyond good and evil'. Therefore Zoroaster
is the very person to point out the truth that good and evil, which as
world-defining categories he once invented, have turned out to be
disastrous untruths. Laurence Lampert in his uniquely detailed
and helpful *Nietzsche's Teaching – An Interpretation of 'Thus Spoke
Zarathustra'* emphasises that Zarathustra is one who teaches *and*
learns, is sick and recovers great health.[13] Thus Zarathustra is
'human', makes mistakes, has moments of error, puzzlement and
weakness. He is 'ideal', purely in the sense of lacking all triviality

and pointlessness. He fights off the Spirit of Gravity (the Dwarf), but not because he is evasively frivolous; rather because he perceives the evasiveness of gravity itself. Likewise, while he might sometimes appear to be a composition of dissonances, he must in the end be seen as a wonderfully complex harmony. It is this very diversity that makes Zarathustra what we may as well call 'ideally non-ideal'. It also makes him inimitable.

Zarathustra is sometimes joyful and observes comedy in many places, but is not in the least a creature of comedy. On the contrary when Zarathustra's return from the mountains is first mentioned in *The Gay Science* this event is prefaced by the words, '*Incipit tragoedia*'.[14] Zarathustra's observations and self-development comprise some sort of tragedy. Nevertheless the work is different from anything previously called a tragedy, not because it ends 'happily', that is to say in a sunrise of triumph, but because the tragic spirit has now been transformed from the grave to the adventurous. The world is far more subtle and elaborate in Zarathustra's eyes than it was in the eyes of Aeschylus and Sophocles, but it is not less painful. In fact by his comportment Zarathustra reveals what sort of art and philosophy the new tragic age will unfold. The tragic, as we have known it, will be 'stood on its head', will become a 'gay science', without losing its fated and worldly character. The Fates, the three sisters, will still – and always – hold universal sway.

It must still appear to many readers that we are dealing with a set of opinions, eccentric and unwelcome opinions at that. In a special sense we undoubtedly are doing so, since Nietzsche, especially in his guise as Zarathustra but elsewhere too, is anything but a dogmatist. As I have mentioned, he positively expects the worthy reader to oppose Zarathustra. For all that, Nietzsche, like Socrates (and most likely in emulation of Socrates), is merely prodding us along a path some of us would choose for ourselves, if we had the wit to discern it. The nihilism of which he so often speaks is certainly upon us and is feebly disguised by references to a recovery of old values, a return to tradition, and so forth. The old values *are* old, that is the point; they are no longer fresh and creative. If these values cannot grow, enhance themselves, in other words *change*, they are dead or dying anyway. Living things keep growing, adapting and appreciating, and do not merely survive: growth is all-important. For the self-same reason Nietzsche speaks of a 'revaluation of values'. Such is not exactly 'his opinion' any more than the arguments of Socrates and Plato to the effect that the world required human analysis were simply their opinions. Nietzsche means that since nihilism has such firm roots, it cannot be uprooted or corrected by references back to Plato and Christ. On the contrary, human culture hitherto has normally been built on nihilism in one form or another, and indeed Plato and Christ stand as the major originators of *our* nihilism, because each postulated the erroneousness of the world. The world needed to be corrected, which is as much as to say replaced, either by intelligent human thought or by the kingdom of heaven (which is within us). Now Nietszche's viewpoint is not a footnote to Plato, or perhaps it is the final footnote to Plato. He sets out to show (not to argue but to *show*) that nihilism must be transmuted. We cannot rid the world of nihilism as such, since we no longer believe in *being*, in simple absolute being; there is nothing outside Plato's cave. The entire universe and all conceivable universes constitute 'the cave', if we still wish to insist on this simile. Alternatively, we might say that we are already outside, and everywhere we look we see nothing but the flames of Heraclitus. What is all-important is that we should move nihilism from a negative to a positive pole of life and value.

This shift of nihilism requires someone who can see reality as it is. Nietzsche writes as follows in *Ecce Homo*:

> It is here and nowhere else that one must make a start to comprehend what Zarathustra wants: this type of man that he conceives, conceives reality *as it is*, being strong enough to do so; this type is not estranged or removed from reality but is reality itself and exemplifies all that is terrible and questionable in it – *only in that way can man attain greatness*.[15]

Such is what Zarathustra wants. But there is scope for confusion here, since it might be supposed that Zarathustra, of all beings, wants what we have spent so much time showing up as unattainable: 'reality as it is'. We now need to stress the difference between reality as it is and truth, for it is the latter which is illusory. 'Reality as it is' means reality as we perceive it. Thus it is certainly not truth, or else it is a new kind of truth. All earlier forms of truth have in common that they are something other than appearances. Once truth meant the Forms. Then it meant the ways of the great religious leaders. Later truth became positivistic or scientific and this mode was held to be anti-metaphysical. What of the equally, or more virulently anti-metaphysical truth of the workings of society as disclosed by dialectical materialism? What of the preference of modern British philosophy for verifiability over truth? The point is that in all these schemes and procedures the one thing truth cannot be is what I presently perceive in the world around me. That perception (or, if someone insists, that product of perception and interpretation) is plainly unreliable, unverifiable and fundamentally sensuous. It is a sort of 'body-truth', usually mediated through ideas and language. It is therefore exactly what truth, in the ancient and most modern senses, is supposed to explain, rigidify or countermand. In brief, even among the opponents of Plato truth is still predominantly 'Platonic': it is a denial or a denigration of individual experience.

Contrariwise, Nietszche's phrase, 'reality as it is', refers to experience: Nietzsche has in mind honest representation of what one has experienced. Heidegger calls this Nietzschean sort of truth '*homoiōsis*', meaning the similarity of phenomenon and representation, or the assimilation of phenomenon to representation.[16] The obvious questions to ask are as follows. What is the criterion of such truth as this? What is to stop one from 'misrepresenting' things? How can *homoiōsis* have value, especially for philosophers?

The answer to questions of this sort is that all conceptual falsifications are attempts to fixate what we now recognise as becoming, as Heraclitean fire. Thus traditional truth, and indeed what is still commonly thought of as truth, is nothing other than the human desire to command the world, as it were 'from the outside'; to exercise human will as though it were apart from the from the processes of nature. This desire is what Nietzsche, through the agency of Zarathustra, sets out to reverse. For the superior will, namely the will to power, might certainly employ some device (for example the principle of verifiability) but would do so in full knowledge that the procedure is nothing other than an exercise of power, and indeed a projection of the complexity we have learned to call the 'ego'. To use such devices without such knowledge is to yield to what Nietzsche calls the Spirit of Gravity. On the other hand, will to power understands that verifiability, for instance, is one of *nature's* dodges. In Nietzsche's eyes one attains greatness not by believing in one's own cozening devices but by acknowledging them and all devices for what they are. So one attains greatness not by conquering nature (which is utter nonsense) but by tragically and joyfully restoring oneself to nature. Man is a prodigal as well as a lost son and may return to his proper home. If we use the words 'conquer nature' with implicit reference to man's *natural* capacities all is well and we do not deceive ourselves. No other creature or thing *knowingly* employs its tricks or is able to think of so many tricks as man. So long as we understand that we are natural forces who exploit or subdue other natural forces, as, for example, when we journey through space or split the atom, then we are not misled. Plainly, though, we cannot master nature in the old metaphysical sense of holding ourselves aloof from nature – or of believing for one moment that our techniques and goals somehow keep nature at bay.

For all that, it is especially interesting that Nietzsche sees man, a wholly natural or worldly being, as having a unique function, which is to 'redeem the world'. Man is not to be redeemed by God but the world is to be redeemed by man. How can this be? The matter is not a side-issue but one central to our enquiry.

We broached this question in the first chapter but now need to explore it further in order to explain Nietzsche's belief about the necessity of tragedy. Our immediate source is the section, 'Of Redemption', in Part Two of *Thus Spoke Zarathustra*. There are many 'inverted cripples'in society (as distinct from actual cripples who, Zarathustra makes plain, are not his concern). An inverted cripple is one who does his best to confine his entire, variegated nature to one function, for example, he has cultivated his sense of hearing so that one might caricature him by drawing an immense ear attached to a mere stalk of a body. Such a cripple is 'over-specialised', as we say, and if in consequence he displays what we call 'genius', his ability is in fact the sign of degeneration. Indeed society is utterly composed, not of men and women but of fragments of men and women. Not only that, but history and learning are likewise fragments. The past is strictly speaking fragmented, since our ways of combining past events into one sort of history or another are without a mythic foundation. Modern man, lacking such a myth, relies partly on his bits and pieces of information but chiefly on a reductive sense of human together-ness, a notion that whatever we do, sink or swim, we do together. As always, the evil ones are those who stand apart. Literary people are familiar with this view of the modern predicament through T. S. Eliot's *The Waste Land*. Eliot personally resolved the problem through joining the Church, while Zarathustra, looking resolutely forward – that is *away from the Church* – sees it as his task to mould all fragments into a *new* design.

This is indeed humanity's redemptive task: we may, and perhaps sooner or later must, redeem the world by giving it a unified design in contrast to the disconnected pseudo-meanings exhibited by the modern world. Zarathustra's emphasis, however, is upon a temporal rather than a spatial unification. He mainly seeks a temporal unity, because he assumes that of all forms of fragmentation the splitting of life into past, present and future is the most devastating and perhaps ultimately ruinous.

It appears that Zarathustra has no wish to impose upon us a notion of simultaneity, so that a thousand ages in our sight should be like an evening gone. On the contrary, the dynamic universal procedure is for one event to unfold into the next. Further, after Einstein it seems incorrect to think of events in space as occurring simultaneously, since there is no constant time, no universal clock. Successions and growth are the universal facts, bearing in mind that the 'growth' commonly takes the form of dissolution. And when a thing has entered into a new combination it cannot come again in its earlier form.[17] Nevertheless that earlier form is preserved and endlessly repeated as part of the world-process. Having once been, it cannot depart in the sense of vanishing for ever, as it were 'in a puff of smoke', or by getting itself steam-rollered into dust by subsequent events. It inalienably belongs to the world-process in its first form. I am of course simplifying, indeed falsifying, by speaking of a 'first form'. There are no rigid forms, not even a series of such forms, but only endless metamorphosis. Our Apollonian constitution forces us to isolate forms in the midst of the stream of metamorphosis, but we should realise that this is no more than our human procedure and 'strategy for survival'. Each form we thus isolate or 'bring forward' from the rolling pageant 'goes back' into the pageant but also remains forever as it momentarily appeared to be. Therefore each event contains an infinity of earlier events, or as Nietzsche says in *Daybreak*, 'The becoming drags the has-been along behind it'.[18]

It is convenient and in keeping with the rest of this book to think this thought of Nietzsche by means of an aesthetic analogy, say the analogy of an incomparable narrative poem. But we must understand at the outset that this is no more than a tool of thought, since the universe is anything but aesthetic. It exhibits no comprehensive design and in Nietzsche's opinion is simply chaos. 'The world,' he says, 'is a unity neither as sensorium nor as spirit . . . .'[19] And 'The total character of the world, however, is in all eternity chaos – in the sense not of a lack of necessity, but of a lack of order . . . '.[20]

Now the point of our analogy lies precisely in the necessity of all cosmic events as compared with the necessity we can so clearly see in the development of our poem. (Obviously the poem itself is a tiny cosmic event.)

In such a work of art one deed, thought, experience, plainly follows another; in short, the poem *evolves*. Each section of the poem and indeed every word, punctuation mark and moment of rhythm is vitally necessary in exactly the place it occurs. But what really matters about this sequence is that the later words would be meaningless and empty if they were not 'impregnated', so to speak, by all the preceding words. Thus a new episode in our lives is composed of all the foregoing episodes in world-history and freshly created also. Something new is created at every turn, yet the something is a product of all that has gone before.

Despite the faults of this analogy (for example, the poem has a clear beginning and end), to regard the world in this way approximates to Nietzsche's own endeavour. This is certainly a simplified and over-theoretical version of his endeavour, but it will serve us in good stead as an approach to the question of tragic significance. Nietzsche takes it for granted that the human organism constructs whatever it contemplates. Therefore we are obliged to construct the past, since there is no other way to make use of the past, to 'cope with' it. (To view the past 'objectively' is just a particular, limited way of determining the past.)

Nietzsche of course wants people to see themselves, correctly, as entering the universe at a certain point. But thereafter they should *knowingly* make a significance of the universe, naturally including whatever they learn (in other words, come to believe) about its past. Unknowingly we do this anyway, for we assume that we progressively discover the universe. Nearly always (that is, when we are not carefully contemplating the matter) we believe the past took more or less the form we now confer upon it. This is roughly correct but also deceptive, since the element of interpretation of past events is inescapable and scarcely perceptible. After all, we *are* our interpretations. If the past included, as it must, certain terrible events, then these too are here and now 'made', which is to say interpreted or qualified by us. That something resembling such terrible events actually occurred is neither here nor there, because all we know or care about them is freshly willed into being here and now. At the very least an old interpretation is stubbornly or sluggishly retained – and this too is an act of will. It is possibly more important that the terrible quality of those old happenings (some of them very old indeed) is the unknown part of us. Whether the quality works in us as a hidden element in our basic design or whether we produce that quality in the form of our present evaluation of the past, we will the quality now, in the present.

Thus we *will* the past. But Zarathustra famously says that 'the will cannot will backwards'.[21] He means that one cannot sensibly will against what, for some reason or other, one supposes happened. It is not sensible to will against an insult received yesterday or, for the sake of argument, the First World War – though in fact we constantly carry out such emotional manoeuvres. On the other hand, there is the 'creative will' which says, 'But I willed it thus'.[22] This is the will to power and 'must will something higher than any reconciliation.'[23] I can say 'Yes' to my honest perception of the Great War and yesterday's insult. It is certainly possible to will backwards in an affirmative spirit. The spirit and direction of will to power thus match what is, anyway, part of one's inherited make-up. Now one lives with the grain of life instead of against it. True, there are many people today who regard such an affirmative will as weakness, even cowardice: one must combat evils, including even past evils. But such numerous people are degenerate in Nietzsche's sense, which is to say they are types who have fallen away from their natural constitution and make a virtue of their fall. By electing to will backwards in a negative spirit they also make a virtue of their own senselessness. In effect they tell themselves that it doesn't matter if they seem to be foolish, since they are assuredly in the right.

The affirmative will, incorporating past, present and future, is the route to the summit of Zarathustra's advocacy. This is how man, uniquely among beings, may redeem the world. He must overcome his desire for revenge against the past. No one says in so many words, 'I seek revenge upon those historical and autobiographical events that have hurt me.' To speak so displays a lunatic perversion. Yet this is our regular human lunacy which we disguise and rephrase as follows: 'I aim to build a future which shall exclude the pains and injustices of the past.' Since Socrates spoke in this vein in the dialogues we have continued to do so, and the spirit of revenge was by no means lacking in the tragic culture destroyed by Socrates and Euripides. Revenge and falsely willing backwards have been the normal human procedures. When we do this normal, entirely human thing, we are trying to correct moments that have irretrievably gone by. The trick is to tell oneself that similar or even identical moments might come in the future and *they* must be prevented. But this is what never happens: reality is not the sameness of moments but rather their endless variety. It is our abstracting minds alone that place the Punic Wars and modern wars in one category of warfare. We cannot now make up for agonies of war actually experienced by producing a future free from war. Such a future might be contrived but could not compensate for the past, and in fact it would not be 'better' in the sense of less painful – for suffering comes in a thousand insidious forms.

The notion of 'progress' in its post-Renaissance sense depends upon an exact repetition of circumstances, with but some features, that is to say, the hurtful features, removed. We even think of the 'bad' as a finite list of experiences that may be progressively reduced, while in truth the bad is hydra-headed, as is the good. An even better truth is that the hydra of human experience constantly puts forth both good and bad heads, handsome and ugly countenances, so that to want to live means to welcome all of them. Living in the other fashion means living resentfully; that is Nietzsche's point. One presumably wants 'to live' – but to alter unalterable conditions of living.

It follows, then, that to 'redeem the world' does not mean to correct it, and, indeed, redemption is nearly the opposite of correction. According to that celebrated remark in *The Birth of Tragedy* we redeem, or to be accurate we *justify* the world by treating it as an aesthetic phenomenon: 'for it is only as an *aesthetic phenomenon* that existence and the world are eternally *justified*'. In *Human, All Too Human* Nietzsche goes further, finding it 'audacious, uncanny or unbelievable', but not in the least objectionable, that Homer believes the suffering of mankind takes place so that poets shall have something to sing about:

> *How paradoxical Homer can be* – Is there anything more audacious, uncanny or unbelievable shining down on the destiny of man like a winter sun than that idea we find in Homer:
>> Then did the gods make resolve and ordain unto men *destruction, that in after times too there might be matter for song.*
> Thus we suffer and perish so that the poets shall not lack *material.*[24]

In general Nietzsche argues that we should treat purely as an aesthetic matter what we normally take to be absolutely not aesthetic. Our usual assumption is that 'existence and the world' may be viewed aesthetically but are not 'themselves' aesthetic. We further assume that to view them in such a fashion (to arrange them beautifully) is, or often can be, an evasion. To put the matter plainly, we believe worldly things must be judged in either a scientific or a moral light. Nietzsche's belief is, to the contrary, that more often than not science and ethics are precisely the distortions, while *aesthesis* in the original Greek sense implies healthy perception of the world. Of course in *The Birth of Tragedy* Nietzsche is discussing and analysing something quite other than modern realism (or impressionism, or post-impressionism); something which formally and quite artificially points to the underlying reality of what has been perceived. The word 'aesthetic' in Nietzsche carries an overtone, not of casting a beautiful haze over a terrible reality, but rather of beautifying the terrible *as both terrible and universal*. Thus the particulars of a horror are not allowed to obscure its universality. By this means, while a new tragic art will possibly be more mimetic than Aeschylean or Sophoclean tragedy, it will still be at variance with non-aesthetic experience. The beauty of the representation remains as the only human way of facing the universality of the horror. At the same time the entire representation will be fundamentally 'truer' than any non-aesthetic experience. For in life, as opposed to art, we immediately transform all terrible things (not forgetting merely jarring or unwelcome things) into *things to be put right*. On this view 'aesthesis' does not falsify or at least it has no need to do so, but our scientific-ethical colouring of day-to-day experience constantly misleads us. (It will be understood that I am referring not to science in its intellectually austere forms, but to science applied for the purpose of curing ills.) The healthy attitude towards life would regularly include a recognition that unwelcome things cannot actually be excluded. For, as Heraclitus maintains, 'Couples are wholes and not wholes, what agrees disagrees, the concordant is discordant. From all things one and from one all things.'[25] Surely this is not so enigmatic a remark as has been supposed, since Heraclitus simply means that our perceptions are shifting, 'goal-oriented' and without what we think of as 'validity'. So reality changes yet stays the same, is multiple and conflicting but also unified and harmonious. The point is that we exclude from our observations whatever we choose. This is a vital, if misleading, pychosomatic process, while the artifice of tragedy is above all not misleading. We need to ask the question: how far can this recognition be extended to a philosophy of life, not kept apart in the artistic sphere of tragedy? How vital is it for us to be misled in order to survive? Somehow or other, it seems, we shall acquire the capacity to 'mislead' ourselves *at will*, knowing that beyond our human devices there is a far vaster – and largely unseen – world of competing devices. To put the matter another way: we shall contrive to have faith in our knowledge, not on the grounds that it is correct but because it is *ours* – our strategy and path through the wilderness. This is of course a tragic idea and a tragic form of loyalty. The underlying attitude is not one of subservience to an ideal of correctness but of loyalty to something loved. The application of the artistic idea of tragedy to life as a whole is most effectively expressed in the following words of Nietzsche:

> If ever you wanted one moment twice, if ever you said; 'You please me, happiness, instant, moment!' then you wanted *everything* to return!
>
> You wanted everything anew, everything eternal, everything chained, entwined together, everything in love, O that is how you *loved* the world.[26]

So Zarathustra speaks towards the end of Book Four. He simply but rapturously reminds all who have experienced one moment of unqualified joy that to wish for it again is to wish all things again. 'All things' means all history, pre-history and the cosmic entirety. Nietzsche is taking literally the announcement of Heraclitus: 'From all things one.' Is this because Heraclitus is somehow 'right'? I do not think it would be a very difficult exercise to demonstrate that all things are entwined together in the fashion we earlier contemplated; thus to argue that the chain may not be broken, and never is broken. But Nietzsche knows that such a logical argument (which incidentally uses logic for the opposite purpose to that world-correcting purpose for which it was intended) would give deceptive pre-eminence to logic. Now only that would seem correct which is logically verifiable. Nietzsche's contrary purpose is to downgrade logic by suggesting that it doesn't matter how one argues – or *if* one argues – since argument is but a trifling human technique. All things are entwined together anyway. Moreover it is hard for the unifying human mind to contemplate 'all things' as sundry items tossed about in space. The minute we contemplate 'everything' we picture an immense unity. That may be what Heraclitus meant and it is certainly a reasonable assimilation of *whatever he meant* to the way modern minds work.

But this normal procedure of the mind, specifically that it makes whole whatever it seizes upon (including, as Gilbert Ryle has shown us, the diversity of 'mind' itself[27]) is attributed by Nietzsche to the 'creative will'. Roughly the same idea is familiar to literary people in the form given it by Coleridge, who speaks of the 'primary imagination', which is 'the living power and prime agent of human perception'.[28] As for Nietzsche, or, correctly, Zarathustra, he announces that

> All 'It was' is a fragment, a riddle, a dreadful chance – until the creative will says to it: 'But I willed it thus!'
>
> Until the creative will says to it: 'But I will it thus! Thus shall I will it!'[29]

Here it is easy to be deceived. So far as possible we already manipulate the past and divest it of its nature as a fortuitous and necessitous unfolding of events. We do this by making sense of it all. We *make* the sense; it was not already there to be found by historians. But the sense we contrive includes our resentment, because we do not acknowledge our creative role. Therefore Zarathustra means that one should decide in favour of the past – as an *acknowledged* product of one's own will. In the end we can master the past, which is to say incorporate it, only by giving it our full and joyous assent. Only the will robs chance of its dreadful aspect and solves all the riddles. And this sort of will is supremely 'realistic', not just because the past has indisputably happened, but because we ourselves *are* it.

All this way of thinking on Nietzsche' part aims to get rid of teleology and the usual ideas of 'progress'. It also aims at restoring 'greatness' in some form. I fancy that the desire for greatness, for qualities to admire, was Nietzsche's prime motivation from childhood, though this did not lead him to construct a purely wish-fulfilling philosophy. On the contrary, he appeciated that the greatness he sought could not come about except through an acknowledgement of the futility, or at least the deceptiveness of simple wishes. Even so, greatness is presented (logically and convincingly) as the sole answer to modern nihilism as a possible means of attaining it. Nihilism is upon us anyway; Nietzsche cannot be said to have fostered it for his own gratification. Nevertheless he saw straight away that the advantage of nihilism is that it sooner or later discourages crass cultures, pseudo-great men and all ideals. Nietzsche wanted Zarathustra wants: a type 'not estranged or removed from reality who is reality itself and exemplifies all that is terrible and questionable in it'. In consideration of Nietzsche's desire we return now to *The Birth of Tragedy* and to those supreme early attempts to be 'reality itself', the Prometheus of Aeschylus and the Oedipus of Sophocles.

When we discussed Aeschylus and his Prometheus in Chapter 2, we were not in a position to consider how the conception of the Titan might be modified by a modern artist to gratify Zarathustra's wishes. The Prometheus of Aeschylus defies Zeus, meaning the brute and arbitrary power of nature, because the Titan has an overwhelming sense of justice. In other words, the genius of Aeschylus is a genius for justice. Now in our ears the word 'justice', has strong moral overtones because we are heirs to the ages of morality. However, it had no such meaning for Aeschylus, and Nietzsche too, though he rarely uses the word, uses it without a moral emphasis. His most expansive reference is as follows:

> There is, to be sure, a quite different species of genius, that of justice; and I cannot in any way persuade myself to regard it as lower than any kind of philosophical, political or artistic genius. It is the way of this kind of genius to avoid with hearty indignation everything that confuses and deceives us in our judgment of things; it is consequently an *opponent of convictions*, for it wants to give to each his own, whether the thing be dead or living, real or imaginary – and to that end it must have a clear knowledge of it; it therefore sets every thing in the best light and observes it carefully from all sides. In the end it will give to its opponent, blind or shortsighted 'conviction' (as men call it – women call it 'faith') what is due to conviction – for the sake of truth.[30]

'What confuses and deceives us in our judgment of things' includes not only the posturing of tyranny and the images produced by culture, but also, most insidious of all, the popular wish to be at one with others. In the grip of this last desire it is common to believe that justice is what 'our side' fights for.

Nietzsche's view and the Aeschylean way are alike correct in their implications. No wonder Aeschylus' reputation among the Athenians was one of pride and perversity! It would be so today. Justice of the Aeschylean sort requires genius and is not in the least popular. Then there is the sting in the tail of Nietzsche's remarks, for even the truth about 'blind or short-sighted "conviction"' must be recognised by both the tragic hero and the tragic philosopher. They should be fair even to those who place their convictions before their perceptions, in a word, the *unjust*. The last thing such a tragic individual can expect is popular justice for himself – but there is no scope for bitterness here. On the other hand, there is here a perennial theme for tragedy. I am thinking of the tragedy of the just person (a sort of genius) among the unjust majority and, Prometheanly, in the face of blind nature. There is no conceivable Socratic or scientific cure for tragedy of this sort.

Now the type of man Zarathustra wants is 'reality itself and exemplifies all that is terrible and questionable in it'. Because we realise that nature, apart from the human race, is wild and heedless of justice, we might be tempted to assume that Zarathustra wants precisely an untamed man. And of course that has been the vulgar misconception of the *Übermensch*. But Zarathustra also wants a person who furnishes himself with his own good and evil and is able to be the judge of himself and avenger of his own law.[31] I have just adapted certain words of Zarathustra which indicate what a difference there is between the mindlessness of nature and the supreme self-determination of the man Zarathustra wants. It is not the lawlessness of extra-human nature that is required but *one capable of producing his own law*.

Will not such a man be godlike in the sense that he has an ability formerly attributed to the gods? So far as I know, the only person to speak in all seriousness of man replacing a god has been Aeschylus: this is the ultimate vision of *Prometheus Bound*. The secret of Prometheus which he will not share with Zeus is that one day Zeus will produce a half-mortal offspring. In line of descent from this child of Zeus will come a human being to rival, indeed to overthrow Zeus himself. For the present, however, Prometheus can do no more than aim to bring Zeus into 'bond and amity' with him.[32] According to our modern understanding both the partnership of Zeus and the Titan and, alternatively, the mortal whose ancestor is Zeus amount to the same figure, specifically one who works with nature rather than against it. This is the man Zarathustra wants, a creature of nature whose intelligence and foresight are simply parts of nature; not powers over reality but constituents of it. His gifts and his mortal superiority over nature must certainly bring him to seek justice in the Heideggerean sense of *homoiōsis*. But he will seek justice joyfully; his wisdom will be a gay science. There is no hint here of the normal human resentment against the world for not readily accommodating itself to human wishes; no suggestion that nature can somehow be forced to conform to human ideas of justice, or that man can confine himself within his own secure and humanised territory, fending off the attacks of wilful nature. Rather the Fates will now and then come over to the newcomer's side, as the Eumenides finally accede to the acquittal of Orestes. And the newcomer will not groan over his condition, as Prometheus groans. Instead he will welcome his condition afresh every morning as Zarathustra welcomes the sun, aspiring not after happiness but after his *work*.

Now it is time to face the question of the point of such tragedy. What raises it far above the category of the 'absurd', to which sophisticated modern people would otherwise consign it? Such people would detect only the tragedy of injustice in the familiar moralistic sense. They must be numbered among the enemies of the tragic hero – enemies to be forgiven and granted their measure of justice also. The point is that tragedy of this new kind takes the 'magical circle of effects', as Nietzsche calls it, to a higher level. Such an elevation is not 'progress', because the same old painful and petty things keep happening; the Fates continue to hold sway and the same mass-minds contribute their gadfly varieties of injustice. For all that, the circle of effects is further elevated above the mud of mere physical existence and the dreary lives of animals. This would be our greatest enhancement since we emerged as a species. For the first time human beings would take everything into their care, instead of giving prime responsibility to spirits, to gods, to God, to the moral law, or to 'objective' nature. Someone replies that this is insane arrogance? But what have we been doing all along when we created superhuman surrogates for our wishes and fears? The frightfulness of the new way lies in casting off all surrogates and openly taking charge. Of course such taking charge could only be effected in a tragic culture that recognises the sheer impenetrability of all things – especially human nature. The paradox in the above remarks is unavoidable, since we cannot but arrange what is really in the hands of the Fates. Up to now we have just pretended to ourselves that the uncontrollable is controlled by some power other than the capricious *Moirai*.

The elevation of mankind is also glimpsed by Sophocles, of whose *Oedipus* plays Nietzsche uses the phrase 'magical circle of effects'. Nietzsche's interpretation of Oedipus (the character and the myth) might be formulated as follows: Oedipus, through an excess of wisdom, sees into the heart of nature and there discovers utter blackness and ferocity. The blackness annhilates all knowledge, the ferocity consumes all decency. So Oedipus breaks the 'spell of past and future'[33] and indeed overwhelms all significant distinctions. He becomes one who, as Nietzsche says of Hamlet, knows the truth that his actions can change nothing 'in the eternal nature of things'.[34] Therefore he is a figure of noble passivity, the sufferer of the world's actions. He is that sufferer because he is the supreme knower: to know all is to suffer all. For the knowledge of Oedipus is anything but theoretical. Oedipus, the godlike, knows that 'everything goes, everything returns; the wheel of existence rolls for ever'.[35] These words of Zarathustra's animals make Zarathustra smile, not because the words are literally untrue but because they are too glib and uncaring. They are true, if understood rightly.

Presumably tragedy reaches its zenith towards the end of *Oedipus at Colonus*. Can we not say, therefore, that the man Zarathustra wants must be able to combine Dionysian wisdom with Apollonian tricks of conquest? When he creates, he will do so as an expression of his own Apollonian law, but he will know that the law and the act of creation have value only as ripples in the sea of coming-to-be and passing-away. Nevertheless those ripples have the purpose of justifying the whole, and there is nothing outside the whole.

Notes and References

The place of publication is London unless otherwise stated.

1 APOLLO AND DIONYSUS

1. F. Nietzsche, *The Will to Power*, (*WP*) trans. Walter Kaufmann and R. J. Hollingdale, ed. Walter Kaufmann (New York: Vintage Books, A Division of Random House, 1968) Section 1050, p. 539.
2. Ibid.
3. For an interesting discussion of the superficiality of both consciousness and language, and their near-identity (anticipating Freud and Wittgenstein) see Section 354, Book Five, *The Gay Science* (*GS*) trans. with commentary by Walter Kaufmann (New York: Vintage Books, A Division of Random House, 1974).
4. F. Nietzsche, *The Birth of Tragedy* (*BT*) and *The Case of Wagner* (*CW*), trans. with commentary by Walter Kaufmann (New York: Vintage Books, A Division of Random House, 1967) Section I. p. 33.
5. Ibid., p. 34.
6. Ibid., 'Attempt at a Self-Criticism', p. 19. This 'attempt' was added to the edition of 1886.
7. Ibid., Section 1, p. 36.
8. Ibid, Section 1, p. 37.
9. F. Nietzsche, *Human, All Too Human – A Book for Free Spirits* (*HAH*), trans. R. J. Hollingdale, with an intro. by Erich Heller (Cambridge University Press, 1986) Section 114, p. 66.
10. *BT*, Section 3, p. 41.
11. Martin Heidegger, *Nietzsche, Volume Two – The Eternal Recurrence of the Same*, trans. with notes and an analysis by David Farrell Krell (San Francisco: Harper and Row, 1984) p. 8.
12. *BT*, Section 4, p. 45.
13. F. Nietzsche, *Beyond Good and Evil – Prelude to a Philosophy of the Future* (*BGE*), trans. with commentary by Walter Kaufmann (New York: Vintage Books, A Division of Random House, 1966); 'On the Prejudices of Philosophers', Section 14, p. 21.
14. G. F. Else, *The Origin and Early Form of Greek Tragedy* (Cambridge, Massachusetts, 1965).
15. *BT*, Section 4, p. 46.
16. Ibid.
17. H. D. F. Kitto, *Greek Tragedy – A Literary Study* (Methuen, 1939) p. 139.
18. Ibid.
19. *BT*, Section 5, p. 52.
20. *BT*, Section 7, p. 57.

21. Ibid., p. 60.
22. F. Nietzsche, *On the Genealogy of Morals* (*GM*) and *Ecce Homo* (*EH*), trans. Walter Kaufmann and R. J. Hollingdale (New York: Vintage Books, A Division of Random House, 1969); *EH*, 'Why I am a Destiny', Section 9, p. 335.
23. *Sophocles* Volume I, The Loeb Classical Library, *Oedipus at Colonus*, trans. F. Storr (Cambridge, Massachusetts: Harvard University Press, and London: William Heinemann Limited, 1981) p. 291. First printed 1912.
24. Aristotle, *On the Art of Poetry*, trans. Ingram Bywater with a preface by Gilbert Murray (Oxford University Press, 1954) p. 31.
25. M. S. Silk and J. P. Stern, *Nietzsche on Tragedy* (Cambridge University Press, 1984). First published 1981.
26. Ibid., p. 187.
27. Ibid., p. 367.
28. Gilles Deleuze, *Nietzsche and Philosophy*, trans. Hugh Tomlinson (The Athlone Press, 1983) p. 3. First published as *Nietzsche et la philosophie* (Presses Universitaires de France, 1962).
29. F. Nietzsche, *Twilight of the Idols* (*TI*) and *The Anti-Christ* (*AC*), trans. with intro. and commentary by R. J. Hollingdale (Harmondsworth: Penguin Books, 1968); *AC*, Section 30, p. 142.
30. *BT*, Section 10, p. 75.
31. Ibid.
32. Ibid., p. 76.
33. *WP*, Book One, Section 2, p. 9.
34. F. Nietzsche, 'Schopenhauer as educator', *Untimely Meditations* (*UM*), trans. R. J. Hollingdale, with an intro. by J. P. Stern, (Cambridge University Press, 1983) p. 141.
35. *BT*, Section 11, p. 77.
36. Ibid., p. 79.
37. *TI*, Section 4, p. 31.
38. Plato, *The Republic*, trans. with intro. by Desmond Lee (Harmondsworth: Penguin Books, 1979) Part Seven, p. 270.

2 AESCHYLUS

1. *WP*, Book Four, Section 796, p. 419.
2. *GM*, Third Essay, 'What is the Meaning of Ascetic Ideals?' Section 4, p. 100.
3. Ibid., p. 101.
4. *HAH*, Section 170, p. 90.
5 *WP*, Book Three, Section 681, p. 361.
6. This idea is central to the argument of *The Case of Wagner*.
7. Richard Schacht, *Nietzsche* (Routledge and Kegan Paul 1985) p. 228. First published 1983.
8. *HAH*. Section 160, pp. 84f.
9. See Lou Andréas-Salome, *Frédéric Nietzsche*, traduit de l'allemand par Jacques Benoist-Méchin (Gordon and Breach) pp. 34f. First edition Paris: Bernard Grasset, 1932.

10. *WP*, Book Three, Section 645, p. 339.
11. *WP*, Book Four, Section 1019, p. 527.
12. Heraclitus, *On The Universe* Fragment 55, see *Hippocrates* Volume IV and *On The Universe* with an English trans. by W. H. S. Jones (Cambridge, Massachusetts: Harvard University Press and London: William Heinemann, 1979) p. 503. First printed 1931.
13. F. Nietzsche, *Daybreak – Thoughts on the Prejudices of Morality (D)*, trans. R. J. Hollingdale with intro. by Michael Tanner (Cambridge University Press, 1982) Book I, Section 9, p. 9.
14. *Aeschylus*, Volume II, The Loeb Classical Library, *The Libation Bearers*, trans. Herbert Weir-Smyth, ed. Hugh Lloyd-Jones (Cambridge, Massachusetts: Harvard University Press and London: William Heinemann 1983) p. 185. First printed 1926.
15. Goldhill, Simon, *Reading Greek Tragedy* (Cambridge University Press, 1986) p. 56.
16. H. D. F. Kitto, *Greek Tragedy – A Literary Study* (Methuen, 1939) p. 66.
17. *Aeschylus*, Volume II, *Agemamnon*, p. 7.
18. Ibid., p. 27.
19. Ibid., p. 79.
20. Ibid., p. 119.
21. Ibid., *The Libation-Bearers*, p. 163.
22. *Aeschylus*, Volume I, The Loeb Classical Library, *Prometheus Bound* trans. Herbert Weir Smyth (Cambridge, Massachusetts: Harvard University Press and London: William Heinemann, 1973) p. 261. First printed 1922.
23. *UM*, 'Schopenhauer as educator', p. 127.
24. *BGE*, 'On the Prejudices of Philosophers', Section 19, p. 25.
25. Ibid.
26. *WP*, Book One, 'European Nihilism', Section 90, p. 55.
27. *WP*, Book Two, 'Critique of the Highest Values Hitherto', Section 136, p. 86.
28. *Aeschylus* (see note 22), *Prometheus Bound*, p. 283.
29. Ibid., p. 233.
30. *BT*, p. 70.
31. *Aeschylus* (see note 22), *Prometheus Bound*, p. 239.

3 SOPHOCLES

1. *BT*, Section 9, p. 70.
2. *AC*, Section 51, p. 168.
3. *BGE*, 'What is Religion?', Section 49, p. 64.
4. *TI*, 'The Four Great Errors', Section 8, p. 54.
5. *EH*, 'Why I am So Clever', Section 10, p. 258.
6. Max Stirner, *The Ego and Its Own*, trans. Steven Byington with intro. by Sidney Parker (Rebel Press, 1982).
7. *HAH*, 'On the History of the Moral Sensations', Section 107, pp. 57f.
8. R. J. Winnington-Ingram, *Sophocles: An Interpretation*, (Cambridge University Press, 1980) p. 19.
9. Ibid., p. 156.

10. *Sophocles*, Volume II, The Loeb Classical Library, *Ajax*, trans. F. Storr (London: William Heinemann and New York: G. P. Putnam's Sons, 1929) p. 49.

11. Ibid., p. 119.

12. G. W. F. Hegel, *The Phenomenology of Mind*, trans. with an intro. and notes by J. B. Baillie (George Allen and Unwin, 1966) p. 477. First published in Gret Britain 1910.

13. Ibid., p. 476.

14. A. C. Bradley, *Oxford Lectures on Poetry* (Macmillan, 1959). First edn. 1909.

15. *WP*, Book Four, 'Discipline and Breeding', III. 'The Eternal Recurrence', Section 1066, p. 549.

16. *Sophocles* Volume II, *Antigone*, p. 321.

17. Ibid., p. 381.

18. *WP*, Book Two, 'Critique of the Highest Values Hitherto', no. 379, p. 204.

19. Jan Kott, *The Eating of the Gods*, trans. Boreslaw Taborski and J. Czerwinski (Eyre Methuen, 1974) p. 139.

20. B. M. W. Knox, *Oedipus at Thebes* (Oxford University Press, 1957) p. 116.

21. *BT*, Section 9, pp. 67f.

22. *Sophocles*, Volume I, *Oedipus at Colonus* p. 147.

23. Ibid., p. 183.

24. H. D. F. Kitto, *Greek Tragedy – A Literary Study* (Methuen, 1939) p. 401.

25. *Oedipus at Colonus*, p. 361.

26. Heraclitus, *On the Universe*, trans. W. H. S. Jones (Cambridge, Massachusetts: Harvard University Press and London: William Heineman, 1979).

27. Ibid., Fragment 41, p. 483.

4 IMPIOUS EURIPIDES

1. F. Nietzsche, 'On the uses and disadvantages of history for life', *Untimely Meditations (UM)*, trans. R. J. Hollingdale with intro. by J. P. Stern (Cambridge University Press, 1983) p. 59.

2. See *HAH*, Volume I, 'A Glance at the State', no. 475, pp. 174f.

3. Ibid., no. 473, p. 173.

4. Ibid., p. 174.

5. *WP*, Book One, 'European Nihilism', Section 1, p. 7.

6. *BT*, Section 10, p. 75.

7. For an illuminating discussion of this possibly central factor in human psychology, see Gilles Deleuze's *Nietzsche and Philosophy*, trans. Hugh Tomlinson (Athlone Press 1983) Chapter 5, part 8. 'Is Man Essentially Reactive?' pp. 166ff.

8. *TI*, 'The Problem of Socrates', Section 5, p. 31.

9. *BT*, Section 10, pp. 75f.

10. Aristotle, *On the Art of Poetry* (Oxford University Press, 1954) p. 51.

11.   *Euripides,* Volume IV, *Alcestis,* trans. Arthur S. Way (Cambridge, Massachusetts: Harvard University Press, and London: William Heinemann, 1980) line 558, p. 455.
12.   See H. D. F. Kitto, *Greek Tragedy – A Literary Study* (Methuen, 1939) Chapter XI, A. M. Dale's edn of *Alcestis* (Oxford University Press, 1954) and D. J. Conacher, *Euripidean Drama – Myth, Theme and Structure* (University of Toronto Press, 1967) Chapter 19.
13.   Victor Ehrenberg, *From Solon to Socrates – Greek History and Civilization during the 6th and 5th centuries B.C.* (Methuen, 1967) p. 349.
14.   Euripides, *Collected Plays* (George Allen and Unwin, 1954) *Medea,* p. 285, line 18.
15.   Ibid., line 15.
16.   Ibid., pp. 307f, lines 292–315.
17.   Ibid., p. 331, line 618.
18.   Ibid., *Hippolytus,* pp. 7f.
19.   H. D. F. Kitto, *Greek Tragedy – A Literary Study* (Methuen, 1939)
20.   Gilbert Murray, introductory note to *The Trojan Women, Collected Plays of Euripides* (see note 14) p. 7.
21.   Ibid.
22.   See F. Nietzsche, *Thus Spoke Zarathustra – A Book for Everyone and No One* (Z), trans. with intro. by R. J. Hollingdale (Harmondsworth: Penguin Books, 1980) Part Four, 'The Sign', p. 336.
23.   *AC,* Section 7, p. 118.
24.   Albin Lesky, *Greek Tragedy,* trans. H. A. Frankfort with a foreword by Professor E. G. Turner (London: Ernest Benn, and New York: Barnes and Noble Books, 1965), p. 171.
25.   G. M. A. Grube, *The Drama of Euripides* (Methuen, 1941) p. 314.
26.   See above, Chapter 2, pp. 27ff.
27.   *Euripides,* Volume III, *The Bacchanals,* trans. Arthur Way (New York: William Heinemann, and London: Macmillan, 1932) line 310, p. 29.
28.   Gilbert Murray, *Collected Plays of Euripides* (see note 14) *The Bacchae,* p. 20.

5   NATURE AND PURITY IN THE RENAISSANCE

1.   *AC,* Section 15, p. 125.
2.   F. Nietzsche, *The Gay Science (GS),* trans. with commentary by Walter Kaufmann (New York: Vintage Books, A Division of Random House, 1974) Book Five, 'We Fearless Ones', Section 372, p. 333.
3.   *TI,* ' "Reason" in Philosophy', Section 1, p. 35.
4.   Ibid., 'How the "Real World" at last became a Myth', p. 40.
5.   Ibid., 'The Problem of Socrates', Section 2, p. 29.
6.   Karl Popper, *The Open Society and its Enemies,* Volume 1, *The Spell of Plato* (Routledge and Kegan Paul, 1945). See especially Chapter 6, 'Totalitarian Justice'.
7.   See *The Republic,* Part XI, 'The Soul Immortal'.
8.   See above, Chapter 1, pp. 8ff.

9. *UM*, 'Schopenhauer as educator', Section 5, p. 160.
10. Herschel Baker, *The Wars of Truth* (Cambridge, Massachusetts: Harvard University Press, 1952) p. 5.
11. *WP*, Book Four, 'Discipline and Breeding', no. 882, p. 471.
12. *Z*, Part One, 'Of the Tree on the Mountainside', p. 69.
13. Ibid., Part Two, 'Of the Tarantulas', p. 125.
14. Aristotle, *On the Art of Poetry* (Oxford University Press, 1954) Section 14, p. 52.
15. *GM*, First Essay, 'Good and Evil', 'Good and Bad', Section 6, pp. 32f.
16. *Z*, Part One, 'Of the Despisers of the Body', pp. 61f.
17. René Descartes, 'Meditations' 4, 'Of Truth and Falsehood', *Discourse on Method and other writings*, trans. with intro. by Arthur Wollaston (Harmondsworth: Penguin Books, 1960) p. 139.
18. Ibid.
19. See Benedict de Spinoza, *The Chief Works of Benedict de Spinoza*, trans. from the Latin with intro. by R. H. M. Elwes (New York: Dover Publications, 1955; 'The Ethics', Part I, especially propositions 26–32, pp. 66ff.
20. *BGE*, Part One, 'On the Prejudices of Philosophers', Section 21, p. 29.
21. Sophocles, *Oedipus at Colonus*, lines 1226–9. See above Chapter 3, p. 68.
22. *AC*, Section 29, p. 141.
23. *BT*, Section 5, p. 52. See above, Chapter 1, p. 12.
24. The reference is especially to Anna Freud's *The Ego and the Mechanisms of Defence*, trans. Cecil Baines (The Hogarth Press, 1966).
25. *EH*, 'Why I am So Clever', 4, p. 246.
26. John Keats, *The Letters of John Keats*, ed. Hyder Edward Rollins (Cambridge University Press and Harvard University Press, 1958) Volume I, Letter 118, p. 387.
27. William Wordsworth, Preface to the second edn of *Lyrical Ballads*.
28. W. B. Yeats, *Autobiographies* (Macmillan, 1955) p. 522.
29. *BT*, Section 12, p. 82.
30. Ibid., Section 17, p. 108.
31. Ibid., Section 7, p. 60.
32. Ralph Berry, *The Art of John Webster* (Oxford University Press, 1972) p. 50.

6 IBSEN AND HARDY, NATURE'S LOST SONS

1. *BT*, Section 1, p. 37.
2. *BGE*, Part One, 'On the Prejudices of Philosophers', Section 14, pp. 21f. See also above, Chapter 1, p. 9f.
3. *WP*, Book Four, 'Discipline and Breeding', no. 1050, p. 539.
4. See above, Chapter 2, p. 47.
5. See Martin Heidegger, *Nietzsche, Volume 1 – The Will to Power as Art*, trans. from the German with notes and an analysis by David Farrell Krell (Routledge and Kegan Paul, 1981).

6.   *The Times*, Letters, 28 November 1919.

7.   See Michael Meyer's *Ibsen* (Harmondsworth: Penguin Books, 1974) p. 572.

8.   Henrik Ibsen, The Oxford *Ibsen*, Volume vi, 'An Enemy of the People', trans. and ed. James Walter McFarlane, (Oxford University Press, 1960).

9.   See F. Nietzsche, *Daybreak – Thoughts on the Prejudices of Morality* (*D*), trans. R. J. Hollingdale with an intro. by Michael Turner (Cambridge University Press, 1982) Book 1, Section 18, pp. 17ff.

10. The Oxford *Ibsen*, Volume i, *Early Plays*, trans. and ed. by James Walter McFarlane and Graham Orton (Oxford University Press, 1970) 'Introduction', p. 1.

11. Bernard Shaw, *Everybody's Political What's What* (Constable, 1944) p. 2.

12. Henrik Ibsen, The Oxford *Ibsen*, Volume i, *Catiline*, Act Three.

13. *WP*, Book Two, 'Critique of the Highest Values Hitherto', no. 351, p. 192.

14. *BGE*, Part Nine, 'What is Noble', no. 259, p. 203.

15. Henrik Ibsen, The Oxford *Ibsen*, Volume i, *The Vikings at Helgeland*, Act Three.

16. See *AC*, Section 29, p. 141 and above, Chapter 5, p. 105f.

17. Ibid., Section 39, p. 151.

18. See The Oxford *Ibsen*, Volume iii, trans. J. Kirkup and G. Fry, ed. James Walter McFarlane (Oxford University Press, 1970) p. 21. Letter of 28 October 1870.

19. See Michael Meyer, *Ibsen* (Harmondsworth: Penguin Books, 1974), abridged version of biography published by Rupert Hart-Davis, p. 395.

20. Henrik Ibsen, The Oxford *Ibsen*, Volume vii trans. Jens Arup and James Walter McFarlane ed. James Walter McFarlane (Oxford University Press, 1966). *The Master Builder*, Act One.

21. Henrik Ibsen, The Oxford *Ibsen*, Volume vi, *Rosmersholm*, Act One.

22. *WP*, Book One, 'European Nihilism', Section 1, p. 67.

23. See Meyer, *Ibsen*, pp. 373ff. Letter to Brandes of 4 April 1872.

24. See *EH*, 'Why I Write Such Good Books', Section 5, p. 267 where Ibsen is called a 'typical old virgin', one of those who 'aims to *poison* the good conscience, what is natural in sexual love'. As the editor, Walter Kaufmann, remarks, Nietzsche cannot have known many of Ibsen's works.

25. *BGE*, 'Our Virtues', no 230, pp. 161ff.

26. Henrik Ibsen, The Oxford *Ibsen*, Volume vii, trans, and ed. James Walter McFarlane, *John Gabriel Borkman*, Act Four (Oxford University Press, 1977).

27. *WP*, Book Three, 'Principles of a New Evaluation', no. 503, p. 274.

28. F. R. Southerington, *Hardy's Vision of Man* (Chatto and Windus, 1971) p. 69.

29. Ibid., p. 70.

30. See Robert Gittings, *Young Thomas Hardy* (Penguin Group, 1988), Chapter 17, 'Moule'. Originally published by Heinemann Educational Books, 1975.

31. Thomas Hardy, *The Return of the Native*, Book Second, Chapter III.
32. Ibid.
33. Ibid., Book Second, Chapter VI.
34. Ibid., Book Third, Chapter I.
35. *HAH*, 'On the History of the Moral Sensations', no. 107, p. 57.
36. Thomas Hardy, *Tess of the D'Urbervilles*, Phase the Fourth, Chapter XXXI.
37. Ibid., Chapter XXXVI.
38. Barbara Hardy, *The Appropriate Form*, (Athlone Press, 1964) pp. 70f.
39. Thomas Hardy, *Jude the Obscure*, Part Sixth, Chapter III.
40. Ibid.
41. See Thomas Hardy, 'Literary Notebook', III, XIV (not published but kept in the Dorset County Museum).

7 ZARATHUSTRA AND THE REBIRTH OF TRAGEDY

1. *BT*, Section 19, p. 121.
2. Ibid., Section 23, p. 137.
3. Ibid., Section 17, p. 109.
4. *BGE*, Part Nine, 'What is Noble', no. 257, p. 201.
5. *WP*, Book One, 'European Nihilism', Section 1, p. 7.
6. F. Nietzsche, 'On Truth and Lies in a Nonmoral Sense', *Philosophy and Truth – Selections from Nietzsche's Notebooks of the early 1870s*, trans. and ed. with intro. and notes by Daniel Breazeale, with a foreword by Walter Kaufmann (New Jersey: Humanities Press, and Sussex: Harvester Press, 1979) p. 79.
7. *GS*, Book Four, 'Sanctus Januarius', no. 324, p. 255.
8. Heraclitus, *On the Universe*, trans. W. H. S. Jones (Cambridge, Massachusetts: Harvard University Press, and London: William Heinemann, 1979) Fragment 20, p. 477.
9. F. Nietzsche, *Philosophy in the Tragic Age of the Greeks*, trans. with intro. by Marianne Cowan (Chicago: Regnery Gateway, 1962) pp. 58ff.
10. *TI*, 'How the "Real World" at last Became a Myth', pp. 40f.
11. See Martin Heidegger, *Nietzsche, Volume Two – The Eternal Recurrence of the Same*, Part Two, 'Who is Nietzsche's Zarathustra?', trans. from the German with notes and an analysis by David Farrell Krell (San Francisco: Harper and Row, 1984) pp. 211ff.
12. *EH*, Why I Write Such Good Books', p. 261.
13. Laurence Lampert, *Nietzsche's Teaching – An Interpretation of 'Thus Spoke Zarathustra'*, (New Haven and London: Yale University Press, 1986). See, for instance, p. 3: 'The scope of the new Zarathustra's ambition – or of what Nietzsche wanted to do – is measured by the ancient Zarathustra's achievement'.
14. *GS*, Book Four, no. 342, p. 274.
15. *EH*, 'Why I am a Destiny', 5, p. 331.
16. Martin Heidegger, *Nietzsche, Volume Three – The Will to Power as Knowledge and Metaphysics*, trans. from the German by Joan

Stambaugh, David Farrell Krell, Frank A. Capucci, ed. with notes and an analysis by David Farrell Krell (San Francisco, Harper and Row, 1987). See especially pp. 139ff.

17.   It is true that according to one formulation of 'eternal return', that the key doctrine of Zarathustra and indeed of all Nietzsche, things do come again in exactly their earlier forms, but this is the version that the most thoughtful modern commentators (I am thinking especially of Heidegger, Schacht, Lampert and Joan Stambaugh) find unacceptable or unnecessary.

18.   *D*, Book I, Section 49, p. 47.

19.   *TI*, 'The Four Great Errors', no. 8, p. 54.

20.   *GS*, Book Three, no. 109, p. 168.

21.   *Z*, Part Two, 'Of Redemption', p. 161.

22.   Ibid., p. 163.

23.   Ibid.

24.   *HAH*, 'Assorted Opinions and Maxims', no. 189, p. 260.

25.   Heraclitus, *On the Universe* trans. W. H. S. Jones (Cambridge, Massachusetts: Harvard University Press, and London: William Heinemann, 1979) no. 49, p. 489.

26.   *Z*, Part Four, 'The Intoxicated Song', no. 10, p. 332.

27.   Gilbert Ryle, *The Concept of Mind*, (Hutchinson, 1949).

28.   S. T. Coleridge, *Biographia Literaria*, Chapter VII.

29.   *Z*, Part Two, 'Of Redemption', p. 163.

30.   *HAH*, Volume One, 'Man Alone With Himself', no. 636, p. 202.

31.   *Z*, Part One, 'Of the Way of the Creator', p. 89.

32.   Aeschylus, *Prometheus Bound*, p. 233.

33.   *BT*, Section 9, p. 68.

34.   Ibid., Section 7, p. 60.

35.   *Z*, Part Three, 'The Convalescent', p. 234.

Bibliography

The place of publication is London unless otherwise stated.

Aeschylus Volume I, The Loeb Classical Library, ed. E. H. Warmington, trans. Herbert Weir Smyth (Cambridge, Massachusetts: Harvard University Press, and London: William Heinemann, 1973).

Aeschylus Volume II, The Loeb Classical Library, ed. Hugh Lloyd-Jones, trans. Herbert Weir Smyth (Cambridge, Massachusetts: Harvard University Press, and London: William Heinemann, 1939).

Andréas-Salomé, Lou, *Frédéric Nietzsche*, traduit de l'allemand par Jacques Benoist-Méchin (Paris: Bernard Grasset, 1932).

Aristophanes – Four Comedies, ed. William Arrowsmith, trans. Douglas Parker and Richard Lattimore (University of Michigan Press, 1977).

Aristotle *On the Art of Poetry*, trans. Ingram Bywater with a preface by Gilbert Murray (Oxford University Press, 1954).

Arnott, Peter D., *An Introduction to the Greek Theatre*, foreword by H. D. F. Kitto (Macmillan, 1961).

Aylen, Leo, *Greek Tragedy and the Modern World* (Methuen, 1964).

Baker, Herschel, *The Wars of Truth – Studies in the Decay of Christian Humanism in the Earlier Seventeenth Century* (Cambridge, Massachusetts: Harvard University Press, 1952).

Bayley, John, *Shakespeare and Tragedy* (Routledge and Kegan Paul, 1981).

Berry, Ralph, *The Art of John Webster* (Oxford University Press, 1972).

Bowra, C. M., *Sophoclean Tragedy* (Oxford University Press, 1944).

Bradbrook, M. C., *Themes and Conventions of Elizabethan Tragedy* (Cambridge University Press, 1935).

Bradley, A. C., *Oxford Lectures on Poetry* (Macmillan, 1959).

Brandes, George, *Friedrich Nietzsche*, trans. A. G. Chater (William Heinemann, 1914).

Conacher, D. J., *Euripidean Drama – Myth, Theme and Structure* (University of Toronto Press, 1967).

Corneille, Pierre, *Polyeuctus, The Liar, Nicomedes*, trans. with intro. by John Cairncross (Harmondsworth: Penguin Books, 1980).

Deleuze, Gilles, *Nietzsche and Philosophy*, trans. Hugh Tomlinson (The Athlone Press, 1983).

Descartes, René, *A Discourse on Method and other Writings*, trans. and intro. by Arthur Wollaston (Harmondsworth: Penguin Books, 1960).

Else, G. F., *The Origin and Early Form of Greek Tragedy*, (Cambridge, Massachusetts: Harvard University Press, 1965).

Euripides Volume II, The Loeb Classical Library, trans. Arthur S. Way (Cambridge, Massachusetts: Harvard University Press, and London: William Heinemann, 1978).

Euripides Volume III, The Loeb Classical Library, trans. Arthur S. Way (New York: Macmillan, and London: William Heinemann, 1932).

Euripides Volume IV, The Loeb Classical Library, trans. Arthur S. Way (Cambridge, Massachusetts: Harvard University Press, and London: William Heinemann, 1980).

Euripides, *Collected Plays of Euripides*, trans. with commentaries and notes by Gilbert Murray (George Allen and Unwin, 1954).

Ehrenberg, Victor, *From Solo to Socrates – Greek History and Civilization during the 6th and 5th Centuries B.C.* (Methuen, 1968).

Freud, Anna, *The Ego and the Mechanisms of Defence*, trans. Cecil Baines (The Hogarth Press, 1966).

Gittings, Robert, *Young Thomas Hardy*, (Heinemann Educational Books, 1975).

Goldhill, Simon, *Reading Greek Tragedy*, Cambridge University Press, 1986).

Grube, G. M. A., *The Drama of Euripides*, (Methuen, 1941).

Hardy, Barbara, *The Appropriate Form*, (Athlone Press, 1964).

Harrison, G. B., *Shakespeare's Tragedies*, (Routledge and Kegan Paul, 1951).

Hegel, G. W. F., *The Phenomenology of Mind*, trans. with intro. and notes by J. B. Baillie (George Allen and Unwin, 1966).

Heidegger, Martin, *Nietzsche, Volume One – The Will to Power as Art*; trans. from the German with notes and an analysis by David Farrell Krell (Routledge and Kegan Paul, 1981).

——, *Nietzsche, Volume Two – The Eternal Recurrence of the Same*, trans. from the German with notes and an analysis by David Farrell Krell (San Francisco: Harper and Row, 1984).

——, *Nietzsche, Volume Three – The Will to Power as Knowledge and Metaphysics*, trans. from the German by Joan Stambaugh, David Farrell Krell and Frank A. Capuzzi (San Francisco: Harper and Row, 1987).

Ibsen, Henrik, *Works* in the Oxford Edition, 8 volumes, ed. James Walter McFarlane (Oxford University Press, 1957–77).

Kaufmann, Walter, *Hegel – Reinterpretation, Texts and Commentary* (Weidenfeld and Nicholson, 1965).

Kitto, H. D. F., *Greek Tragedy – A Literary Study* (Methuen, 1939).

Knox, B. M. W., *Oedipus at Thebes* (New Haven: Yale University Press, and London: Oxford University Press, 1957).

Kott, Jan, *The Eating of the Gods – An Interpretation of Greek Tragedy*, trans. Boleslaw Taborski and Edward J. Czerwinski (Eyre Methuen, 1974).

Lampert, Laurence, *Nietzsche's Teaching – An Interpretation of Thus Spoke Zarathustra* (New Haven and London: Yale University Press, 1986).

Lesky, Albin, *Greek Tragedy*, trans. H. A. Frankfort with a foreword by Professor E. G. Turner (Ernest Benn, 1965).

Levin, Harry, *Christopher Marlowe – The Overreacher* (Faber and Faber, 1961).

Lucas, F. L., *Greek Drama for the Common Reader* (Chatto and Windus, 1967).

Meyer, Michael, *Ibsen* (Harmondsworth: Penguin Books, 1974). First published in 3 volumes by Rupert Hart-Davis in 1967 and 1971.

Millgate, Michael, *Thomas Hardy – A Biography* (Oxford University Press, 1982).

Montaigne, Michel de, *Essays*, trans. and intro. by J. M. Cohen (Harmondsworth: Penguin Books, 1966).

Nietzsche, Friedrich, *Beyond Good and Evil – Prelude to a Philosophy of the Future*, trans. with commentary by Walter Kaufmann (New York: Vintage Books, A Division of Random House, 1966).

——, *The Birth of Tragedy* and *The Case of Wagner*, trans. with a commentary by Walter Kaufmann (New York: Vintage Books, A Division of Random House, 1967).

——, *Daybreak – Thoughts on the Prejudices of Morality*, trans. R. J. Hollingdale with an intro. by Michael Tanner (Cambridge University Press, 1982).

——, *Dithyrambs of Dionysus*, Bilingual Edition, trans. and intro. by R. J. Hollingdale (Anvil Press Poetry, 1984).

——, *The Gay Science*, trans. with commentary by Walter Kaufmann (New York: Vintage Books, A Division of Random House, 1974).

——, *On the Future of Our Educational Institutions* and *Homer and Classical Philology*, trans. with intro. by J. M. Kennedy (T. N. Foulis, 1909).

——, *On the Genealogy of Morals*, trans. Walter Kaufmann and R. J. Hollingdale and *Ecce Homo*, trans. with commentary by Walter Kaufmann (New York: Vintage Books, A Division of Random House, 1967).

——, *Human, All Too Human – A Book for Free Spirits*, trans. R. J. Hollingdale with intro. by Erich Heller (Cambridge University Press, 1986).

——, *Philosophy in the Tragic Age of the Greeks*, trans. with intro. by Marianne Cowan (Chicago: Regnery Gateway, 1962).

——, *Selected Letters of Friedrich Nietzsche*, trans. A. N. Ludovici, ed. and intro. by O. Levy (Soho Book Company, 1985).

——, *Thus Spoke Zarathustra – A Book for Everyone and No One*, trans. with intro. by R. J. Hollingdale (Harmondsworth: Penguin Books, 1980).

——, *Twilight of the Idols* and *The Anti-Christ*, trans. with intro. and commentary by R. J. Hollingdale (Harmondsworth: Penguin Books, 1978).

——, *Unpublished Letters*, trans. and ed. by Karl F. Leidecker (Peter Owen, 1960).

——, *Untimely Meditations*, trans. R. J. Hollingdale with intro. by J. P. Stern (Cambridge University Press, 1983).

——, *The Will to Power*, trans. Walter Kaufmann and R. J. Hollingdale, ed. with intro. by Walter Kaufmann (New York: Vintage Books, A Division of Random House, 1968).

Pascal, Blaise, *The Thoughts of Blaise Pascal*, trans. from the text of M. Auguste Molinier by C. Kegan Paul (Kegan Paul, Trench, 1938).

Pickard-Cambridge, A. W., *Dithyramb Tragedy and Comedy* (Oxford University Press, 1927).

Plato, *The Republic*, trans. with intro. by Desmond Lee (Harmondsworth: Penguin Books, 1979).

——, *The Trial and Execution of Socrates*, trans. with intro. by Peter George, drawings by Michael Ayrton (The Folio Society, 1972).

Pocock, Gordon, *Corneille and Racine – Problems of Tragic Form* (Cambridge University Press, 1973).

Popper, Karl, *The Open Society and its Enemies, Volume I – The Spell of Plato* (Routledge and Kegan Paul, 1945).

Racine, Jean, *Complete Plays*, trans. with a biographical appreciation by Samuel Solomon, intro. by Katherine Wheatley (New York: Random House, 1967).

Ryle, Gilbert, *The Concept of Mind* (Hutchinson, 1949).

Schacht, Richard, *Nietzsche* (Routledge and Kegan Paul, 1983).

Silk, M. S., and Stern, J. P., *Nietzsche on Tragedy* (Cambridge University Press, 1981).

Sophocles Volume I, The Loeb Classical Library, trans. F. Storr (Cambridge, Massachusetts: Harvard University Press and London: William Heinemann, 1981).

Sophocles Volume II, The Loeb Classical Library, trans. F. Storr (New York: G. P. Putnam's Sons, London: William Heinemann, 1929).

Spinoza, Benedict de, *The Chief Works of Benedict de Spinoza*, trans. from the Latin with intro. by R. H. M. Elwes (New York: Dover Publications, 1951).

Southerington, F. R., *Hardy's Vision of Man*, (Chatto and Windus, 1971).

Steane, J. B., *Marlowe – A Critical Study* (Cambridge University Press, 1964).

Stirner, Max, *The Ego and Its Own*, trans. Steven Byington with intro. by Sidney Parker (Rebel Press, 1982).

Tejera, V., *Nietzsche and Greek Thought* (Dordrecht: Martin Nijhoff, a member of the Kluwer Academic Publishers Group, 1987).

Vickers, Brian, *Towards Greek Tragedy – Drama, Myth, Society* (Longman, 1973).

Winnington-Ingram, R. J., *Sophocles: an Interpretation* (Cambridge University Press, 1950).

Index